The Playwright
and the Pirate

The Playwright
and the Pirate

Bernard Shaw and Frank Harris:
A Correspondence

1856-1950

edited, with an introduction, by
Stanley Weintraub

The Pennsylvania State University Press
University Park and London

Library of Congress Cataloging in Publication Data

Shaw, Bernard, 1856–1950.
    The Playwright and the Pirate.
    1. Shaw, Bernard, 1856–1950—Correspondence.
2. Harris, Frank, 1855–1931—Correspondence.
3. Dramatists, English—19th century—Correspondence.
4. Authors, English—19th century—Correspondence.
I. Harris, Frank, 1855–1931. II. Weintraub, Stanley, 1929–   . III. Title.
PR5366.A464   1982   822'.912   82-468
ISBN 0-271-00310-3   AACR2

Published in the United States of America by The Pennsylvania State University Press

Published in Great Britain by Colin Smythe Limited, Gerrards Cross, Buckinghamshire

Contents

Introduction

In his dozens of bantering, yet benevolent, letters to Frank Harris over more than thirty years, Bernard Shaw regularly inserted references to Harris as "buccaneer" and "ruffian," and the old pirate objected. But, reduced to living off nostalgia for the good years past, and begging letters that deflated the pride in the old buccaneering sails, Harris protested too much. The mostly well-earned reputation that had helped to do him in was, in his last decades, his only negotiable currency.

In one letter Harris reminded Shaw that both had emerged as forces on the London intellectual scene almost at the same time, in the early 1880s, as journalists and reformers, and had achieved fame on the same journal, Harris as editor-proprietor of *The Saturday Review* and G.B.S. (as he signed his columns) as its highly visible—and quotable—theatre critic. Yet Harris, for once, had been deliberately modest, perhaps a gesture aimed at drawing Shaw's support for one of the pirate's dubious propositions at a time when Shaw was world-famous and Harris was down and out.

In truth Shaw had striven for years after his emigration from Ireland (at twenty, in 1876) to find a measure of literary success, but did not see his first play produced, and that unsuccessfully, until he was thirty-six. He was nearly forty when he joined Harris's paper. Harris, on the other hand, was a boy-immigrant from Ireland—"born in Galway of pure or impure Welsh parents," he told Shaw—who became an American citizen and then returned to the Old World to make his fortune. By 1885, when he and Shaw were both twenty-nine, Harris was the upstart young editor of the London *Evening News*. Shaw, who had been an unemployed writer of unsaleable novels, in 1885 had finally acquired the opportunity to write anonymous reviews of third-rate books for the *Pall Mall Gazette* and equally poorly paid musical notices for *The Dramatic Review*. Two years later Shaw was still writing reviews of third-rate books, and was also tramping the galleries for unsigned art columns in *The World*. Meanwhile Harris, already a pompous, commanding figure in London, had married a widow of forty-eight with wealth and social position, was editor of *The Fortnightly Review*, and contemplated standing for Parliament.

Later, when Shaw had play royalties pouring in, and Harris, grasping in his old age for something to publish, sent his old friend a questionnaire, Shaw answered, "You want to know what it feels like to be a rich man. Well, you should know; for if you are not a millionaire at this moment, you have been one for an afternoon, or for a week, or if rumor be true, for perhaps a year when you married a lady in Park Lane and spent all your money consorting with Randolph Churchill and Edouard Sept." Shaw was applying salt to the old wound, for in almost every way it had been downhill for Harris after that, and a precipitous ascent for Shaw as critic, playwright and social philosopher; yet at one point their careers had converged. In the mid-nineties Harris had taken over the moribund *Saturday Review*, hired clever but largely unknown writers like H. G. Wells, Arnold Bennett, Robert Cunninghame Graham, John Runciman and D. S. MacColl to write for him, and turned out a weekly that was the most lively in London. For his drama critic Harris wooed away from *The World* a music critic who had begun in yet another paper under the pseudonym of *Corno di Bassetto* and was then writing as *G.B.S.* As music critic Shaw had achieved his aim of making even philistine stockbrokers who cared nothing about the arts read his column. As drama critic for Frank Harris he was the most feared and respected, as well as the most entertaining, columnist in London; and he consolidated his reputation to such an extent that when he turned over his assignment to Max Beerbohm in 1898 he could write in a valedictory column,

> For ten years past, with an unprecedented pertinacity and obstination, I have been dinning into the public head that I am

an extraordinarily witty, brilliant, and clever man. That is now part of the public opinion of England; and no power in heaven or on earth will ever change it. I may dodder and dote; I may potboil and platitudinize; I may become the butt and chopping-block of all the bright, original spirits of the rising generation; but my reputation shall not suffer: it is built up fast and solid, like Shakespear's, on an impregnable basis of dogmatic reiteration.

Shaw had taken his leave of Harris just in time. By 1900 Harris was clutching at any opportunity to retrieve his fortunes. He had lost *The Saturday Review* and would edit a series of journalistic disasters, beginning with *The Candid Friend*, each a greater money-loser than its predecessor. It was rumored that Harris recouped his losses, and sustained his high living, by quietly blackmailing other high-living Londoners with the threat of exposure in his seldom-successful magazines, which became increasingly ridden with scandal. One libel suit, which resulted when, as proprietor of *Modern Society*, he published something he should have only threatened to publish, even put him in jail. He had lost his wife, who was jealous of his affairs with younger women even before they happened, and they did happen—again and again. He was publishing his own fiction—some of it, like *Montes the Matador and Other Stories*, not bad for its time—but few critics noticed, and few readers bought any copies. A career as a playwright would end after one significant play—significant primarily because Harris had purchased the scenario from Oscar Wilde at a time when Wilde would have sold anything for a few pounds; and indeed Oscar sold *Mr and Mrs Daventry* to several would-be dramatists, each transaction conferring exclusivity to the purchaser. Harris's few later plays fizzled.

Shaw, meanwhile (having married an Irish millionairess in 1898), was arriving as the leading playwright in the language, and one of his era's major public personalities. Harris was hurtling headlong in the other direction. Never quite respectable, he had been tolerated—even courted—as an amiable vulgarian when he was a rising star. His booming voice and four-letter language, his inability to look like anything other than an Albanian highwayman even when dressed in tails, his gluttonous gormandizing and insatiable womanizing, quickly made

Shaw inscribed this portrait: "To Frank Harris, from G. Bernard Shaw, Nice, 1928."

Frank Harris and Nellie (Humanities Research Center, University of Texas at Austin).

him a pariah in the circles where his income had been found, and as his opportunities as editor and writer dwindled during the Edwardian years, he took on a paranoid air. It was English hypocrisy and philistinism that was bringing him down, he insisted, not the inability of Frank Harris to rein in his gift for self-destruction. And no help came from the pretty young Nellie O'Hara, who called herself Mrs Harris all her life and had expensive tastes which kept Harris in debt. Only when the real (and long estranged) Mrs Harris finally died at a great age in 1927 could Frank make an honest woman of Nellie, but Shaw through the years politely referred to her as if she and Harris were living together with full benefit of clergy; and termagant as she could be, she nevertheless tolerated Harris's indulgence of his sexual itch among servants, sub-editors, and assorted females who wandered into his wide orbit. ("Sex," Harris assured his young assistant on *Modern Society*, the future novelist and playwright Enid Bagnold, "is the gateway to life," and she duly went through the gateway.)

Before Harris became a literary confidence man, and let his journalistic hand falter, he possessed the confidence and the aplomb of the successful late-Victorian man of letters. Yet there was a vulgarity about him which Shaw chose not to see. Harris had, Shaw wrote in his preface to *The Dark Lady of the Sonnets* in 1910, "a range of sympathy and understanding that extends from the ribaldry of a buccaneer to the shyest tenderness of the most sensitive poetry," and could be all things to all men. "To the Archbishop he is an atheist, to the atheist a Catholic mystic, to the Bismarckian Imperialist an Anacharsis Klootz,* to Anacharsis Klootz a [George] Washington, to Mrs Proudie a Don Juan, to Aspasia a John Knox: in short to everyone his complement rather than his counterpart, his antagonist rather than his fellow creature. Always provided, however, that the persons thus affronted are respectable persons."

The lines explain much about the Shaw/Harris relationship. Shaw was cool, scrupulous, precise, generous, humane. Beneath the pose of self-advertising egoist he was a shy man; beneath the clown's motley he masked a philosophic mood; beneath the Bunyanesque preacher he was a sentimental Irish romantic.

*Jean Baptiste Klootz (or Clootz), who called himself Anacharsis, after the 6th century B.C. Athenian friend of Solon, was a German revolutionary guillotined in Paris in 1794.

While Shaw's sexual temperature was low, the Irish-born Harris, who fancied himself a sentimental romantic, possessed a compulsion for lechery that, when he became impotent in later years, became transmuted into erotic "autobiography" which was more fantasy than fact.

Harris's finer feelings often did him credit. Yet the real Harris he could never recognize in himself was more often unscrupulous and ungenerous. While Shaw was quick to own up to the "pantomime ostrich" he played, beneath the pose of good samaritan and altruist was a self-indulgent Frank Harris who saw himself only as model human being. When he claimed that he had offered to help Oscar Wilde in his extremities, he really thought he had, although he had grossly exaggerated his assistance *ex post facto*. When he offered to assist Harold Frederic's mistress at her trial for manslaughter (she had treated Frederic's fatal stroke with Christian Science), and pay half the court costs, he actually did sit with her at the trial, and write a *Saturday Review* editorial defending her. That he stayed away at the end, and failed to remember his offer to pay her bills, never occurred to him as a flaw in his character. So it went through his life. "Frank Harris," Wilde concluded in a prison letter, "has no feelings. It is the secret of his success. Just as the fact that he thinks other people have none either is the secret of the failure that lies in wait for him somewhere on the way of Life."

Major Barbara's father in Shaw's play was always embarrassing his wife by doing the right thing for the wrong reasons, as Shaw might have done; Harris was always doing the wrong thing for the wrong reasons, yet claiming that both were somehow right, and that he was following his conscience. Perhaps he was an attractive personality to Shaw exactly because he was Shaw's complement rather than his counterpart, because there were qualities in him, exaggerated to be sure, that Shaw saw the lack of in himself. To Shaw, Harris was not "vulgar, mean, purblind, spiteful," which he was to other men—and women. And to Shaw, Harris lacked humor "because scorn overcomes the humor in him." Later, he would see a pathetic humor in Harris, but contented himself in his *Dark Lady* preface with the prophetic line about his old friend, "Nobody ever dreamt of reproaching Milton's Lucifer for not seeing the comic side of his fall."

In Harris's dealings with others in person and in print Shaw often thought he saw "a capacity for pity," but it would become an obsessive self-pity when each attempt to recoup his fortunes would end in misfortune. Harris had immense capacities for bouncing back after defeat, but each resurrection required some help from his friends, and soon there were few friends who could stand the strain of such a friendship. The longest-standing friendship remained Shaw's. But it required lending no money and seeing Harris in person as little as possible while keeping Harris at arm's length via correspondence. Their exchanges of letters kept the relationship going, and at the level Shaw was willing to tolerate—not only for old times' sake. Harris was a walking melodrama, and Shaw enjoyed the roles he had created for the two of them, although Harris would regularly try to break out of his because he did not know he was playing Frank Harris. Had he known, his pride would not have permitted it. When Harris once objected to Shaw's jocularly accurate descriptions of him, Shaw rose to the bait:

> You must not take my comments on your personal characteristics as sneers and disparagements. If you do you will find me an impossible man to have any relations with. I tell you you are a ruffian exactly as an oculist might tell you that you are astigmatic. I will tell you now more precisely what I mean—if I have done so already you have brought the reputation on yourself.
>
> Somebody in London society who likes interesting people meets you and invites you to dinner. He asks you to take in a bishop's wife. You entertain her with deep-voiced outpourings of your scorn for the hypocrisy and snobbery of the Church, finishing up with a touch of poetry about Mary Magdalene and her relations with Jesus. When the poor lady escapes to the drawing-room and you find yourself between the bishop and Edmund Gosse, you turn the conversation on to the [pornographic] genius of [Felicien] Rops, and probably produce a specimen of his work, broadening your language at the same time into that of the forecastle of a pirate sloop.
>
> And if you observe the least sign of restiveness or discomfort on the part of the twain, you redouble your energy of expression and barb it with open and angry scorn. When they escape upstairs in their turn, they condole with one another. Gosse says, "My God, what a man!" The bishop says, "Oh, impossible; quite impossible!"

Now though this particular picture is a fancy one, it is not founded on any lies that people have told me. I have seen and heard you do such things; I have been condoled with, and have had to admit that you are a monster, and that clever as you are, it is impossible to ask anyone to meet you unless they are prepared to stand anything that the utter-most freemasonry of the very freest thought and expression in the boldest circles can venture on. . . .

"You can't write to me or about me without calling me names," Harris complained with unfeigned concern; "I have never felt this inclination towards anyone and so cannot understand it in you. . . . What you call my 'ruffianism' is revolt against convention which you incarnated almost as strongly in London as I did. You . . . seem even more unconscious of it in yourself than I am." The "sex business" which he confessed he had trouble getting printers to print was as essential to *his* art as he knew it was to Shaw's, but somehow Shaw managed to safely tuck it between the lines. He did not have that alternative, he told Shaw, for "you cannot know a man without knowing his faith and practice in this respect; and I wanted to state them about the men I knew. . . . You, on the other hand, seem to have no difficulty in this matter."

Not seeing any possible relationship between Harris's principles and her husband's practice, Charlotte Shaw insisted that the first volume of Harris's notorious *My Life and Loves* be burnt, page by page, in the fireplace; and she would neither tolerate another volume, nor Harris. G.B.S. patiently indulged his old companion-in-arms of *Saturday Review* days, sometimes paying a heavy price for permitting the often-desperate Harris to exploit him. In part Shaw sincerely wanted to assist Harris, who was helpless to help himself; and since Shaw had been forced by his excess of public visibility to restrict the character of his benevolence, he wanted to furnish assistance within the confines he permitted himself. He would not write prefaces which might enable authors to peddle bad books. He would not recommend bad business bargains to London publishers on the strength of his name. He would not provide outright charity, which he felt broke the spirit. But he indulged Harris within characteristically Shavian limits, permitting him to publish letters which had been composed as disguised articles or prefaces or afterwords, and when autograph G.B. Shaw letters began bringing substantial prices from collectors and Harris was even more down and out than usual, Shaw would carefully write a long, entertaining letter by hand rather than mail a typed letter that would bring less in the marketplace.

The gaps in correspondence, especially between 1908 and 1915, suggest that some letters are missing. Yet Harris obviously saved all or most of Shaw's letters and Shaw regularly filed his correspondence. Some letters may have been pilfered by secretaries or maids; some may yet be in private collections. It is clear, however, that these were years when the two had fallen out of sympathy and out of most contacts. Harris had moved from magazine to magazine, and Shaw had ceased furnishing him with copy as the journals became more gossip-ridden and scandalous, and Harris's financial speculations leaned more and more over the edge of the law.

After he had produced his Shakespeare play, *The Dark Lady of the Sonnets*, and Harris had accused Shaw of pilfering from his own play about the Bard, *Shakespeare and His Love*, Shaw reviewed the book in the *Nation* (24 December 1910), owning up to cribbing from everyone who had ever written on the subject, including Harris. But Harris's work was "impoverished by his determination not to crib from me. . . ." What was, to Shaw, most Harrisian was not the picture of Shakespeare as an Elizabethan Frank Harris but Harris's picture of himself as Shakespearean disciple. "This remarkable portrait has every merit except that of resemblance to any Frank Harris known to me or to financial and journalistic London. I say not a word against finance and the founding of weekly journals; but if a man chooses to devote to them what was meant for literature, let him not blame me for his neglected opportunities. The book . . . with a preface accusing me of having trodden a struggling saint into darkness so that I may batten on his achievements, might just as well have been published fifteen years ago. If they have been suppressed, it has been by Mr Harris's own preoccupation with pursuits which, however energetic and honorable, can hardly be described as wrestling with angels in the desert in the capacity of one of 'God's spies.'" Harris's non-literary activities (including amorous ones) had been sufficiently questionable to have provoked regular comment in the press, and Shaw did not need to detail them to his readers. "I have never disparaged his activities, knowing very little about them except that they seemed to me to be ultra-mundane; but I feel ill-used when a gentleman who has been warming both hands at the fire of life, and enjoying himself so vigorously that he has not had time to publish his plays and essays, suddenly seizes the occasion of a little *jeu d'esprit* of my own on the same subject . . . to hurl them, not into the market, but at my head. If he has been neglected, he has himself to thank." But Shaw was not finished. Dropping personalities, he concluded that if Harris wished "to keep in the middle of the stream of insult which constitutes fame for fine artists today" he had to furnish the public with "plenty of masterpieces to abuse," rather than a few desultory works "of the kind that our Philistine critics and advertisement managers do not understand even the need of reviewing. . . . "

Such sharp words, however witty and well-meant, could only drive Harris farther apart from Shaw, but Shaw was in no mood to condone the fruits of Harris's Edwardian years. It would only be when both Shaw and Harris, for widely different reasons, found themselves in the wartime wilderness in 1915, that there was a reason for a rapprochement. And it came when Shaw defended Harris's unpopular views in the *New Statesman*. The result would be a growing Harrisian dependence on a now-benevolent but cautious Shaw, and a burgeoning correspondence, which would only end with Harris's death in 1931.

The First World War left Harris a shipwreck. He barely escaped England ahead of his creditors and critics, the latter having multiplied because Harris, half out of bitterness with John Bull and half out of affection for the Germany he had known for several years as a student, had taken to observing publicly and often that England might be as war-guilty as Kaiserdom. In New York he struggled with yet another magazine, *Pearson's*, which he turned to socialism, sensationalism, and pro-Germanism, and which only survived because whenever *Pearson's* was forbidden entry into the U.S. mails it received a new wave of publicity and Harris pocketed a few more handouts from supporters. Although he could no longer find publishers for his books in the U.S. or abroad, he nevertheless wrote volume after volume of reminiscences of the great men he had known (or, in rare cases, read about), his *Contemporary Portraits*. They were not, Shaw told him in 1915, "like anybody else's attempts at the same kind of thing. They are really much more like what used to be called Characters than the sort of stuff we do nowadays. I doubt if any of our Savile Club scribes would venture to defend them." But, Shaw praised, "When you tackle a great man, you really do know the sort of animal you are dealing with. . . ." Among the less savory aspects of the "portraits" were not only Harris's pioneering emphases (for reasons less historical than commercial) on his subjects' sex lives, but his suggestions, few with any validity, that he had more than a little to do with the success of his subject. Contemplating his own inevitable biography, Shaw torpedoed that treatment in advance with a letter which included a hilarious spoof, "How I Discovered Frank Harris," where a penniless and starving Harris is discovered huddled on a bench on the Embankment and catapulted to fame by an insistent G.B.S. Then Shaw followed up Harris's portrait with a lengthy one of his own, "How Frank Ought to Have Done It," in which, in the third person, he parodied Harris's style. It was meant as fun, but Harris seized on the jocular letter, published it, and accepted the dollars it brought without embarrassment.

At the very last, Shaw had to rescue Harris, after some concern that he had confessed too much too explicitly to the old pirate, by permitting him to secure a large advance from an American publisher in order to concoct a G.B.S. biography largely out of Shaw's many autobiographical letters, texts of which Shaw censored and bowdlerized for publication, sometimes to Harris's great disappointment. But Harris made use of whatever he could, sometimes changing the first person to the third person and sometimes making no change at all. Yet even that turned out in the end to be not enough help to the failing Harris (who was beyond help) and his ghost writer Frank Scully. When Harris died in the south of France, in self-exile both from England and America, Shaw felt that he not only had to complete the book but rewrite it—in the pompous Harrisian style—to pay for Harris's obsequies and provide for the aging Nellie's uncertain future. Then he wrote a characteristically paradoxical postscript in his own name to give the book a further push.

It was a curiously appropriate end to a relationship that had been less than a friendship but undescribable by any other name. For a moment in time they had been valuable to each

other professionally. After that the two flamboyant self-pub-
licists were linked only by the conscious need of one for the
propping up of a faltering ego and a fading reputation, and the
unconscious desire of the other for basking in his hard-won
self-esteem and preening himself via his own memoir-writings
while helping a down-and-out colleague who had been unable
to cope with his too-quick success. Grasping at straws at the
end, the ill and increasingly desperate Harris even suggested,
since he had preserved most of his letters from Shaw (who had
earlier urged Harris to sell them while the market was right),
that all their correspondence be published, as was Shaw's with
Ellen Terry. Shaw was cool to the idea. "We have never had a
correspondence in that sense," he explained to Harris on a postcard: "my occasional attempts to persuade you that the world
is not yet populated exclusively by Frank Harrises would not
make a book even if they were fit for publication."

Piteously, Harris appealed, "Such a threat [to forbid quo-
tation] is worse than unfair. I have already months ago entered into a contract and received the money from the publisher for giving him my life of you and some of your own
letters. Now 6 months afterwards you forbid me to use a word.
Three months ago you wrote: 'I have written the information
you want in my own hand; sell it and have a spree with Nellie.'
And now you forbid and threaten me. . . . What am I to do? I
cannot rewrite the whole book. . . . Do be sensible. You talk
of Henderson's 600 pages as the only authorized biography.
There is hardly a gleam of Shaw in the whole tome. . . . If
you had put 'private' at the head of any letter I would have
regarded it as an order. . . . You say you have 5 to 10 thousand
£s a year—I have nothing. . . ."

Such a close to the affair, with Shaw teasing the hard-up
and ailing Harris with the prospect of making his book from
Shaw's letters, and then alternately withdrawing permission
to quote and restoring it; censoring the mildly objectionable—
and hardly Harrisian—parts after tantalizing the pathetic Harris with them at Harris's request; and finally (in an excess of
guilt or self-protectiveness, or both) rewriting the book as well
as seeing it through the press for Harris's widow, suggests an
unsatisfactory side of Shaw. Perhaps it is an unappetizing aspect of all of us reflected in much of the Shavian side of the
exchange. That he was toying with his old friend while making

efforts to help him suggests an element of unrecognized cruelty in the underside of benevolence. But this is for the reader to decide about these letters, which may be less a correspondence than a tragicomedy.

In the editing of the letters, a few typographical errors, where of no consequence, have been silently corrected. Idiosyncratic spellings and punctuation, including Shaw's personal way with contractions and his general refusal to italicize or otherwise set off titles, have been left as written.

The editor is grateful for the cooperation, in making manuscript letters available, of the George Arents Research Library, Syracuse University, the Humanities Research Center, University of Texas at Austin, the Library of Congress, the Morgan Library, the British Library, the Houghton Library of Harvard University, and the Pattee Library of The Pennsylvania State University. For lending their expertise he is also grateful to Dan H. Laurence, Charles W. Mann, Martin Quinn, Shirley Rader, and Suzanne Downs.

List of Abbreviations

The code used below is based upon that employed by Dan H. Laurence in the *Collected Letters of Bernard Shaw*. Where a source credited below has not yet been awarded a number in the Laurence edition I have indicated alternative symbols.

Collected Letters code

A   Holograph letter
C   Holograph postcard
E   "Compliments of Bernard Shaw" enclosure card
H   Typewritten letter
U   Photographic reproduction
X   Published text
YY Cablegram

1   Privately held or unlocated
2   British Library (British Museum)
4   T. E. Hanley Collection, Humanities Research Center, University of Texas at Austin
6   Houghton Library, Harvard University
10 Library of Congress
213 American Art Association, Anderson Galleries, Catalogue of Henderson Sale, 30 January 1930

Published letters and ms. sources not in Laurence, vols. I and II

CP   "How Frank Ought to Have Done It," appendix to Harris's *Contemporary Portraits* (New York, 1919)

FH Frank Harris's *Bernard Shaw* (London, 1931)

G-SH letter published in Sheila Hodges, *Gollancz. The Story of a Publishing House, 1928–1978* (London, 1978)

MB George W. Bishop, *My Betters* (London, 1957)

ML Morgan Library

NS *New Statesman*

PS The Pennsylvania State University, Pattee Library

SY George Arents Research Library, Syracuse University

TLS [London] *Times Literary Supplement*

The Playwright
and the Pirate

SHAW to HARRIS

Earlier letters than the first included here almost certainly existed. When, in 1895, Harris invited Shaw to write a weekly article for The Saturday Review, *Shaw apparently replied in "a letter somewhat after this fashion," Harris later wrote,*

> How the Dickens you knew that my thoughts had been turning to the theater of late and that I'd willingly occupy myself with it exclusively for some time to come, I can't imagine. But you've hit the clout, as the Elizabethans used to say, and, if you can afford to pay me regularly, I'm your man so long as the job suits me and I suit the job. What can you afford to give?

According to Harris his answer was "equally prompt and to the point":

> I can afford to give you so much a week, more, I believe, than you are now getting. If that appeals to you, start in at once; bring me your first article by next Wednesday and we'll have a final pow-wow.

No such exchange has turned up, but it is likely to have happened. Once G.B.S. began visiting the Saturday *office (each Wednesday) with each theatre article there were no occasions for letters. The magazine Harris created became a lively one, and with Shaw as drama critic, John Runciman as music critic, and H. G. Wells, Max Beerbohm and others of large later reputations writing for him, the years through 1898 were the high water of the editor's reputation. A predilection for libel suits and bad investments, however, forced Harris to look for ready cash, and his only asset was the* Saturday.

HARRIS to SHAW [A/2]

[Harris had pencilled a new address above the Palace Hotel, Monte Carlo letterhead.

Shaw had been reading Harris's draft of the book which became The Man Shakespeare. *The "pulpit" which Harris had given up was his proprietorship of the* Saturday Review. *Shaw had been his drama critic until 21 May 1898, when he resigned because an infected foot which required surgery had made it difficult for him to get around to theatres. Busy with politics, playwriting and marriage—he had wed Charlotte Payne-Townshend on 1 June—he was also grateful for the excuse to quit regular journalism.*

Valiant-for-Truth appears in John Bunyan's Pilgrim's Progress, *one of Shaw's favorite books.]*

Limehurst, Roehampton Vale, S.W.
30th November 1898

My dear Shaw,

Excuse this pencil-scrawl; but my nerves won't stand the stooping that pen-&-ink demand and I want to answer your incomparable letter without delay in order perhaps to get another from you before I start southwards (The Palace Hotel, Monte Carlo will be my winter address). Of course your correction of my stuff was right. It was Enobarbus (the nearest Shakespeare ever came to a Greek chorus by the way) & not Caesar who called Antony "Sworder," the emendation, however, strengthening my argument which is all I care for. Facts are to me the dust of things to be laid with the watering-machine of any tolerable theory.

Your reminder that Valiant-for-Truth was a real fighting man is more valuable still: the passage *was*, too, one of my favourites but it was pushed out of my memory-sieve probably by some Shakespeare verses not half so good. I shall incorporate the passage in my book & so you'll again reap the gratitude of my readers. By the bye I intend to incorporate in the Book all your criticism (given to me in a previous letter) of "Othello" & of "Measure for Measure"; have I your permission to so decorate & adorn my drab garment? Silence, Sir, on your part will be construed to mean permission.

You ask me why I gave up the pulpit? First, because they (the True-blue Conservatives) offered me more for that antique objet d'art than it was worth. Secondly, because I *needed* the money. Thirdly, because I wanted nerve-rest. Fourthly, because following your example I want to try my hand at books & plays & stuff more enduring than articles. Have I given you reasons enough?

The longing for sunshine I feel in me gives me a sort of unspoken promise of unswerved health; I'm off.

Why don't you feed up that foot of yours? Your ascetic combat with a thousand generations of flesh-eating beer-ale & wine bibbing ancestors may be amusing (to others) but it's distinctly trying to you & your friends & lovers of whom I profess myself one [and who] beg you to relinquish the struggle at once. You have done enough to show your courage & obstinacy. Now return to conventions & common sense for a season at least, if for nothing else [than] to get up your strength. I could talk more solemnly to you but not more sympathetically.

Ever Yours

Frank Harris

P.S. I cannot tell you how much your praise meant to me: it refreshes like rare wine. Yours, Fr. Harris

SHAW to HARRIS [H/6]

[Shaw had gone to see Harris's play Mr and Mrs Daventry, *based upon a scenario which Harris had purchased from Wilde in the days of Oscar's adversity. Max Beerbohm had succeeded Shaw as* Saturday Review *drama critic. Shaw's first play had been* Widowers' Houses *(1892). "Mrs Pat" is actress Mrs. Patrick Campbell, who played Mrs. Daventry.]*

Piccard's Cottage, Guildford

4th November 1900

Dear Harris

The moment the Borough Council Election was over, I went to the Royalty. The play is good, and successful (which is not always the same thing) in exact proportion as it is Frank Harris. Before the curtain went up George Moore informed me that I should see at a glance that the whole play was by Oscar Wilde. What I did see was that this was George's honest opinion, because you have undoubtedly amused yourself by writing some imaginary conversations on Wilde's lines; and George, who has no sense of humor, cannot see the underlying difference. Here I think you should not encourage yourself, because it is not natural to you to play with an idea in Wilde's way, and make people laugh by showing *its* absurdity: your notion of gambolling is to unexpectedly fix your teeth in the calf of some sinner and hold on. And you cannot help yourself out by observation in this instance, because English society is not in the least witty, and always runs curiously to see a wit like Wilde's exactly as it sits down eagerly to *look at* a man playing the piano. The fact is, life does not *amuse* you as it amuses the humorist. You perceive its ironies with a mordant sensation about the corners of your mouth that may feel like laughter; but when your teeth snap, they close, not on the irony, not even on the unfortunate mortal who is the subject of it, but on the spectator whom you are getting at. Please observe that this is a perfectly legitimate comedic operation when it is done in your own manner. But when it is done by one of the impossible drawingroom epigrammatists of the Wilde theatre, one feels at once that the fun is not real fun—it hurts; and that the epigrammarian ladies are figments. Wilde was careful to provide an ideal husband to keep them in countenance; the whole force of your play comes from the reality of the husband. This is what sets Max Beerbohm trying to express his feeling by the bull in the china shop. The prattling ladies are very like china shepherdesses trying to play up to a real shepherd. I speak feelingly on this point because we all make the same mistake at first; the more connoisseurship we start with, the more certain we are to begin with a mixture of genres—of those which have struck our fancy with that which is our original own. In the first version of my first play I introduced a lot of funny trifling of the Robertson-to-Pinero comic relief kind. The effect was perfectly frightful—like patching a suit of armor with a cheap chintz. Now Wilde's manner is immeasurably nearer akin to the new manner than the old comic relief was: consequently your drawingroom conversations produce no such disastrously hideous effect as my japes did; and you have saved the situation further by pure style; but still the incongruity is there, and it will come through and shew on the surface in a few years time, through the difference in wear between the two genres.

Fortunately for you, the play is a real beginning. You have hardly dug a foot into the vein as yet. The husband's suicide is all my eye. What you must do now is to begin a sequel to the play as follows:—

The shot does not kill Daventry (I have known a man recover and live for a long time after shooting himself straight between the eyes and lodging the bullet in the back of his skull). He sends a hurried note to the pair apologizing for the failure and warning them not to marry until he has divorced the lady, as he has, on reflection, become too curious to see how their marriage will turn out to reshoot himself more efficiently. His point is, that the lady's claim, carefully examined, is only a claim to a fool's paradise, and that her charge against him is simply that he has confronted her with a view of life which prevailed over her's, in spite of her prejudice against it, because the facts supported it and contradicted hers. Her feeling that the millionaire has restored her ideals means that she has met a young fool like herself, with money enough to make love's young dream seem for a moment like a real paradise even in such a sink as Monte Carlo. Therefore, says Daventry, I am going to wait until you are forty and see how a woman of your sort comes out when her imaginative illusions are gone. Already I have shattered—with my pistol—your fundamental illusion that the vileness of the world is only the vileness of my view of it. Further, I have shattered your notion that I am a mere animal because I am intelligent enough to keep the animal in me separate from the rudimentary poet and philosopher, and that you have attained a higher place than I because you scrupulously confuse your consciousness of the impulses which led you to hunt down and capture your millionaire. As you admit, I am a better man than you thought. It seems a simple thing to say *now*; but when you are my present age you will perceive that this is no mere sentimental-magnanimous admission, but a sinking away of the entire moral continent from under your feet into the depths of the sea, leaving you buffeting the waves for a moral foothold. Your millionaire has shewn himself so far the perfect dupe of the morality which can only justify itself by my proving a villain because I have kissed a coarser woman than my wife. The hole in my head goes straight through that morality; and whenever you return to it I shall point to the scar as the saints in the pictures point to their stigmata. And so on.

On this basis you get your drama, ending either in redivorce and remarriage (which would be *my* ending) or a *ménage à trois* like the Nelson-Hamilton one, but on a fleshless basis. Moral: the one woman who should be sacred to a man is his wife. That is the true reductio ad absurdum of marriage.

If you go and sit out the play again you will find that the husband is the interesting person in it, and that it is strong whilst he is on a positive basis and weak whilst he is on an apologetic basis. As a rascal redeemed by an act of self-sacrifice he is not worth halfprice at nine o'clock. As a moralist claiming a real basis for morals, he is worth all the money and more. It is his instructive clutches at the positive position that give the play its drive. It is the lapses from this that land it among epigrams and duels and reverence for the pretty lady's ideals and the like anachronisms. Only make good your footing on the new moral ground and you will spout enthralling plays as profusely as Calderon for the next twenty years. You have swallowed more life than a thousand ordinary playwrights: what you want is a new philosophic digestion that will make bone and muscle of the realities which the old drama excreted, and excrete the sentimentalities which the old drama assimilated. This could be more briefly expressed, but not more elegantly.

I have seen you twice since I collapsed in '98. The first time you were in such a transport of laughter, apparently at some anecdote you were telling to the man with you, that I had not the heart to interrupt the conversation. The second time you were in a hansom. I send this to the Royalty, not knowing your address. Somebody told me you had left Roehampton for Kingston.

yours ever
G. Bernard Shaw

P.S. An observation which I have not been able to work in above is that adultery is the worst of themes for shewing an author's range; and your range is what is more astonishing to people accustomed to the dramatists of commerce.

Also that your supremacy over all Macbeth commentators

does not justify you in making Mrs Daventry express herself in the style of Duncan. I think I heard Mrs Pat say something about "measureless content."

HARRIS to SHAW [H/2]

Melbury Lodge, Kingston Hill, Surrey
27th November 1900

My dear Shaw,

Thanks for your excellent letter.

All you say about the difference between Wilde's beautiful kindly humour and my sardonic bitterness is absolutely true— or at least seems so to me. You think I imitated him in the first act, and perhaps I did—at any rate it is certain that the first act is the weakest of the lot. The second act I think is spoiled by bad stage management; but then all we novices have to suffer at the hands of the actor or actress who knows that a part is greater than the whole.

You think the shooting of Daventry all wrong; you dismiss it as contemptuously as Archer does. Well, here is my idea of it.

The decay of Christianity and the belief in a future life has had for chief consequences 1st the demand on the part of the people for a better life on this earth—socialism—and 2nd the demand by the other oppressed class, woman, for a larger satisfaction of her instincts in this world. This new woman wants nothing but love, whatever form she may individually affect, affection or passion. I have taken her to demand affection in this case. But this new woman has been done before. Quite true; and it remains to be seen whether Mrs Daventry is 5% better or 5% worse than the new woman that other dramatists in our time have created. But I am the first to put opposite this new woman the old conventional view of sexual morality which is the husband's view and which I have here incorporated in the husband Mr Daventry.

Now I have been more than fair to this old convention. So far from making him brutal I have allowed him to repent on the stage, promise reformation &c. in order to win your sympathies. Now how should he end? I maintain the old convention dies of its own falseness, kills itself, in fact, and that is what

Daventry does. If you tell me that the individual man of this sort, Daventry, would not kill himself, I say you are mistaken. He is a man of forty who has had all the best of life. Almost for the first time he has failed. He has got himself into an impasse. It is your disappointed realist who does blow out his brains—not your idealist whose soul is wide enough to have sympathy for others.

But there I could discuss the matter for ever. The truth is that naked intelligence is no good in judging a work of art. A verdict of the public is—I mean the best public; and the opinion of the half dozen who do count—is that Mrs Daventry is a creation and Daventry about as good.

I am glad to be able to tell you that this view of the matter is borne out by the box office.

I am measureably content—which is not an imitation of Duncan.

Yours sincerely,
Frank Harris

P.S. I cannot tell you the pleasure it has given me to see your fist again. I only wish we could foregather. If I had seen you as you saw me, in a hansom or in a café, I would have come up and spoken; but I am blind, or at least very short-sighted.

I hardly venture to show myself a critic to so good a critic; but why do you not give us another Candida—a piece I think worthy of Goldsmith (a fact which shows how little use intellect is in creative work).

SHAW to HARRIS [A/4]

[Shaw's play receiving its first performance was Captain Brassbound's Conversion. *Harris had just published* Montes the Matador and Other Stories, *in which "Sonia" was based on the assassination of the Czar by a bomb thrown by revolutionaries. "Sonia" is Sophia Perovskaia, one of those hanged for the deed, who in a last letter to the narrator writes, "Do you remember once saying to me that ideas were better than deeds, that deeds had always some of the dirt of the world on them? How true that is! . . . but the thing had to be done and that must be enough for me." Henry Blanchamp had been managing editor of Harris's*

Saturday Review. *The Irish politician and writer Justin Mc-Carthy was then seventy but would turn out journalism for twelve more years.*

Hooleyisms *may be explained in the note to Shaw's letter of 27 September 1918.]*

10, Adelphi Terrace, W.C.
16th Dec., 1900

My dear Harris

I am for the moment a done-up man: I must fly to the country for Xmas and rest. They are doing a play of mine tonight at the Stage Society; and the rehearsing (a month's work compressed into one wild week) has demoralized and destroyed me—that and unlimited Borough Council and Fabian Society together. So we must either put off the lunch, or you must take it at Piccard's Cottage, St. Catherines, Guildford.

Thank you for the autographed copy of Montes. When I wrote last I had only read half of it: otherwise I should of course have been full of Sonia, which is a very fine shot at a star, and a bullseye at that. In Sonia and Mrs. Daventry you are shewing the top end of your range. Why you want to plunge back into the journalistic mudbath again, Lord knows! You are the most extraordinary chap, with your genius and your shiny hats and Cafe Royal lunches and Hooleyisms and all sorts of incongruities! And now you want to give your struggling soul a final good chance of damnation by "coming into a Paper," with sixteen pages by Blanchamp, one by me, no advertisements, and a note by you every two months or so. All pure waste of time: even parliament would be better. We're too old for it: journalism is not for men over forty, unless they are Justin McCarthys. What you have to do now is to make your will, so to speak, in a series of dramas, tales or what you will.

Piccard's Cottage is attainable by the main Portsmouth Road south from Guildford. A short mile from the town is St. Catherine's post office. Turn to the right round the corner of that post office; go up the hill; and the last cottage on the right at the top is Piccard's. My wife, who turned up her nose at Montes, and said it was only a superior style of penny dreadful, capitulated before Sonia and is curious to see what sort of monster you may be.

As ever
G. Bernard Shaw

SHAW to HARRIS [C/PS]

[While Shaw was busy capturing the Edwardian stage, Harris went through a succession of magazine proprietorships. The Candid Friend *appeared on May 1, 1901, with society photographs, gossip, political and theatrical articles—and advertising. Shaw even contributed an article, "All About Myself," to an early issue. When even practical advice to ladies on coiffures and costume, competitions and prizes, failed to pick up circulation, Harris added exposé articles. After Countess Cowley sued for libel when Harris claimed in print that she demonstrated "contemptible snobbery" by retaining her title after her divorce and remarriage,* The Candid Friend *went under, although the court awarded her only £100. The last issue was August 9, 1902.*

Harris, as Shaw had suggested, turned to playwriting. Shakespeare and His Wife *(later* Shakespeare and His Love*) secured him an option from Beerbohm Tree for £500, but the play was never produced, and was only published in 1910.* Black China *would have the hero a thief, a role Tree refused to play. It was neither published nor produced. Eventually there would be* The Bucket Shop, *given a Stage Society production at the Aldwych in 1914, and* Joan la Romée, *privately printed in Nice in 1926, but Harris's career as playwright was, after* Mr and Mrs Daventry, *as futile as Shaw's was successful.*

Turning again to magazines, Harris began an Automobile Review *which never published an issue. What resulted, however, was* Motorist and Traveller, *which he began editing in 1905 with backing from the Dunlop Tyre Company. The blend of gossip and travelogue, however, failed to hold together. When the venture ended in 1906, with it ended Harris's £500 annual salary. Quickly he turned to other friends, and made £400 editing and peddling to Macmillan Winston Churchill's biography of his father. By then Shaw had ceased hectoring Harris, since the attempts were useless.]*

The Old House, Harmer Green, Welwyn
22 December 1904

I have no doubt the first two numbers of the Automobile Review, which you will really edit & write, will become classics in motor journalism. The next ten will be edited by your chauffeur, and will perhaps be readable, as he will see you pretty frequently. The last three will not be edited at all.

Cant you let the Stage Society have the Shakespear play, or the carpenter one? I shall not encourage you to journalize any more. Give it up; and give up finance. Literature is your business. To the deuce with your Automobile Reviews & Candid Friends & the like! Waste of *your* time—not that you will give them much of it.

G.B.S.

SHAW to HARRIS [H/4]

[Despite editorial failures and frustrations, Harris persisted. With promises of borrowed money—none of it from Bernard Shaw—he attempted to get back into magazine or newspaper publishing through the purchase of an existing organ. Among others, the proprietors of The Times *declined the offers, but Harris did land the struggling* Vanity Fair, *producing his first issue early in 1907. To keep it from toppling into bankruptcy he even regally revisited the United States, in search of funds and of copy. Only the latter materialized, and he published his accounts of the Far West in his own journal, later turning them into his purported memoirs of cowboy days,* On the Trail. *Chicago also provided the material for his novel about the 1886 Haymarket Riot,* The Bomb. *Meanwhile Harris cultivated lawsuits—on behalf of his shaky investments and alleged libels, piracies and persecutions. A number of them added to his notoriety as blackmailer; some cost him money he did not have. The* Bomb, *which he wrote in two months of furious activity, was designed to recoup his fortunes. Seeking praise, he sent an advance copy to Shaw.*

John Altgeld had been governor of Illinois at the time of the Haymarket trials; Mrs. Lucy Parsons was the widow of one of the alleged Haymarket anarchists—a labor organizer—executed for the crime.]

10 Adelphi Terrace, W.C.
7th October 1908

My dear Harris,

I have just found your letter here on my return to London. I am confronted by such a monstrous heap of arrears of work, both professional and friendly, that I know perfectly well that if you send me a manuscript, it will lie on my hands and on my conscience for two years if I am really to give my mind to it and read it with the horrible responsibility of having to give an opinion for serious business use afterwards. So be warned; and dont press me with it, though if I saw it advertized as actually published I should certainly order it and read it at once.

I have forgotten the details of the Chicago business of 1886. At the time I was so much interested in it that I tried to get signatures to a petition for the reprieve of the men. Outside the Socialist League and other circles in which it was signed as a matter of course, the only name I got was that of Oscar Wilde. It was really a very handsome thing of him to do, because all the associations of the thing were vulgar and squalid, and Oscar, as you know, was a snob to the marrow of his bones, having been brought up in Merrion Square, Dublin. I do not know whether you saw anything of Mrs Parsons when she came to this country to exploit our sympathy with the men who were executed: if not, your book may lack an element of comedy which she was eminently qualified to supply. If I recollect aright, Governor Altgeld some years afterwards published a book which I did not read, but which was reviewed in the Socialist press as a vindication of the hanged anarchists and a blighting exposure of their prosecutors.

By the way, on looking at your letter again to see whether I have left anything unanswered, I see that you have actually sent me the book. Heaven only knows where it is: I have not yet got through half of the sackful that was waiting for me. When I reach it, I will communicate further.

Yours ever,

G. Bernard Shaw.

P.S. I have routed out the book, and find myself unable to part with it until I have read it.

HARRIS to SHAW [H/4]

Vanity Fair
33, Strand, W.C.
26th October, 1908

My Dear Shaw,

A fortnight ago you wrote me saying that you would read my book, "The Bomb" and tell me what you thought of it; but you have not written, and now the book is on the eve of publication. It will be published this week. I wanted you to write a review of it which I should be very proud to publish in "Vanity Fair" if no better medium suggested itself.

"The Bomb" is a sort of confession of faith, the first reasoned defence of anarchy I have seen in print. Read it, my dear Shaw, and tell me what you think of it, even if you will not consent to review it over your own name.

Yours sincerely,
Frank Harris

SHAW to THE EDITOR,
THE NEW STATESMAN [X/NS]

[It took the war to initiate the interchange which would continue unabated until Harris's death. The beginning was not a letter from one to the other but Shaw's spirited defense of his old friend's war stance—which Shaw used to indirectly defend his own embattled position resulting from his iconoclastic supplement to The New Statesman *the previous November, "Common Sense About the War." Harris, who had re-emigrated to the United States shortly after the war began, had contributed a number of articles on the war to the* New York Sun *which were then revised and issued as a book,* England or Germany? *On June 19, 1915, although the book bore the imprint of a New York publisher, it was reviewed in* The New Statesman, *where both Harris and the book were condemned. Since Harris was considered an Englishman in America, the review declared,*

his "decidedly mischievous" anti-British writings were widely quoted. As a contribution to controversy the book was derided, but "as an event or symptom it has, by reason of the author's personality and career, a certain international significance." Harris's career was then recounted, including the seamy side. Between literary enterprises, the reviewer wrote, "Harris would appear in the courts in connection with cases of a curious shadiness; and about a year ago he closed his career in England with a short spell in a London prison." (His comments in Modern Society *on a divorce case had resulted in a judgment of contempt of court, and bankruptcy had followed while he was in prison and young Enid Bagnold was editing the magazine for him. Trying to fill the pages with pieces by writers of some standing, to help save the magazine, she appealed to Shaw, among others. Shaw had refused.)*

"It is extraordinary, we may agree," the review went on, "that a man like Frank Harris should be able in any circumstances to attain a position which invests with importance the things he does and says; but so it happens in this world of incalculable chance." Harris, it concluded, "a fugitive from England, is an advocate of German civilisation and German sins. There is, to be sure, nothing original in his articles or his book, except the impassioned denunciation of English law and the English prisons—product of a painful personal experience."

Shaw reacted in a letter to the editor of The New Statesman, *published in the issue of June 19, 1915. It would take more than a month before a copy would reach Harris across the Atlantic.]*

The Adventures of Frank Harris

To the Editor of THE NEW STATESMAN.

Sir,—Your article on Frank Harris gives me an excuse for a comment on his book and on himself which may perhaps supply a needed touch or two to the portrait of the man. I have just read the book, and am struck by its intense British feeling. It is a consistent and indignant attack on England, a plea for Germany, and an express repudiation of the author's connection with England (Frank declares himself a naturalized Member of the United States Bar); and yet it all through expresses a wounded concern for England, and a high, if bitterly disappointed ideal of England, which, unreasonable as it may seem in its application to the war, makes it more bearable to seriously proud Englishmen than most of the professedly patriotic explosions with which so many of us are now relieving our feelings at the expense of making our country ridiculous, besides informing the enemy loudly of his mistakes, a service which, one would think, we might offer first to our own side.

The book must be read with due discrimination. For instance, the chapters which deal with the author's personal misadventures in our courts must obviously be taken goodhumoredly as the petulances of a sensitive man who never could be got to understand that illiterate Philistines have rights as against men of genius. When Frank Harris really edited a paper, he edited it very well, as the files of the *Fortnightly* and the *Saturday* shew. But when, pre-occupied by more fascinating activities, he left the office boy to edit it, the results were disastrous. The office boy, plunging recklessly into finance, would express an opinion that such and such a bank was a rotten concern, not knowing how easily a bank and its customers can be ruined by a run provoked by the idlest rumor. Or the boy tried his hand at smart society gossip, and playfully attributed conduct to highly placed and blameless persons which, if true, would have made them socially and politically impossible for life. Harris was always ready to apologize for these "accidents," as he calls them in his book, in a tone which showed how trifling he thought them; and he could not understand why, in spite of this simple settlement between one gentleman and another, he should be cast in heavy damages, with the judges sternly approving instead of protesting, and even finally thrown into jail for a perfectly natural (to him) contempt of court. But the perfect candor with which he states these grievances, and the obvious sincerity of his expectation that everyone will agree with him in his disgust at the insensibility of the judges to his point of view, and at the general uselessness and oppressiveness of the laws of England for the purposes of men of genius, must disarm every reader with any kindliness of humor, and cannot mislead even the stupidest.

Harris's history as an editor, as far as I know it, is that after the *Fortnightly* and the *Saturday* episodes, he was in demand in that capacity. He founded the *Candid Friend*, and edited quite two numbers of it, after which it was looked after for him by a clever lady (since deceased) of high social position, whose stock of photographs of royal and noble personages, and reminiscences of their circles, prolonged the agony of the paper's inevitable dissolution for many months. After the *Candid Friend* I did not take in the papers that were "edited by Frank Harris," because I knew Frank's style, and the office boy could not take me in even when, greatly daring, he actually signed his articles with Frank's name. I do not deny Frank's responsibility nor defend his neglect. I give him away (guessing the truth rather than knowing it) because his real failings, though inexcusable, are much more amiable than the ostensible ones which so shocked our judges.

Finally let me say that there is not the slightest inconsistency between Harris's attacks on Germany when all the world feared her, and his defence of her now that she is fighting for her life at desperate odds, with no reasonable chance of escape from the mighty enemies that beset her on every side except in a resistance so desperate that it may pay her enemies better to come to some sort of terms with her than to do their worst. The under dog in a fight has always had Harris's sympathy: he is a martyr to pity. It may seem strange to those whose sympathies are purely sensational that the sanguinary melodrama of Belgium should move him less than the tragedy of Germany, which has not yet reached its final act. But the horrors of war, whether they culminate in Belgium or in Galician Jewry, are mere horrors and nothing else. The true tragic theme of the war is the issue between England and Germany. And it is entirely characteristic of Harris that, having hated the official Prussian spirit, when it threatened the world, he should remember only the virtues of the Germans when the Prussian spirit has led them to the verge of the abyss. No doubt he rather forgets our own virtues; but so many writers are busy reminding us of them that the omission is hardly likely to prove serious. At all events, as one of Harris's old *Saturday* staff, I do not like to leave his reputation precisely where your article left it, though I quite admit that the article serves Frank right, and by no means presses its view of him as far as it might be pressed by a writer disposed to make the worst of it.
—Yours, etc.,

G. Bernard Shaw.

HARRIS to SHAW [H/4]

St. Regis Hotel, New York
August 25, 1915

My dear Bernard Shaw:

I don't thank you for your chivalrous defence of me in "The New Statesman": thanks are not needed between us; but the mere mention of your name always calls alive in me the old kindliness towards you, the current in a spate of memories.

This book "Contemporary Portraits" that I send you will show you that I have been working and I think you will say to some effect, for although the critics don't know it, these seem to me about the best portraits of living men ever done.

I know that whatever insight I may have I have spared no labour in getting the souls of my subjects on paper. I should like to know what you think about them, very very much. You have never written about my work, a criticism I mean of it. Why not try your hand at these? It would be very helpful to me because I find that I am almost unknown in America and not likely to be appreciated unless helped by authority. You talk about my talents as an "editor" being in demand; they have never been in demand yet: I have never been able to get decently remunerative work unless I found it for myself and in America I find it almost impossible to discover.

One thing I want to say to you: I wrote a screed about you in the "Smart Set," accepting their assurance that they wouldn't alter a word, and they gave it the silly title and the almost insulting flip at the end in spite of their promise. I had ended it by saying that you had continued to write for me for some months at very great pecuniary loss to yourself, a thing I thought very generous in you at the time and worth recording. These cursed journalists won't even let us pay our debts generously.

I remain in all good fellowship and friendship,

Yours sincerely,
Frank Harris

P.S.—By the bye, when you have read this book perhaps you would let John Harris have it to read. You know the man

I mean—John F. Harris, Camden Place, Stafford, England. I would send him a copy but I have not got any by me.

Remember me to yr wife and believe me Sincerely
Frank Harris

SHAW to HARRIS [H/4]

[Harris's newest book, Contemporary Portraits, *included a life of Wilde in which he laid claim to greater intimacy with Oscar than could possibly have been the case in life. He was writing prolifically, hoping to seize upon a subject which would capture the public's attention. It was Shaw who first suggested an autobiography, which would become the scandalous* My Life and Loves. *Harold Hodge was Harris's successor as editor of* The Saturday Review *(1898–1913), inheriting many of Harris's debts. George Moore's version of the life of Jesus was his novel* The Brook Kerith. A Syrian Story *(Edinburgh, 1916).]*

10 Adelphi Terrace, London, W.C.
11th November 1915

My dear Frank Harris

Your book reached me some time in September, when I was in Torquay. I have a friend there, Carlos Blacker, who was a friend of Oscar Wilde's: and he pounced on the book at once. As others followed his example, and as anything I dont do at once is generally either not done at all or horribly delayed, John Harris has had to wait until this month for the book.

Has it been published in England yet? I have seen one review of it, and a few patriotic imbecilities about it: but I forgot to note whether the review referred to an English edition or to the one you sent me. The allusions remind me very much of the conventional allusions to Rousseau. You disconcert the conventional reviewer very much as Jean Jacques disconcerted the whole of Europe. It is a sort of criticism that began, ironically, with Hamlet. The world most potently and powerfully believes, but holds it not honesty to have it so set down.

But there are two things worth saying about these Contemporary Portraits. First, when you tackle a great man, you really do know the sort of animal you are dealing with, which I suppose establishes your claim (if you make it) to be one of the species yourself. Second, they are not like anybody else's attempts at the same kind of thing. They are really much more like what used to be called Characters than the sort of stuff we do nowadays. I doubt if any of our Savile Club scribes would venture to defend them. Neither would they venture to defend the Memoirs of St Simon. Which means that you can draw the bow of Ulysses, and they can not.

In your letter you allude to an article in The Smart Set. I didnt see it; but I know too well the incredible things they still do in America to accept anything that is put forward even over an individual signature except on overwhelming evidence of style, sentence for sentence. It was perhaps, however, as well that they smudged out your generous reference to my pecuniary loss. The truth is, I didn't lose anything in the long run. When the paper changed hands, I came upon the scene as a creditor, but not a pressing one, as Harold Hodge conveyed to me that if I could possibly hold on for a time it would make matters easier for him and for everybody else; so I said there was no hurry, and took no further steps until a longish time after—it may have been a couple of years then—I saw that the paper had passed into the hands of a gentleman who was quite well able to pay his way. I then wrote to Hodge and asked him whether I could put in my claim without affecting him in any way. He said I could; and it was then paid. So you may write that off your conscience. The delay never really cost me the slightest inconvenience. From 1894, when I ceased to live from hand to mouth and began to draw money from the theatre, I always had more money at the bank than I wanted; consequently the debt, which was no great matter after all, never reached me: my banker has so much the less to play with: that was all. In 1898, my play The Devil's Disciple made quite a lucrative success in America. Also in that year I got married to a lady who was considerably more than self-supporting. So you see there really was no pecuniary loss at all, nor even the most momentary inconvenience.

It seems to be my destiny to dog your footsteps with apparent plagiarisms. The Shakespear effort was bad enough: but you now tell me that you are doing the life of Jesus. I am doing exactly the same thing by way of preface to Androcles and the Lion, which is a Christian martyr play: so you must hurry up.

They tell me that what I have gathered from the gospel narratives and the rest of the New Testament, which I have read through attentively for the first time since, as a boy, I read the whole Bible through out of sheer bravado, is much the same as Renan's extract. I do not know whether this is true; for I have never read the Vie de Jesus, though I will look it up presently. Anyhow, it is rather significant that you and I and George Moore should be on the same tack. The main thing that I have tried to bring out, and indeed the only thing that made the job worth doing for me, is that modern sociology and biology are steadily bearing Jesus out in his peculiar economics and theology.

Your most interesting book will be your autobiography. People often ask me to tell them about Frank Harris: who he was, where he came from, was he an American, was he a German Jew, was he a Welshman, was he an Irishman, was he an Englishman; and I have to confess that though I am as interested as they are I have not the remotest idea of what the answers to all these questions may be, and that when I first met you you were an accomplished, unaccountable, and amazing fact, totally obscuring your past by the intensity of your present and the awestruck speculations suggested by your future.

I am called away, and must break off suddenly.

Yours ever

G. Bernard Shaw.

HARRIS to SHAW [H/4]

[Harris had found a job with the Chesapeake and Ohio Railroad, which would be short-lived. His militant pro-Germanism and inability to work with others made him impossible as a subordinate. The biographical details he furnished Shaw were largely correct, although his two years as a cowboy was mostly fiction. He had some experience of the frontier in his teens, but learned about cows from being in the meat trade in Kansas with his brother before he went to college. Henry Mayers Hyndman was the founder of the Social Democratic Federation and an important figure in Socialism when Harris was a young newspaperman.

The James Stephens referred to was an Irish nationalist in-volved with the militant Irish Republican Brotherhood. Arrested in Dublin in 1865, he escaped to New York.]

3 Washington Square, New York City
December 4, 1915

My dear Shaw:

Your gorgeous characteristic letter about my *"Contemporary Portraits"* reached me in due course—a rare draught of the wine that's meant for souls. Before I speak of it, I want to remind you that you never acknowledged my best book of short stories, *"Unpath'd Waters,"* which I sent you and that I've re-ceived nothing of yours for years. Now and again I go to the theatre; it reminds me of encaustic work as compared with painting and the personalities of the actors perpetually deform-ing the conception of the artist, drive me crazy. But I have seen *Fanny's First Play* and *Pygmalion* and now *Androcles and the Lion* and enjoyed them all immensely: the humour is of the intellect, the sort that engages and pleases me most intimately. What a gift it is! And what a master of it you are! I have only the sardonic sort and that only by sparks out of the clash of characters—a poor endowment.

I have just finished my book: *"Oscar Wilde: his Life and Confessions"* in 2 vols: it's the best thing I've done yet: there are pages in it I can reread with pleasure, which does not often happen to me. I'll send you a copy early in the new year, I hope.

What you say about your work on Jesus interests me of course prodigiously: with one glance you have seen as far as can be seen with one glance and doubtless it is the most profitable glance which has shown you the depth and sureness of His vision. As I have said again and again in these last ten years: not one jot or one tittle of his word shall ever pass away. To me the deepest & sincerest soul that has left any portrait of himself in recorded time. When I think of his age, and dis-abilities, and shining certitude, I doubt whether my love is this side idolatry: but I wish I could divine his—But one of these days you will see what these fifteen years of study of him has brought me: I think I can show you how his soul grew and that is to raise him from the dead.

Meanwhile I am the Advertising Manager of an American Railway. I cannot beg and the office-boys who direct American papers and magazines don't know Joseph and won't have anything to do with me because their paymasters have put it about that I am a pro-German as I was once a pro-Boer! And this public is just as purblind and snobbish and truffle-nosed as the Cockney born within hearing of Bow Bells. The two great combative peoples, both of German stock, both with the same false ideals of courage and chastity, may fight to an issue for all I care: I only wish France and Ireland and Russia and Italy were safe out of the *melee*.

You are reported as having said recently that the war must go on till the German is awakened out of his dream: my dear Shaw, you know as well as I do that we are never beaten or driven out of our dreams: that is the real portion of our lives which can never be taken away from us. But probably you have been misreported: if so, forgive me.

You ask me whether I am a Jew or an Irishman, and Englishman or an American? I had thought you knew. I was born in Galway of pure or impure Welsh parents: my father and mother Welsh as far back as I can trace them—pure Pembrokeshire Kelts. My father was in the British Navy and brought it to a Commander's rank, I believe—About eleven I got into sympathy with the Catholic Irish, strangely enough while at the Royal School at Armagh, and even at that age was a violent Fenian sympathizer and pored over proclamations offering money for the betrayal of James Stephens, the Head-Centre (the words thrilling me!) and cursed the English and Black Protestants (of whom I was one) with "the curse of Crummle!"

My father sent me at 12 to Ruabon Grammar School in North Wales (co-religionists of his having sons there!) and there I stayed three years learning a little Vergil and Greek accidence, some Algebra and conic sections and much more Walter Scott, telling stories the while at night, getting into hot water with the masters for continual talking and learning to despise my English schoolfellows as much as I had liked my Irish ones. At fifteen (thanks to Fenimore Cooper and Mayne Reid) I bolted to America instead of South Africa tho' I long weighed the two in romantic balance. There I learned life: hotel-clerk and brakesman on a railway: cowboy for two gorgeous years: the second summer I took down with me Carlyle's *"Heroes and Hero Worship"* and Mill's *"Political Economy."* At eighteen, violent, shrewd, inordinately conceited, argumentative, thought-loving,

I met my good genius: a professor of Greek at Kansas University, one Byron C. Smith, who seemed to me to know everything—a genius, one of the Shining Band! I think now a charming nature and really good scholar. He set me to work: I studied under him two years, working like a fiend; he fired my ambition already inordinate, by his praises, and when he went away to die untimely in consumption, kissed me declaring that I must go to Germany as he had gone and to Athens where he had studied, and ultimately do the great work he had longed to do—a consecration. Have I made good? Not yet altogether perhaps; but life still beckons mysterious and beautiful as when I was sixteen. I was admitted to the Bar at Lawrence, Kansas, '76, became an American citizen and practiced law for nearly a year. In the meantime, Smith had gone to Philadelphia for his health: one day I read some Emerson: gave up my practice incontinently and went off to Philadelphia to consult with Smith. The end of it was spent round the world: then to Paris and spent all my money: back to Brighton College to earn some more: going to London on Sundays to meet Carlyle; and then back to Germany and Italy and Greece and Russia for five years more of poverty and study and occasional feasts when some article was accepted.

In London at 28; got hold of *Evening News* as Editor: made a success: went to Rome for a winter: got *Fortnightly Review*: six years later bought the *Saturday Review* with borrowed money: the rest you know—There, is a complete and most veracious skeleton for you that tells you nothing of my being in Cape Town or Sydney or Buenos Ayres or of the impressions this wonderful world had made upon me. Had I only been wise and gone, as I fully intended to go, from *The Saturday Review* with £20,000 in my pocket to the centre of China and stayed there studying for five years, I might have realized all my youthful dreams, which were to know more and see further than any other man and yet keep perfect balance of soul in spite of imperious wilful temper. Well, if I win here and make a little money, I intend yet to have a shot at it and see if China can teach me anything I don't know. *But?* I have my Gospel according to St. Thomas to write, and five or six volumes of Autobiography, and I'm sixty odd. What after all is age? Time itself only a mode of thought and space a figment of our imagination! I am on fire with dreams, intoxicated with visions, all throbbing with ambitions, younger and more hopeful than I was at twenty, which proves perhaps that I have lived in the main rightly, or that my Welsh parents gave me a rarely good constitution!

But I shut up, lest I weary you: you brought it on your own head, this confession of mine. I should infinitely like to have yours. Send it me; will you? At points we touch: I talked Socialism in the Parks in 83–4 and so did you: you and I made *The Saturday*, and incidentally ourselves, famous from 94 to 98. I have no idea where you were born or learned to read or what your early reading tastes were. You got hold of music, too, as I never did, tho' I knew Lohengrin and Tannhauser in 78–9 already. I am very curious to know how you came to see Socialism and the evils of competition so clearly! Hyndman didn't understand Socialism when I first met him. Won't you tell me all this? When a man who has an *ego* talks about himself, he is always most interesting, and I think you owe me a letter. I'll tell you about America one of these days.

Best Greetings to your wife. My wife is a hot British partisan—which keeps the house lively.

Yours ever,
Frank Harris

P.S.—Even in this long epistle I have not told of how as a boy my Irish-Fenian sympathies and the fact that in the English School I was always called "Pat," gave me the Irish angle from which I saw and ridiculed all things English! Later I got the American democratic squint on the Briton and finally attained the German (Heine) viewpoint, sharpened by personal passion infiltrated into me by the British lyings and murderings in Egypt and South Africa.

Yours ever
Frank Harris.

SHAW to HARRIS [U/1]

[Knowing that Harris needed a Shavian dimension to his copy to help sell it, Shaw provided it in the guise of a long letter which he invited Harris to attach to his biography of Wilde. In printing it Harris added the title, "My Memories of Oscar Wilde," his editorial commentary in the form of footnotes, and Shaw's

rebuttal notes (in italics). In reprinting it in his own Pen Portraits and Reviews *Shaw removed all the footnotes, but did not
restore his original text. Although it has Shaw's imprimatur,
Harris's version differs in a number of places from Shaw's
original seventeen-page typescript. Harris edited out the first
sentence, "improved" Shaw's prose in a number of places, and
carefully touched up references to Lord Alfred Douglas and to
Wilde's homosexuality. No page of the published text is without
Harris's alterations.*

*Shaw's references to the need to publish unexpurgated Wilde's
prison letter to Douglas,* De Profundis, *now can be read in con-
junction with the published text (1962). The* Century Guild
Hobby Horse *was an 1890s Arts-and-Crafts journal edited by
connoisseur Herbert Horne; Arthur H. Mackmurdo was an ar-
chitect and designer who founded the Century Guild in 1882.
Stewart D. Headlam, a Christian Socialist minister and founder
of the Guild of St. Matthew, was the man of courage who put up
bail money for Oscar Wilde at the time of his arrest in 1895.
Lady Colin Campbell succeeded Shaw as art critic on* The World
*and was part of the 1880s world of London journalism which
Harris and Shaw knew. T.C.D. is the "insider's" abbreviation
for Trinity College, Dublin. Harris's slip for* Dark Lady of the
Sonnets *in his footnote is surely deliberate, a humorous poke at
Shaw alluding to Harris's contention that Shaw had lifted the
idea for his play from Harris's own work on Shakespeare. Harris's "Fair Lady" corruption of Shaw's title is repeated in subsequent correspondence.*

*In this long letter Shaw recalls for Harris six occasions during
which he was in Wilde's company—all G.B.S. is able at the time
to remember. However a seventh is described in an earlier letter—one to Harris dated 7th October 1908, in which he describes
asking Wilde in 1886 to sign a petition on behalf of the condemned Haymarket Riot prisoners in Chicago. Shaw recalls it
later in the present letter without altering his count. There were
almost certainly others.*

*The "naval exhibition" in Chelsea at which Shaw recalls meet-
ing Wilde took place on August 14, 1890. Shaw had gone to it as
music critic, to "see whether there is any music there."*

*One additional note must be supplied here, as it has become
a matter for controversy. Shaw writes early in his memoir that
Wilde's charm was so infectious that "I understand why [Wil-
liam] Morris, when he was dying slowly, enjoyed a visit from*

Wilde more than from anyone else." Morris, however, died at Kelmscott, where Wilde never visited, eighteen months after Oscar had gone to prison. Yet there is no contradiction in Shaw's line, as he had referred to Morris's "dying slowly," and meant that in Morris's last years, when he was clearly failing, the author of The Soul of Man under Socialism *had been a solace to the old socialist partisan and poet.*

Most of the people mentioned in the long letter are recognizable, and some reappear in later correspondence, such as Sir Edmund Gosse (1849–1928), Librarian of the House of Lords and a critic of pompous respectability. Mrs. Charles Calvert (1837–1921), as she was known on the stage, was Adelaide Helen Calvert, a formidable actress for sixty-eight years, husband of the actor-manager of the Prince's Theatre and mother of stage and film actor Louis Calvert. Sir George Alexander (1858–1918), actor-manager of St. James's Theatre, created the title role of Ernest Worthing in Wilde's play; Charles Kean (1811–1868), was the actor-son of actor Edmund Kean. Thomas Power O'Connor (1848–1929) was an Irish-born journalist and Liberal M.P. who founded and edited The Star *in 1888, and employed Shaw as critic. Sir Edward Clarke, Q.C., M.P. (1841–1931), was Wilde's defense attorney in his litigation with the Marquess of Queensberry. "Bosie" Douglas is, of course, the Marquess's youngest son, Lord Alfred Douglas.*

Antoine-Francois Prévost, a Benedictine priest (1697–1763), wrote Manon Lescaut, *an epistolary novel about the chevalier Des Grieux's doomed love for the charming and amoral demimondaine Manon. Théophile Gautier (1811–1872), French poet and critic, was also author of the influential and "pagan" novel* Mademoiselle de Maupin, *a l'art pour l'art manifesto which contributed much to Wilde's creed.*

Blut Brüderschaft is blood-brotherhood; galloping ventre à terre is at full speed.

Shaw dated the letter at the beginning and at the end, from two different places, suggesting that it took him four weeks and more than one venue in which to complete the long letter.]

Ayot St Lawrence, Welwyn, Herts.
7th August 1916

Dear Frank Harris

Do not be revolted by the red ink: the black part of the ribbon is worn out.

I have an interesting letter of yours to answer; but when you ask me to exchange autobiographies, you take an unfair advantage of the changes of scene and bustling movement of your own adventures. My autobiography would be like my best plays, fearfully long, and not divided into acts. Just consider this life of Wilde which you have just sent me, and which I finished ten minutes ago after putting aside everything else to read it at one stroke.

Why was Wilde so good a subject for a biography that none of the previous attempts which you have just wiped out are bad? Just because his stupendous laziness simplified his life almost as if he knew instinctively that there must be no episodes to spoil the great situation at the end of the last act but one. It was a well made life in the Scribe sense. It was as simple as the life of Des Grieux, Manon Lescaut's lover; and it beat that by omitting Manon and making Des Grieux his own lover and his own hero.

Des Grieux was a worthless rascal by all conventional standards; and we forgive him everything. We think we forgive him because he was unselfish and loved greatly. Oscar seems to have said: "I will love nobody: I will be utterly selfish; and I will be not merely a rascal but a monster; and you shall forgive me everything. In other words, I will reduce your standards to absurdity, not by writing them down, though I could do that so well—in fact, *have* done it—but by actually living them down and dying them down."

However, I mustn't start writing a book to you about Wilde: I must just tumble a few things together and tell you them. To take things in the order of your book, I can remember only one occasion on which I saw Sir William Wilde, who, by the way, operated on my father to correct a squint, and overdid the correction so much that my father squinted the other way all the rest of his life. To this day I never notice a squint: it is as normal to me as a nose or a tall hat.

I was a boy at a concert in the Antient Concert Rooms in Brunswick Street in Dublin. Everybody was in evening dress; and—unless I am mixing up this concert with another (in which case I doubt if the Wildes would have been present)—the Lord Lieutenant was there with his blue waistcoated courtiers. Wilde was dressed in snuffy brown; and as he had the sort of skin that never looks clean, he produced a dramatic effect beside Lady Wilde (in full fig) of being, like Frederick the Great, Beyond

Soap and Water, as his Nietzschean son was beyond Good and Evil. He was currently reported to have a family in every farm-house; and the wonder was that Lady Wilde didn't mind—evidently a tradition from the Travers case, which I did not know about until I read your account, as I was only eight in 1864.

Lady Wilde was nice to me in London during the desperate days between my arrival in 1876 and my first earning of an income by my pen in 1885, or rather until, a few years earlier, I threw myself into Socialism and cut myself contemptuously loose from everything of which her at-homes—themselves desperate affairs enough, as you saw for yourself—were part. I was at two or three of them; and I once dined with her in company with an ex-tragedy queen named Miss Glynn, who, having no visible external ears, had a head like a turnip. Lady Wilde talked about Schopenhauer; and Miss Glynn told me that Gladstone formed his oratorical style on Charles Kean.

I ask myself where and how I came across Lady Wilde; for we had no social relations in the Dublin days. The explanation must be that my sister, then a very attractive girl who sang beautifully, had met and made some sort of innocent conquest of both Oscar and Willie. I met Oscar once at one of the at-homes; and he came and spoke to me with an evident intention of being specially kind to me. We put each other out frightfully; and this odd difficulty persisted between us to the very last, even when we were no longer mere boyish novices and had become men of the world with plenty of skill in social inter-course. I saw him very seldom, as I avoided literary and artistic society like the plague, and refused the few invitations I received to go into society with burlesque ferocity, so as to keep out of it without offending people past their willingness to indulge me as a privileged lunatic.

The last time I saw him was at that tragic luncheon of yours at the Café Royal; and I am quite sure our total of meetings from first to last did not exceed twelve, and may not have exceeded six.

I definitely recollect six: (1) at the at-home aforesaid. (2) at Mackmurdo's house in Fitzroy Street in the days of the Century Guild and its paper The Hobby Horse. (3) at a meeting somewhere in Westminster at which I delivered an address on Socialism, and at which Oscar turned up and spoke. Robert

Ross surprised me greatly by telling me, long after Oscar's death, that it was this address of mine that moved Oscar to try his hand at a similar feat by writing The Soul of Man Under Socialism. (4) a chance meeting near the stage door of the Haymarket Theatre, at which our queer shyness of one another made our resolutely cordial and appreciative conversation so difficult that our final laugh and shake-hands were almost a reciprocal confession. (5) a really pleasant afternoon we spent together on catching one another in a place where our presence was an absurdity. It was some exhibition in Chelsea: a naval exhibition, where there was a replica of Nelson's Victory and a set of P. & O. cabins which made one seasick by mere association of ideas. I don't know why I went or why Wilde went; but we did; and the question what the devil we were doing in that galley tickled us both. It was my sole experience of Oscar's wonderful gift as a raconteur. I remember particularly an amazingly elaborate story which you have no doubt heard from him: an example of the cumulation of a single effect, as in Mark Twain's story of the man who was persuaded to put lightning conductor after lightning conductor at every possible point on his roof until a thunderstorm came and all the lightning in the heavens went for his house and wiped it out.

Oscar's much more carefully and elegantly worked out story was of a young man who invented a theatre stall which economized space by ingenious contrivances which were all described. A friend of his invited twenty millionaires to meet him at dinner so that he might interest them in the invention. The young man convinced them completely by his demonstration of the saving in a theatre holding, in ordinary seats, six hundred people, leaving them eager and ready to make his fortune. Unfortunately he went on to calculate the annual saving in all the theatres of the world; then in all the churches of the world; then in all the legislatures; estimating finally the incidental and moral and religious effects of the invention until at the end of an hour he had estimated a profit of several billions: the climax of course being that the millionaires folded their tents and silently stole away, leaving the ruined inventor a marked man for life.

Wilde and I got on extraordinarily well on this occasion. I had not to talk myself, but to listen to a man telling me stories better than I could have told them. We did not talk about Art,

about which, excluding literature from the definition, he knew
only what could be picked up by reading about it. He was in a
tweed suit and low hat like myself, and had been detected and
had detected me in the act of clandestinely spending a happy
day at Rosherville [Gardens] (so to speak), instead of pontificat-
ing in his frock coat and so forth. And he had an audience on
whom not one of his subtlest effects was lost. And so, for once,
our meeting was a success; and I understood why Morris, when
he was dying slowly, enjoyed a visit from Wilde more than from
anybody else, as I understand why you say in your book that
you would rather have Wilde back than any friend you have
ever talked to, even though he was incapable of friendship,
though not of the most touching kindness[1] on occasion.

Our sixth meeting, the only other one I can remember, was
the one at the Café Royal. On that occasion he was not too
preoccupied with his danger to be disgusted with me because I,
who had praised his first plays handsomely, had turned traitor
over The Importance of Being Earnest. Clever as it was, it was
his first really heartless play. In the others the chivalry of the
eighteenth century Irishman and the romance of the disciple of
Théophile Gautier (Oscar was really old-fashioned in the Irish
way, except as a critic of morals) not only gave a certain kindness and gallantry to the serious passages and to the handling
of the women, but provided that proximity of emotion without
which laughter, however irresistible, is destructive and sinis-
ter. In The Importance of Being Earnest this had vanished; and
the play, though extremely funny, was essentially hateful. I
had no idea that Oscar was going to the dogs, and that this
represented a real degeneracy produced by his debaucheries. I
thought he was still developing; and I hazarded the unhappy
guess that The Importance of Being Earnest was in idea a
young work written or projected long before under the influence of [W.S.] Gilbert and furbished up for [George] Alexander
as a potboiler. At the Café Royal that day I calmly asked him
whether I was not right. He indignantly repudiated my guess,
and said loftily (the only time he ever tried on me the attitude
he took to John Gray and his more abject disciples) that he was
disappointed in me. I suppose I said, "Then what on earth has
happened to you?" but I recollect nothing more on that subject
except that we did not quarrel over it.

[1]Excellent analysis. [Ed.]

When he was sentenced I spent a railway journey to the north on a Socialist lecturing excursion drafting a petition for his release. After that I met Willie Wilde at a theatre which I think must have been the Duke of York's, because I connect it vaguely with St. Martin's Lane. I spoke to him about the petition, asking him whether anything of the sort was being done, and warning him that though I and Stewart Headlam would sign it, that would be no use, as we were two notorious cranks, and our names alone would make the thing ridiculous and do Oscar more harm than good. Willie cordially agreed, and added, with maudlin pathos and an inconceivable want of tact: "Oscar was NOT a man of bad character: you could have trusted him with a woman anywhere." He convinced me, as you discovered later, that signatures would not be obtainable; so the petition project [was] dropped; and I don't know what became of my draft. When Wilde was in Paris during his last phase I made a point of sending him inscribed copies of all my books as they came out; and he did the same to me.

In writing about Wilde and Whistler, in the days when they were treated as witty triflers, and called Oscar and Jimmy in print, I always made a point of taking them seriously and with scrupulous good manners. Wilde on his part also made a point of recognizing me as a man of distinction by his manner, and repudiating the current estimate of me as a mere jester. This was not the usual reciprocal-admiration trick: I believe he was sincere, and felt indignant at what he thought was a vulgar underestimate of me; and I had the same feeling about him. My impulse to rally to him in his misfortune, and my disgust at "the man Wilde" scurrilities of the newspapers, was irresistible: I don't quite know why; for my toleration of his perversion, and recognition of the fact that it does not imply any general depravity or coarseness of character, is an acquirement through observation and reflection. I have all the normal violent repugnance to homosexuality—if it is really normal, which nowadays one is sometimes provoked to doubt. Also, I was in no way predisposed to like him: he was my fellow-townsman, and a very prime specimen of the sort of fellow-townsman I most loathed: to wit, the Dublin snob. His Irish charm, potent with Englishmen, did not exist for me; and on the whole it may be claimed for him that he got no regard from me that he did not earn.

What first established a friendly feeling in me was, unexpectedly enough, the affair of the Chicago anarchists, whose Homer you constituted yourself by The Bomb. I tried to get some literary men in London, all heroic rebels and skeptics on paper, to sign a memorial asking for a reprieve of these unfortunate men. The only signature I got was Wilde's. It was a completely disinterested act on his part; and it secured my distinguished consideration for him for the rest of his life.

To return for a moment to Lady Wilde. You know that there is a disease called giantism, caused by "a certain morbid process in the sphenoid bone of the skull—vis., an excessive development of the anterior lobe of the pituitary body" (this is from the nearest encyclopedia). "When this condition does not become active until after the age of twenty-five, by which time the long bones are consolidated, the result is acromegaly, which chiefly manifests itself in an enlargement of the hands and feet." I never saw Lady Wilde's feet; but her hands were enormous, and never went straight to their aim when they grasped anything, but minced about, feeling for it. And the gigantic splaying of her palm was reproduced in her lumbar region.

Now Oscar was an overgrown man, with something not quite normal about his bigness—something that made Lady Colin Campbell, who hated him, describe him as "that great white caterpillar." You yourself describe the disagreeable impression he made on you physically, in spite of his fine eyes and style. Well, I have always maintained that Oscar was a giant in the pathological sense, and that this explains a good deal of his weakness.

I think you have affectionately underrated his snobbery, mentioning only the pardonable and indeed justifiable side of it; the love of fine names and distinguished associations and luxury and good manners.[2] You say repeatedly, and *on certain*

---

[2] I had touched on the evil side of his snobbery, I thought, by saying that it was only famous actresses and great ladies that he ever talked about, and in telling how he loved to speak of the great houses such as Clumber to which he had been invited, and by half a dozen other hints scattered through my book. I had attacked English snobbery so strenuously in my book on "The Man Shakespeare," had resented its influence on the finest English intelligence so bitterly, that I thought if I again laid stress on it in Wilde, people would think I was crazy on the subject. But he was a snob, both by nature and training, and I understand by snob what Shaw evidently understands by it here.

planes, truly, that he was not bitter and did not use his tongue to wound people. But this is not true on the snobbish plane. On one occasion he wrote about T. P. O'Connor with deliberate, studied, wounding insolence, with his Merrion Square Protestant pretentiousness in full cry against the Catholic. He repeatedly declaimed against the vulgarity of the British journalist, not as you or I might, but as an expression of the odious class feeling that is itself the vilest vulgarity. He made the mistake of not knowing his place. He objected to being addressed as Wilde, declaring that he was Oscar to his intimates and Mr. Wilde to others, quite unconscious of the fact that he was imposing on the men with whom, as a critic and journalist, he had to live and work, the alternative of granting him an intimacy he had no right to ask or a deference to which he had no claim. The vulgar hated him for snubbing them; and the valiant men damned his impudence and cut him. Thus he was left with a band of devoted satellites on the one hand, and a dining out connection on the other, with here and there a man of talent and personality enough to command his respect, but utterly without that fortifying body of acquaintance among plain men in which a man must move as himself a plain man, and be Smith and Jones and Wilde and Shaw and Harris instead of Bosie and Robbie and Oscar and Mister. This is the sort of folly that does not last forever in a man of Wilde's ability; but it lasted long enough with Oscar to prevent his laying any solid social foundations.[3]

Another difficulty I have already hinted at. Wilde started as an apostle of Art; and in that capacity he was a humbug. The notion that a Portora boy, passed on to T.C.D. and thence to Oxford and spending his vacations in Dublin, could without special circumstances have any genuine intimacy with music and painting, is to me ridiculous.[4] When Wilde was at Portora, I

[3]The reason that Oscar, snobbish as he was, and admirer of England and the English as he was, could not lay any solid social foundations in England was, in my opinion, his intellectual interests and his intellectual superiority to the men he met. No one with a fine mind devoted to things of the spirit is capable of laying solid social foundations in England. Shaw, too, has no solid social foundations in that country.

This passing shot at English society serves it right. Yet able men have found niches in London. Where was Oscar's?—G.B.S.

[4]I had already marked it down to put in this popular edition of my book that

was at home in a house where important musical works, including several typical masterpieces, were being rehearsed from the point of blank amateur ignorance up to fitness for public performance. I could whistle them from the first bar to the last as a butcher's boy whistles music hall songs, before I was twelve. The toleration of popular music—Strauss's waltzes, for instance—was to me positively a painful acquirement, a sort of republican duty.

I was so fascinated by painting that I haunted the National Gallery, which Doyle had made perhaps the finest collection of its size in the world; and I longed for money to buy painting materials with. This afterwards saved me from starving: it was as a critic of music and painting in the World that I won through my ten years of journalism before I finished up with you on the Saturday Review. I could make deaf stockbrokers read my two pages on music, the alleged joke being that I knew nothing about it. The real joke was that I knew all about it.

Now it is quite evident to me, as it was to Whistler and Beardsley, that Oscar knew no more about pictures[5] than anyone of his general culture and with his opportunities can pick up as he goes along. He could be witty about Art, as I could be witty about engineering; but that is no use when you have to seize and hold the attention and interest of people who really love music and painting. Therefore, Oscar was handicapped by a false start, and got a reputation[6] for shallowness and insincerity which he never retrieved until it was too late.

Comedy: the criticism of morals and manners *viva voce*, was his real forte. When he settled down to that he was great. But, as you found when you approached Meredith about him, his initial mistake had produced that "rather low opinion of Wilde's capacities," that "deep-rooted contempt for the showman in him," which persisted as a first impression and will

---

Wilde continually pretended to a knowledge of music, which he had not got. He could hardly tell one tune from another, but he loved to talk of that "scarlet thing of Dvorak," hoping in this way to be accepted as a real critic of music, when he knew nothing about it and cared even less. His eulogies of music and painting betrayed him continually though he did not know it.

[5] I touched upon Oscar's ignorance of art sufficiently I think, when I said in my book that he had learned all he knew of art and of controversy from Whistler, and that his lectures on the subject, even after sitting at the feet of the Master, were almost worthless.

[6] Perfectly true, and a notable instance of Shaw's insight.

persist until the last man who remembers his aesthetic period has perished. The world has been in some ways so unjust to him that one must be careful not to be unjust to the world.

In the preface on education, called Parents and Children, in my volume of plays beginning with Misalliance, there is a section headed Artist Idolatry, which is really about Wilde. Dealing with "the powers enjoyed by brilliant persons who are also connoisseurs in art," I say, "the influence they can exercise on young people who have been brought up in the darkness and wretchedness of a home without art, and in whom a natural bent towards art has always been baffled and snubbed, is incredible to those who have not witnessed and understood it. He (or she) who reveals the world of art to them opens heaven to them. They become satellites, disciples, worshippers of the apostle. Now the apostle may be a voluptuary without much conscience. Nature may have given him enough virtue to suffice in a reasonable environment. But this allowance may not be enough to defend him against the temptation and demoralization of finding himself a little god on the strength of what ought to be a quite ordinary culture. He may find adorers in all directions in our uncultivated society among people of stronger character than himself, not one of whom, if they had been artistically educated, would have had anything to learn from him, or regarded him as in any way extraordinary apart from his actual achievements as an artist. Tartufe is not always a priest. Indeed, he is not always a rascal: he is often a weak man absurdly credited with omniscience and perfection, and taking unfair advantages only because they are offered to him and he is too weak to refuse. Give everyone his culture, and no one will offer him more than his due."

That paragraph was the outcome of a walk and talk I had one afternoon at Chartres with Robert Ross.

You reveal Wilde as a weaker man than I thought him: I still believe that his fierce Irish pride had something to do with his refusal to run away from the trial. But in the main your evidence is conclusive. It was part of his tragedy that people asked for more moral strength from him than he could bear the burden of, because they made the very common mistake—of which actors get the benefit—of regarding style as evidence of strength, just as in the case of women they are apt to regard paint as evidence of beauty. Now Wilde was so in love with style that he never realized the danger of biting off more than he could chew: in other words, of putting up more style than his matter would carry. Wise kings wear shabby clothes, and leave the gold lace to the drum major.

You do not, unless my memory is betraying me as usual, quite recollect the order of events just before the trial. That day at the Café Royal, Wilde said he had come to ask you to go into the witness box next day and testify that Dorian Gray was a highly moral work. Your answer was something like this: "For God's sake, man, put everything on that plane out of your head. You don't realize what is going to happen to you. It is not going to be a matter of clever talk about your books. They are going to bring up a string of witnesses that will put art and literature out of the question. Clarke will throw up his brief. He will carry the case to a certain point; and then, when he sees the avalanche coming, he will back out and leave you in the dock. What you have to do is to cross to France to-night. Leave a letter saying that you cannot face the squalor and horror of a law case; that you are an artist and unfitted for such things. Don't stay here clutching at straws like testimonials to Dorian Gray. *I tell you I know.* I know what is going to happen. I know Clarke's sort. I know what evidence they have got. You must go."

It was no use. Wilde was in a curious double temper. He made no pretence either of innocence or of questioning the folly of his proceedings against Queensberry. But he had an infatuate hautiness as to the impossibility of his retreating, and as to his right to dictate your course. Douglas sat in silence, a haughty indignant silence, copying Wilde's attitude as all Wilde's admirers did, but quite probably influencing Wilde as you suggest, by the copy. Oscar finally rose with a mixture of impatience and his grand air, and walked out with the remark that he had now found out who were his real friends; and Douglas followed him, absurdly smaller, and imitating his walk, like a curate following an archbishop.[7] You remember it the other

---

[7]This is an inimitable picture, but Shaw's fine sense of comedy has misled him. The scene took place absolutely as I recorded it. Douglas went out first saying—"Your telling him to run away shows that you are no friend of Oscar's." Then Oscar got up to follow him. He said good-bye to Shaw, adding a courteous word or two. As he turned to the door I got up and said:—"I hope you do not doubt my friendship; you have no reason to."

"I do not think this is friendly of you, Frank," he said, and went on out.

way about; but just consider this. Douglas was in the wretched position of having ruined Wilde merely to annoy his father, and of having attempted it so idiotically that he had actually prepared a triumph for him. He was, besides, much the youngest man present, and looked younger than he was. You did not make him welcome: as far as I recollect you did not greet him by a word or a nod. If he had given the smallest provocation or attempted to take the lead in any way, I should not have given twopence for the chance of your keeping your temper. And Wilde, even in his ruin—which, however, he did not yet fully realize—kept his air of authority on questions of taste and conduct. It was practically impossible under such circumstances that Douglas should have taken the stage in any way. Everyone thought him a horrid little beast; but I, not having met him before to my knowledge, and having some sort of flair for his literary talent, was curious to hear what he had to say for himself. But except to echo Wilde once or twice he said nothing.[8] You are right in effect, because it was evident that Wilde was in his hands, and was really echoing him. But Wilde automatically kept the prompter off the stage and himself in the middle of it.

What your book needs to complete it is a portrait of yourself as good as your portrait of Wilde. Oscar was not combative, though he was supercilious in his early pose. When his snobbery was not in action, he liked to make people devoted to him and to flatter them exquisitely with that end. Mrs. Calvert, whose great final period as a stage old woman began with her sudden appearance in my Arms and the Man, told me one day, when apologizing for being, as she thought, a bad rehearser, that no author had ever been so nice to her except Mr. Wilde, the author of A Woman of No Importance.

Pugnacious people, if they did not actually terrify Oscar, were at least the sort of people he could not control, and whom he feared as possibly able to coerce him. You suggest that the Queensberry pugnacity was something that Oscar could not deal with successfully. But how in that case could Oscar have felt quite safe with you? You were more pugnacious than six

[8] I am sure that Douglas took the initiative and walked out first.
I have no doubt you are right, and that my vision of the exit is really a reminiscence of the entrance. In fact, now that you prompt my memory, I recall quite distinctly that Douglas, who came in as the follower, went out as the leader, and that the last word was spoken by Wilde after he had gone.—G.B.S.

Queensberrys rolled into one. When people asked, "What has Frank Harris been?" the usual reply was, "Obviously a pirate from the Spanish Main."

Oscar, from the moment he gained your attachment, could never have been afraid of what you might do to him, as he was sufficient of a connoisseur in Blut Bruderschaft to appreciate yours; but he must always have been mortally afraid of what you might do or say to his friends.[9] You had quite an infernal scorn for nineteen out of twenty of the men and women you met in the circles he most wished to propitiate; and nothing could induce you to keep your knife in its sheath when they jarred on you. The Spanish Main itself would have blushed rosy red at your language when classical invective did not suffice to express your feelings.

It may be that if, say, Edmund Gosse had come to Oscar when he was out on bail, with a couple of first class tickets in his pocket, and gently suggested a mild trip to Folkestone, or the Channel Islands, Oscar might have let himself be coaxed away. But to be called on to gallop *ventre à terre* to Erith—it might have been Deal—and hoist the Jolly Roger on board your lugger, was like casting a light comedian and first lover for Richard III. Oscar could not see himself in the part.

I must not press the point too far; but it illustrates, I think, what does not come out at all in your book: that you were a very different person from the submissive and sympathetic disciples to whom he was accustomed. There are things more terrifying to a soul like Oscar's than an as yet unrealized possibility of a sentence of hard labor. A voyage with Captain Kidd may have been one of them. Wilde was a conventional man: his unconventionality was the very pedantry of convention: never was there a man less an outlaw than he. You were born an outlaw, and will never be anything else.

That is why, in his relations with you, he appears as a man always shirking action—more of a coward (all men are cowards more or less) than so proud a man can have been. Still this does not affect the truth and power of your portrait. Wilde's memory will have to stand or fall by it.

[9]This insight on Shaw's part makes me smile because it is absolutely true. Oscar commended Bosie Douglas to me again and again and again, begged me to be nice to him if we ever met by chance; but I refused to meet him for months and months.

You will be blamed, I imagine, because you have not written a lying epitaph instead of a faithful chronicle and study of him; but you will not lose your sleep over that. As a matter of fact, you could not have carried kindness further without sentimental folly. I should have made a far sterner summing up. I am sure Oscar has not found the gates of heaven shut against him: he is too good company to be excluded; but he can hardly have been greeted as "Thou good and faithful servant." The first thing we ask a servant for is a testimonial to honesty, sobriety and industry; for we soon find out that these are the scarce things, and that geniuses[10] and clever people are as common as rats. Well, Oscar was not sober, not honest, not industrious. Society praised him for being idle, and persecuted him savagely for an aberration which it had better have left unadvertized, thereby making a hero of him; for it is in the nature of people to worship those who have been made to suffer horribly: indeed I have often said that if the crucifixion could be proved a myth, and Jesus convicted of dying of old age in comfortable circumstances, Christianity would lose ninety-nine per cent. of its devotees.

We must try to imagine what judgment we should have passed on Oscar if he had been a normal man, and had dug his grave with his teeth in the ordinary respectable fashion, as his brother Willie did. This brother, by the way, gives us some cue; for Willie, who had exactly the same education and the same chances, must be ruthlessly set aside by literary history as a vulgar fellow of no account. Well, suppose Oscar and Willie had both died the day before Queensberry left that card at the Club! Oscar would still have been remembered as a wit and a dandy, and would have had a niche beside Congreve in the drama. A volume of his aphorisms would have stood creditably on the library shelf with La Rochefoucauld's Maxims. We should have missed the Ballad of Reading Gaol and De Profundis; but he would still have cut a considerable figure in the Dictionary of National Biography, and been read and quoted outside the British Museum reading room.

---

[10]The English paste in Shaw; genius is about the rarest thing on earth whereas the necessary quantum of "honesty, sobriety and industry," is beaten by life into nine humans out of ten.—Ed.

If so, it is the tenth who comes my way.—G.B.S.

As to the Ballad and De Profundis, I think it is greatly to Oscar's credit that, whilst he was sincere and deeply moved when he was protesting against the cruelty of our present system to children and to prisoners generally, he could not write about his own individual share in that suffering with any conviction or sympathy.[11] Except for the passage where he describes his exposure at Clapham Junction, there is hardly a line in De Profundis that he might not have written as a literary feat five years earlier. But in the Ballad even in borrowing form and melody from Coleridge, he shews that he could pity others when he could not seriously pity himself. And this, I think, may be pleaded against the reproach that he was selfish. Externally, in the ordinary action of life as distinguished from the literary action proper to his genius, he was no doubt sluggish and weak because of his giantism. He ended as an unproductive drunkard and swindler; for the repeated sales of the Daventry plot, in so far as they imposed on the buyers and were not transparent excuses for begging, were undeniably swindles. For all that, he does not appear in his writings a selfish or base-minded man. He is at his worst and weakest in the suppressed[12] part of De Profundis; but in my opinion it had better be published, for several reasons. It explains some of his personal weakness by the stifling narrowness of his daily round, ruinous to a man whose proper place was in a large public life. And its concealment is mischievous because, first, it leads people to imagine all sorts of horrors in a document which contains nothing worse than any record of the squabbles of a couple of housemaids; and, second, it is clearly a monstrous thing that Douglas should have a torpedo launched at him and timed to explode after his death. The torpedo is a very harmless squib; for there is nothing in it that cannot be guessed from Douglas's own book; but the public does not know that. By the way, it is rather a humorous stroke of Fate's irony that the son of the Marquis of Queensberry should be forced to expiate his sins by suffering a succession of blows beneath the belt.

Now that you have written the best life of Oscar Wilde, let us have the best life of Frank Harris. Otherwise the man behind

[11]Superb criticism.
[12]I have said this in my way.

your works will go down to posterity[13] as the hero of my very inadequate preface to The Dark Lady of the Sonnets.

Ever,
G.B.S.

Sedbergh
4th September 1916

HARRIS to SHAW [H/4]

[Pearson, then a young actor-turned-journalist, would become, after Army service in the Middle East, a prolific writer of popular biographies, including a fine one of Shaw, in which he was greatly assisted by his subject. Pearson was not unknown to Shaw: he had acted in the premiere of Androcles and the Lion.*]*

3 Washington Square, New York, N.Y.
Sept. 11, 1916

My dear Shaw:—

This is to introduce to you Hesketh Pearson, a good fellow and a dear friend of mine, and an ardent admirer of yours who wants to know you out of purest hero-worship.

He has been filling his letters to me recently with praise of your plays and of you and so I present him to you with all my best wishes.

He will probably bring you one of the copies on vellum of the Oscar Wilde book as your name is "taboo" to the English censor.

Again most cordially yours,
Frank Harris

[13]A characteristic flirt of Shaw's humor. He is a great caricaturist and not a portrait-painter.

When he thinks of my Celtic face and aggressive American frankness he talks of me as pugnacious and a pirate: "a Captain Kidd": in his preface to "The Fair Lady of the Sonnets" he praises my "idiosyncratic gift of pity"; says that I am "wise through pity"; then he extols me as a prophet, not seeing that a pitying sage, prophet and pirate constitute an inhuman superman.

I shall do more for Shaw than he has been able to do for me; he is the first figure in my new volume of "Contemporary Portraits." I have portrayed him there at his best, as I love to think of him, and henceforth he'll have to try to live up to my conception and that will keep him, I'm afraid, on strain.

God help me!—G.B.S.

HARRIS to SHAW [H/4]

[Shaw's preface about Jesus was his introduction to Androcles and the Lion. *Harris's* Contemporary Portraits *were his continuing journalistic series, which he collected regularly in book form. Henry Mayers Hyndman (1842–1921) was the spellbinding founder of the Social Democratic Federation in 1881, and according to Shaw his primary model for John Tanner in* Man and Superman.

Shaw's response to H. G. Wells had followed Wells's proposal that Germany indicate its sincerity about peace by throwing out the Kaiser and installing a republic, and suggesting republican directions for Britain as well.]

3 Washington Square, New York, N.Y.
Sept. 11, 1916

My dear Shaw:—

Here is the best review at short notice I can do on this astonishing preface of yours about Jesus. I hope you will like it though it is by no means yet in its final form. These "Portraits" of mine that you like cost me endless labor and trouble. I have to rewrite them again and again to get them true and good for often in my wish to keep them faithful I fall into harshness as in this sketch of you, perhaps. Words like clothes must not be too close to fact or they become stiff and ungraceful; a little looseness is an excellent thing in writing as in life.

And you especially tempt to caricature.

Now I want you to help me to make a great portrait of you to head the second volume of my "Contemporaries." I want to know why you did not marry early and beget children?

Would you like children now, or are you content to live for yourself alone and your wife and your work?

Do you write rapidly as your letters seem to show and your speaking, or do you write and correct and re-write? Or are you sometimes happy and satisfy yourself in your first sketch and at other times have to re-write and correct and rewrite again?

What are your hours of work?

Does the applause of the many please you as much as the critical praise of the few?

How did you come to be a vegetarian? Was it through indigestion?

Have vegetables kept you in good health? What are their advantages besides cheapness?

How did you become a teetotaller? Have you stuck to that steadily?

Do you read many novels and plays—fiction?

When did you first become a socialist? Was it through Hyndman about the beginning of the old Social Democratic Federation?

When did you study French and German? How much do you know of them? Do you know any other foreign language?

Did Latin and Greek give you anything? What are your views on education?

Why have you not written some music? Why have you not expressed yourself in that art as well as in letters? Things you said about it in the old days interested me hugely.

When did you lose your belief in personal immortality? Was the wrench painful, or did you shed the old creed as a snake his skin quickly and completely with nothing worse than a tickling?

A splendid letter from you appeared to-day making delicious fun of Wells and his ridiculous plan of turning Germany into a republic. Bulldog or Dachshund—there's not much to choose between 'em.

I wrote at the beginning of the war that the Germans could not be beaten; now after years they are still easy winners on points.

But there, I don't want to argue with you but to get at the heart of your mystery and set you down fairly. Tell me all you can and answer please all these questions. I shall excite curiosity about you here in the circles you would wish to be heard in. *Pearson's Magazine* has 125,000 readers—120,000 I should think convinced Socialists. Here you ought to be known. If you will help me I'll do it.

Now a favor. I want you to tell me what you think of my "Life of Wilde." I know you will be frank, but I want you to put your finger on the shortcomings. Of course if you would do a paper on all my work I should be definitely obliged and I hesitate to ask you. I leave the two requests with you. You could do the bigger one even in a couple of days. Just as one writer to another I say I am little known here in the U.S.A. and a study sketch of me or my work by you would do me infinite good at the moment. The whole pro-British press is down on me because I regard Germans as human beings. All the magazines have bought articles and stories of mine and then refused to publish them. I have never been as poor since I was twenty as I have been in New York; too poor to do my work; too poor to do any good work. A boost now I've got a chance would be invaluable to me. I leave it to you. I only say this; that were the position reversed, you know how gladly I would do it for you. *Basta*!

I am sending you two copies of the Oscar Wilde book on Japanese vellum which you subscribed for ages ago. If the binding is not as good as it might be consider that I promised Japanese vellum when it was fifteen cents a pound and now for this I paid eighty cents.

Yours always,
Frank Harris

P.S. I'm sending you the October *Pearson's* with a preliminary paper on you. I hope to enclose with this the article on yr "Jesus" wh. will appear in Nov. If you will give me the data I ask for I will do a third on yr relations to things and thought and men and a sort of summing up or loose classification. Please help me & write soon.

Sincerely Yours Always
Frank Harris

HARRIS to SHAW [H/4]

[John Davidson wrote poems and ballads about the seamy side of the 1890s. Shaw unsuccessfully tried to encourage him to write plays and give up hackwork. George Moore's book on Jesus was The Brook Kerith *(1916).]*

3 Washington Square, New York City
Sept. 29, 1916

My dear Shaw:—

You are the first person I think in my journey through the world who has shown any wish to surpass me in generosity. I thought you mean to me in that Shakespeare business, unwilling to give credit where credit was due. Now you have more than made amends and I am rather ashamed of myself for harboring even a small thought of you. It was very fine and very generous of you to send me this long and superb letter about Oscar Wilde.

You advise me to use it as an appendix, but I want your permission to use it as a preface to my popular edition of Oscar Wilde which will come out in 1917; and I might give with it a photo of Oscar Wilde taken towards the end which is a dreadful illustration of your severe, but I think just judgment of him.

I agree with every word you say about his snobbery. He was snobbish in the most vulgar way possible—incredible. I did not bring it into the portrait because the shadows were already black enough—quite as dark as the lights were high.

Oscar never reached originality except in the "Ballad of Reading Gaol"—that happy accident which, as Burns saw, comes to all us artists sooner or later.

By the way, I wish you would say directly what you imply rather than say in this letter of yours about my Oscar book— that I have made Oscar live for those who did not know him and perhaps have increased the knowledge of those who did know him personally.

Now, though you have given so much I want you to give more. I want you to answer the questions I recently put to you in a letter because I want your portrait to be complete and more or less worthy of the subject, for I want it to head my second volume of "Contemporary Portraits." I want to know all the things I have asked you and a hundred more that I have not ventured to ask. Here is one. You condemn sensuality at times rather contemptuously as Davidson did. Why? To me sexual desire is as good a thing as hunger and infinitely more attractive both in pursuit and gratification, because at its best it involves some self-sacrifice for another. Desire of a woman is as good as desire of wisdom or goodness and more powerful as a driving force. I want to know what you think about this. Please deal with me frankly as I should with you.

My second request is more personal. I want you to write me what you think of this article of mine about your Jesus. I have outlined here the way I am going to treat Jesus. From the outline you will guess a good deal—if not most of it. The best part you will not guess because it is my contribution—not only to our knowledge of Jesus, but to modern thought. As I predicted George Moore's book is negligible—nothing in it worth reading.

Now thanking you again for all your kindness and even more because your generosity increases my estimate of Shaw though it makes the portrait of him more difficult, I remain,

Yours ever,
Frank Harris
September of this Year of *Dis-Grace* 1916

HARRIS to SHAW [H/4]

[Ludwig Boerne was a political journalist in early nineteenth-century Germany, brought into play here because of Heine's crack about Boerne's impenetrable ignorance. Harris, who had studied in Germany, knew the literature well.]

3 Washington Square, New York, N.Y.
Oct. 5, 1916

My dear Shaw:—

You have written about me twice at length—once in the introduction to your "Fair Lady of the Sonnets" and now in regard to my Wilde book. I am exceedingly obliged to you but there is a curious discrepancy between your two pictures. In the one you speak about my extraordinary gift of pity. You even ascribe all my *insight to the pity in me*; and in the latter portrait I have become "a pirate of the Spanish Main."

How can you reconcile this apostle of pity with the pirate? To make a composite portrait out of the pirate and the apostle it seems to me, may test even your extraordinary art.

There is of course no reason why you should see any definite personality in me but the antinomy between "pity" and "pirate" nettles my curiosity. Have you the reconciling word? If you have I wish you would give it to me because I cannot follow your mind in these apparently contradictory flights. I half believe you find the "pirate" in my cocked nose and combative manner and the "pity" in my writings and acts?

Meanwhile please do not forget, too, that I am awaiting your answers to my questions about yourself for I want to complete my portrait of you and set it forth in a third article.

I should also like you to tell me whether you were able to read Moore's book "The Brook Kerith." I promised my readers to read it and do a portrait of Moore probably. Now Moore is quite clear to me. I have known him intimately for thirty odd years, but this book is a nightmare of ignorance and profanity and the profanity is not extravagant enough to make me forgive the ignorance.

Do you remember Heine's verse about Boerne's ignorance?

> "Kein Buch und keine Akademie
> Hat seinen Verstand verdorben
> Nein, seine ganze Ignoranz
> Hat er sich selber erworben."

Do write to me and answer my questions both in this and my previous letters. Your letters are a delight to me in this land where commonplace rages like that unholy wind which Dante describes as blowing the spirits about ceaselessly in the dusk where nothing can be distinctly seen.

Yours ever,
Frank Harris.

P.S. Please tell me what you thought of my critique or appreciation of your work on Jesus. I had no other portrait of you than this caricature of Max: won't you send me a recent photo signed—Please remember me to your charming wife & ask her to pick the photo!

Yours
F.H.

SHAW to HARRIS [H/6]

[Henderson, who had published the first of his three biographies of Shaw in 1911—the last in 1956—was a professor of mathematics at the University of North Carolina in Chapel Hill. T. D. O'Bolger, who had written a Ph.D. thesis on Shaw with the help of voluminous autobiographical letters Shaw sent him, was prevented from publishing the work when Shaw had second

thoughts about exposing some of that autobiography to the public, particularly what he had to say about the parental ménage à trois *with G. J. Vandeleur Lee, Lucinda Shaw's music tutor. G. K. Chesterton and Joseph McCabe had published early books on Shaw (1909 and 1914).*

The one-act play in which Shaw claimed to have put "the physical act of sexual intercourse on the stage" was Overruled *(written 1912), in which a man and woman, each married to someone else, embrace ecstatically, and tumble about upon a large upholstered sofa, but the entire scene is played farcically.*

Shaw discusses his indebtedness to Thomas Tyler for the "Dark Lady" theory (the "identification" of Mistress Mary Fitton) as an explanation of Shakespeare's sonnets, in his preface to his play on the subject. Tyler, a habitué of the British Museum Reading Room in the 1880s, wrote a book on the Sonnets *which Shaw had reviewed anonymously in the* Pall Mall Gazette *on 7 January 1886.*

T. P. O'Connor had founded The Star *in 1888, and, in the new century,* T. P.'s Weekly. *"Willie" Wilde was Oscar's journalist brother and "Robbie" the art critic Robert Ross, who was Oscar Wilde's closest friend and later his executor.*

Hesketh Pearson, who would become, a generation later, one of Shaw's best biographers (again with massive help from G.B.S.), had no connection with the magazine which appeared to bear his name.

By "Ana" Shaw meant a suffix such as in "Shaviana."]

Ayot St Lawrence, Welwyn, Herts
16/10/16

Dear Frank Harris

I have received a budget of letters from you, and another from the enthusiastic Hesketh Pearson, whose general attitude to all men of letters in London who do not instantly throw down their morning's work and devote themselves heart and soul to the modern Christ (alias F. H.), is that they are cads, scoundrels, and ingrates. He is certainly a most wholehearted hero worshipper and disciple: his only heresy is a demand why you and I waste our time in writing about obsolete deaders like Jesus and Shakespear instead of living in our own times. Which is very sensible of him. I will presently try to make an opportunity of seeing him and sizing him up. Meanwhile, make large allowances for youthful impatience if he reports an infamous coldness and slackness on the part of literary London in responding to your biographical masterpiece.

As to your questions—well, hang it all, just look at them! It would involve my sitting down for months to an autobiography, I should not hesitate to do it if I had not done it already, and found that most conscientious snake soon has enough of collecting all his cast skins for a museum.

There is a monumental work on me by Archibald Henderson, Professor of Mathematics at the University of South Carolina, and an inveterate writer on the modern drama, which is indispensable to my future biographers. It contains many mistakes, some of them queer enough; but on the whole it does all the spade work up to its date. I wrote a good deal of autobiography for Henderson, who was as callow as Pearson at the time; for I knew that he would go through with it and that he had literary power enough to impose himself, and that the more he knew the better. Had it been possible for me to find time to read his proofs and correct them, the work would have been an authoritative one; but I delayed and delayed and delayed until at last in desperation he went to press without waiting any longer for me. I was treating him shamefully; but after the first effort I felt like a dog returning to his vomit, and could not bring myself to suspend my current work to read my own history. I did not even check the illustrations; and the result is that one of them which looks exactly like the sort of house a poet might starve in in Montmartre, is a picture of a house in which I never lived. The photographer went down the wrong side of the street and did not notice that he had passed from Osnaburgh St to its continuation under another name and with a new numbering. He photographed number 36; but it was not 36 Osnaburgh St where I actually dwelt, and which unluckily is a most respectable looking house, down the area steps of which no starving poet dare have ventured. This will give you an idea of the extent of my failure to check the final state of the biography. But if you cannot depend on the detail always, you can depend on the mass. I told Henderson when he first approached me with the intention of writing a magazine article about a youth of twenty or so, as he then thought me, that what he was proposing to do was to write a history of the last quarter of the nineteenth century. He tackled that job undismayed, and did it astonishingly well for a very young Southerner whom you would have declared hopelessly unqualified to do it at all.

He really did me a considerable service; for until his book appeared nobody had succeeded in piecing me together. Musicians had a tradition about me; Socialists had a tradition about me; the theatre had a tradition about me; economic cranks had a tradition about me; and all sorts of wild stories were current (mostly lies but not all); yet none of these sections knew the other's tradition; and when Henderson first achieved a conspectus of them all, I at once found myself much more of a person and less of a legend than before.

But I could not allow Henderson to use all the stuff I gave him, because my mother was then alive; and it was altogether beyond the power of so young a man (he was then unmarried) to do justice to the curious *ménage à trois* which made my boyhood so very different from normal bourgeois domestic boyhoods. In my play Misalliance, the hero is a man with three fathers. Well, *I* am a man who had three fathers. There was my actual authentic Shaw father. There was the man of genius, a musician, who, like Coleridge or Ruskin, established his bachelordom in my father's house. And there was in the intervals of his voyages as a ship surgeon, my maternal uncle, whose uproarious blasphemy and profanity knew no *maxima reverentia* for my youth, and who lavished on colloquial obscenity a command of literary expression and a barbarous humor which Rabelais might have envied.

Henderson could not divest himself of the idea that the man of genius was a scoundrel who had seduced my mother. A man who could have done that could have seduced the wooden Virgin in the museum in Nuremberg. My mother could have boarded and lodged the three musketeers and D'Artagnan for twenty years without ever discovering their sex; and they would no more have obtruded it on her than they would have ventured to smoke in her drawingroom.

Henderson said just enough to rouse a good deal of curiosity in other men who shared his interest in me and wanted to write the champion essay on me. Among others there was, and is, an Irishman named Demetrius O'Bolger, also a professor, and now resident at 1621 Green St, Philadelphia, his university being the University of Pennsylvania. Demetrius, intrigued by the unsolved problems raised by Henderson and by my published scraps of autobiography, cast all delicacy to the winds, and asked me a heap of most intimate questions. So again, seeing by these questions what ridiculous constructions and surmises might arise among the fanciers of what they call Ana, I once more sat down and spent a lot of valuable time answering these questions, and describing the curious Shavian cuckoo's nest, and my schooling and reading and so forth, just as the inquisitiveness of Demetrius suggested. And now you want me to start again. I had rather die misunderstood: a doom that has no terrors for me as far as my mere personal history (which I have never admitted as more than the merest accident) is concerned. Demetrius will presently slosh out what I have given him in what will be practically an appendix to Henderson; and then, if you can stand it, and have any more questions to ask, I may gossip some more, as there are matters that would have a special prosperity in your ears. Why not let Demetrius loose in Pearson's by way of expediting him? You see, there is a good deal of mere Dictionary of Biography stuff which you want to know, but out of which you would not make three lines of copy, whilst the others would make volumes of them. Better let them do it for you.

The real difficulty is that you have not read my works. Now it happens that Gilbert Chesterton has written a book about me which is the last word in the sort of book that can be written about me without reading me. Even you will not be able to beat it. McCabe has written a surpassingly bad book about me which shews the extreme danger of dealing with the ideas associated with me instead of the ideas I have expressed. Such books have forced me to recognize that my analytical faculty is exceptional, and that I have a power of dissecting out bundles of ideas that are inseparable in the minds not only of ordinary men but of extraordinary ones who have not followed my analyses very vigilantly. McCabe is a gross instance: he really does not get beyond such rude generalizations as that a man who does not think Darwin the greatest of men must believe in the miracle of St Januarius and exult in the tortures of the Inquisition, or that you, having expressed doubts of the sagacity of Grey, must desire to see your mother and sisters raped by Pomeranian grenadiers; but much more careful critics fall victims in the same way, however finer they may cut it, to mere associations of ideas which I have made it my business to dissolve.

For instance, take this question of yours about sex. I know

of no writer who has dealt as critically with sex as I have. Archer's early complaint that my plays reeked with sex was far more sensible than the virgin-eunuch theory which the half-penny journalists delight in. I was the first to point out that though all our plays professed to be about sex they never dealt with sex at all, but with the marriage law, and with the conventions of cuckoldry and the like. I introduced Don Juan into the third act of Man & Superman to deal with what women had taught him (among other things: that act contains my whole creed). In the tiny one-act farcical comedy I published the other day I actually put the physical act of sexual intercourse on the stage. I have shewn by a whole series of stage couples how the modern man has become a philanderer like Goethe, and how the modern woman has had to develop an aggressive strategy to counter his attempts to escape from his servitude to her. And yet men are so stupid that the critic in Fanny's First Play, solemnly declaring that the play cannot be by me because there is "the note of passion in it; and Shaw is incapable of the note of passion" is echoed even by Frank Harris! But that is because you have not seen my plays nor read them, not to mention their monumental prefaces, which also deal largely with this question of sex. Women never make this mistake except when they are going on mere hearsay and are tempted to try the virtue of Joseph at an unexpected risk to their own. I have never known a woman really interested in my plays and writings and reading them and seeing them who remained in the dark on this point. If you ever read them—and God forbid that I should urge you at your age to attempt such a task: one might as well ask a centenarian to read Shelley right through as it would influence his whole life powerfully—but if you did you would not need to ask a single question. And if you dont, you had better avoid this subject, as you will certainly botch it frightfully.

Of course I have to be, like all live writers, in constant reaction against the excesses of my time. My criticism of Shakespear in The Saturday would have been mere lunacy had they appeared when Shakespear was underrated and apologized for by such an insect as Nicholas Rowe on the ground that he wrote "by a mere light of nature" instead of as a properly educated scholar like Nicholas himself. The infatuated Amorism of the nineteenth century, like its Bardolatry, made it necessary for me to say with emphasis that Life and not Love is the supreme good; that the restriction of the word passion to sexual appetite and its denial to science and philosophy is a modern abuse of the most sickening vulgarity and ignorance; that a man or woman who is preoccupied with sex to more than, say, one twentieth part of the extent (measured in time) during which he is preoccupied with hunger or business or art or science or education or dry living generally is a neurotic degenerate or a pampered idler; that there is no instinct or appetite which can be starved so easily or deflected so whimsically or trivially as the sex instinct in spite of its pretences to be the most imperative of all instincts; and that the people who talk and write most about it betray to the really experienced people that their romance is mere green sickness, and that they have either had no experience or have no capacity for experience and therefore did not notice what they really felt. People seize on scraps like these, and on my vegetarian diet (that of the bull and elephant), to build up a theory of priestly asceticism or physical impotence; and they air it from one to another until at last it passes into the cant currency and trips up even able critics. You must clear all that out of your head when you start on me. Dante, Goethe, and Tolstoy impress the mob as cold ascetics. All three would have been called libertines if their affairs had come into the divorce court. Byron was reviled as a libertine. He was probably a much more abstemious man than his cheesemonger. All four, but especially the first three, knew more about sex than any whore in Piccadilly possibly could, without a fraction of her experience. For, to conclude with a curious observation, though poverty and fastidiousness prevented me from having a concrete love affair until I was twentynine, the five novels I wrote before that date (novels were the only wear then) shew much more knowledge of sex than most people seem to acquire after bringing up a family of fifteen.

I am glad you think the letter about Wilde may be useful. Before letting it loose give me an opportunity of correcting a proof, because I want to modify three passages at least. I want to strike out the name Robbie because Ross hates it, and was called so by Wilde because Wilde knew him as a boy in his mother's house (R's mother). I think it would be fairer to Wilde to put in a word to indicate that his attack on T.P. was not an unprovoked one, though that does not excuse its snobbery. And

I have some remorse about calling poor Willie a vulgar fellow of no account in public, as his widow is no doubt still extant, and it is cruelly true.

I will try to scribble some sort of comment on your Androcles review, for which much thanks; but just now I must go back to my arrears of work.

By the way, what was it that actually happened in that Shakespear business? All I can recollect is that by some means a manuscript of your play got into my hands; and later on Granville Barker and I discussed the possibility of producing it at the Court Theatre, but gave it up because we could do nothing creditable at that time with costume plays. Barker's great productions of Shakespear's plays and of Masefield's Philip were then hopelessly beyond our means; and we had to stick to realistic modern plays with realistic modern scenery and realistic modern people. Long after this Mrs Lyttelton proposed a Shakespear playlet as a *piece d'occasion* to get money for the Shakespear Memorial National Theatre; and I knocked off The Dark Lady of the Sonnets, which was duly performed in your presence. I did all I could to make it a means of advertizing your play: in fact I wrote so much about it that I could not get my stuff published, as it was too long for a weekly paper. I kept it by me and used it as material for my preface to the Dark Lady. That is the whole story as far as I remember it. But I dont remember how the script came into my hands originally, or what interval elapsed between that and my discussion with Barker, with whom I was acting on a quite remote recollection of the play, not on a recent reading of it; so that it seems that the manuscript Barker read was not the one I read.

What still puzzled me is how you got hold of the dark lady theory. My preface was partly a pious duty to Tyler, who rubbed that theory into me for years. I cannot say "Not marble nor the gilded monuments of princes shall outlive this powerful preface"; but I owed him that little tombstone for old times' sake. Also, as you evidently believed that I had got the dark lady from your play, and had simply cribbed her without acknowledgment, I wanted to make it clear to you that Tyler was a real person, and that I had been stuffed with the dark lady before you were born, so to speak, and, in view of Tyler's published volume on the sonnets, never dreamt of her otherwise than as public property. But in any case, I have no more conscience about plagiarizing, or being plagiarized, than Moliere or Shakespear.

I have had as yet only the first Harris Pearson.

G.B.S.

SHAW to HARRIS [H/4]

[Marie Corelli had written about Christ in Barrabas *(1894) and F. W. Farrar published a* Life of Christ *in 1874. The title to the letter was added by Harris.]*

Bernard Shaw & Jesus the Christ
10 Adelphi Terrace, London W.C.
20th Oct. 1916

Dear Frank Harris

Your review of my Androcles preface is very interesting reading, as all your stuff is; but on the subject of the mildness of Jesus you must fight it out, not with me, but with St Matthew. The Sermon on the Mount, even if we could accept it as a genuine open air speech and not a very obvious collection of "sayings", would not afford the slightest presumption that Jesus was himself the sort of person he exhorted his hearers to be.

There is an old story, told sometimes about Mazarin, sometimes about Richelieu, of a minister's antechamber hung with pictures: those on one side being all idyllic landscapes and scenes of domestic sentiment: those on the other scenes of battle and blood and torture. The minister, when he wanted to size up a new man, watched how he took the pictures. If he clung to the battle pictures, the minister knew that he was a timid man of peace, for whom action and daring were full of romantic fascination. If he wallowed in cottage sentiment and the Maiden's Prayer, he was immediately marked down for military preferment and dangerous jobs.

Have you ever known a sportsman who was ferocious? Have you ever known a humanitarian who was not ferocious? You are yourself so in love with the Sermon on the Mount, and with all aspects of gentleness and pity, that people who have never met you possibly imagine you as a Christlike, dove-eyed figure. But has anybody who has met you personally ever described you as "Gentle Francis, meek and mild!" The apparent contradiction of your pity for Sonia and Oscar Wilde by your buccaneering manners and occasionally frightful language is a familiar natural phonomenon.

Suppose I had declared that the gospel of Matthew was incredibly inconsistent because the haughty and vituperative Jesus whom he describes could not possibly be the preacher of patience, kindness, and forgiveness. Surely you would have found such a criticism hasty and shallow, and reminded me that the Shelley who wrote Prometheus Unbound and Laon and Cythna was the same Shelley who poured the fiercest invective on Castlereagh, on Eldon, and on his own father, not to mention the entire tribe of old men. Would you say that Herbert Spencer must have been a lazy man because he warned people so earnestly against the gospel of hard work? On the contrary, you can see very plainly that he gave the warning just because he had been himself unable to keep his industry within prudent bounds, and overstrained himself permanently in working at his First Principles.

Almost everyone who is interested in Jesus has a pet conception of him, and protests against my preface for not reproducing it. But my preface has nothing to do with any modern conception of him. I go to the Bible and I find there four biographies of Jesus. Three of them are called synoptic because they agree roughly as to the course of events in his life; and two of them are at least not contradictory as to his character. The fourth describes a different career and a different man—so different that if he were not named and had not been crucified by Pontius Pilate at the demand of the Jews, he might have been classed as an apostle or even as the leader of a great heresy. The world has mixed these three Jesuses into one Jesus. The great painters have painted the three kings in the stable with the shepherds: an impossible combination which would have scandalized Matthew and irritated Luke. Matthew was a man of books, a chronicler. Luke was a sentimental romancer. John was a man of the world and a politician with a turn for magic and metaphysics, not unlike Paracelsus. Matthew took it for granted that Jesus belonged to the haughty classes; had socially correct views as to the Gentiles; and was offensive as a matter of course to those who disagreed with him. Luke made an operatic tenor of him and gave him charming manners. Neither Matthew nor Luke write as eye witnesses or like men who had ever taken part in political life: they do not know how politicians and priests really talk and behave, *viva voce*. John, on the contrary, writes both as an eye witness and as a man who knew what people are like on committees and at political and religious demonstrations according to their classes. The difference is like that between Anthony Trollope and a provincial novelist who represents the king as always wearing the crown and being addressed by the prime minister in private as "your Majesty." In the end you feel pretty clear as to the sort of man Matthew was, and Luke was and John was. You even have a distinct notion of Mark. But Jesus eludes you, because though nothing could be more definite than the type of man chronicled by Matthew, you perceive that Matthew had no eye for character, and did not understand originality or even unconventionality. Luke's portrait, though good fiction, is too obviously Mozartian to be credible as a bit of realism. And John is making up a figure of the higher Freemasonry, and never takes you behind the scenes of his temple-theatre.

Out of all these I have picked some scraps of doctrine common to the four, and some traits of Bohemian life in which the four records confirm what would be deduced from the circumstances. And I have given the only explanation as yet discovered of the otherwise unaccountable going like a lamb to the slaughter. Beyond this I could not go without dropping into fiction. You can project your ideal Christ on the pages of your next book just as Burne Jones has projected his finest Christ on the window of Speldhurst Church. This Christ is not a bit like Holman Hunt's Light of the World. And Holman Hunt's Christ is not a son of Blake's God in Job. Your Christ will not be like Farrar's or Marie Corelli's. The ideal Christs are of all sorts, from tailor's dummies to reincarnations and revelations; but when you come to the documents, you come back to my preface.

The so-called higher criticism is a bore because it cannot see the man behind the gospel. It does not even tell you that Matthew and Mark were chiffoniers; it insists that there were no such persons and that the wind blew the chiffons into a heap and thus produced a gospel. That is only the useless part of the truth: I have sifted the heap for the cinders, not for the dust.

In haste, as usual
ever
G. Bernard Shaw

PS This, as you may see, is a duplicate. I keep the original copy lest this should be torpedoed, as several of my letters have been in previous submarine eruptions.

HARRIS to SHAW [H/4]

[Shaw of course had written his "Jesus" letter as a gift to Harris, and was not surprised that it was being prepared for publication in Pearson's Magazine.*]*

3 Washington Square, New York
Nov. 9, 1916

My dear Shaw:—

Another magnificent letter from you—one of the most humorous and truest I have ever seen.

I treated you a little harshly in the first of my articles on you but I shall make amends. I certainly must admit your generosity and chivalry; but you repeat in this letter a mistake you have made several times. I allege, you say, that you copied your play from mine. I never made any such statement. I say that you have, wittingly or unwittingly, taken your "Fair Lady of the Sonnets," not from the Sonnets, but from my book on Shakespeare, especially from my picture of Mary Fitton where as Cleopatra she is depicted as jealous, hot tempered and masterful. You are so scrupulous in most ways that any little slip stands out like scar on a cheek. But one would forgive you worse faults for the bigness in you and for your infinite humor. Perhaps I appreciate this latter quality more than most men, for I have no genial humor in me at all, and very little even of the sardonic sort.

I cannot attempt to answer your letter in a letter.

Your say I have "buccaneering manners and frightful language." I know one or two people—women even—who declare that I have charming manners and am infinitely amiable. Both appreciations are false and both true perhaps. You are a dreadful realist with almost a woman's sharpness of eye for foibles and little whimsicalities of manner and character. You are generous too, and kind—kinder to others than to yourself. There is both the east wind and the southwest in you and I have seen it blow from both points of the compass within the same moment's time. But the essence of you is that you are a big man and have an intellect of the first quality. And that Jesus had too, but you won't see it. Pretend indeed that he is not distinct to you. He is distinct and he is a miracle of insight—not into the weaknesses and vices of men, but into their nobilities.

Your estimate of the "Brook Kerith" is very nearly my own. It is a preposterously dull book. I had to flog myself again and again to get through it and even then I only read it superficially. It is a wretched picture of the chief character.

I am sure you have written the letter "Bernard Shaw and Jesus" for publication, so I shall publish it. I must thank you for both it and the noble letter that will be published with my next edition of the Wilde book, and make it famous I think.

I want you to like Hesketh Pearson. I think he probably overestimates both of us. We are to him the great twin brethren; but I have had so little of such outspoken hero-worship in my life and I have needed it so badly in these last two years that I feel grateful for his extravagant admiration.

One more serious word. I wish you would fight for peace. The Germans are no nearer exhaustion than England. The war is an endless stupid butchery. Get that stupid bellicosity out of the papers and out of the English mind. Every handicap increases the Germans' power. The blockade has enormously increased their industrial efficiency and the idea of an economic blockade of them after the war is worse than mad.

Good bye, Shaw for the moment. I use a bludgeon and you the bladders of the jester, but the result is much the same and we are fighting on the same side—more power to you!

Yours ever,
Frank Harris

HARRIS to SHAW [H/4]

[Harris, in the close of his letter, betrayed an inflated assessment of Shaw's public impact upon the first years of the war. His speeches urging a negotiated peace before more millions were killed often went unreported in the

press. Not until late in 1917 did the public mood begin to shift.]

3 Washington Square, New York
Dec. 23, 1916

My dear Shaw:—

I just want to send a word to wish you Christmas greetings and all luck and happiness in the new year.

I wanted to thank you for the great kindness you have shown me. I have not had occasion to be grateful often in my life but I delight in the feeling and hug it to my heart. I am very glad to think of Bernard Shaw as full of the milk of human kindness.

I believe too, that he is working for peace as I am, and there is no other cause at this moment so worthy. I can hardly bear even to think of the brutal war—an insult to human reason. I stretch hands across the sea to Shaw and thank him with all my heart, and am proud to hail him as a great captain in the liberation war of humanity.

Ever yours,
Frank Harris

P.S. I am holding this to send you my answer to your most interesting paper entitled "Bernard Shaw and Jesus." It should have been ready before; but I'll get a pull next Tuesday. By the way please send me a good signed photograph so that I may not be forced to use caricatures of you. Yours ever, Frank Harris.

SHAW to HARRIS [H/4]

[Although Shaw had been attacking the war since his thirty-page "Common Sense About the War" in 1914, he did become a War Loan subscriber, however not for the interest gains he described to Harris. As he wrote in 1918, in a piece for the American press urging citizens to subscribe to the Liberty Loan, "War is a horrible business, and to contribute money to its prosecution wrenches the best instincts of the best men as no other sort of financial transaction can. But there is no way out of war but the fighting way until the establishment of a supernational court of justice, a supernational legislature, and a supernational police, making an end of the existing international anarchy."

Uncle Pumblechook, Joe Gargery's uncle and the torment of young Pip's life in Dickens's Great Expectations, *is forever attempting, through bullying methods, to improve Pip's character.* Max Beerbohm *is the Stage Society speaker. The playlet which Shaw was rehearsing was the satire on wartime red tape and bureaucracy,* Augustus Does His Bit.

Lady Colin Campbell, a journalist as well as a noted London beauty (Whistler did her portrait), succeeded Shaw as art critic on The World.*]*

10 Adelphi Terrace, London W.C.
15th January 1917.

Dear Frank Harris

I have just received your letter enclosing the proof of my comment on your J.C. criticism and your rejoinder.

I can scrawl only a hasty reply, as I am rehearsing a play, and there is some question of my going to the front immediately afterwards to see the show.

I feel anxious about your future when I find you still insisting on your heroes having the consistency of the stage sailor, who never says or does anything "out of character". Your Jesus is a stage sailor; your Shakespear is a stage sailor; and because you cant make a stage sailor out of me, you are puzzled and say you cannot reconcile this and that in me. What would you do if you had to write portraits of Paganini and Turner, who both made presents of enormous sums of money in lumps of five figures, and were both among the meanest of men? Or Paul Jones, the bravest of naval heroes, who was terrified out of his wits when a jealous husband pursued him in Spain? Or of Frank Harris, as delicate as Shelley, and as coarse as a bushranger. Your characters with "assorted" qualities are ridiculous: somebody will call you a literary grocer, and serve you right. You are like a woman "matching" colors in a haberdasher's shop, with your "consistencies". I wish I could find a few more insults to stir you up; but I havnt time. You must learn to put vinegar in your salads. Not venom, mind; but vinegar.

You should read my Common Sense About the War. There you will find why I intend neither Hohenzollern nor Guelph to exploit my pen in this war.

The explanation of my investment is 4½%. In your reminiscences you note that I am careful about money, and belong to the "thou shalt starve ere I starve" brigade. I am never more generous than I can afford to be. I have never found that the stage sailor's five pound notes did much good. The few I have distributed certainly did a great deal of harm, and made an enemy apiece for me, very properly.

Oscar Wilde used to say of me "Shaw hasnt an enemy in the world; and none of his friends like him." And one evening at a public dinner of the Stage Society, when I had to propose the health of the critics and Max had to acknowledge, he came to me before the speechmaking began and said, "You are going to say, aren't you, that you yourself are a critic." I said very likely I should. "But you *must*", said Max; "for my reply depends on it." So I promised to say it, and did. Then Max got up, and began his speech like this. "When I was at school, the head-master made a speech to us every year, which always began by asking us to remember that he was 'one of *us*.'" A chuckle from the audience shewed that the point had gone home.

Now I am going to schoolmaster you a bit. You are a very unAmerican man: quite intensely European in your culture and your vein; and you will find that the Americans will ask you more and more for stories about the Europeans you have known, as they come to feel that you cannot write as an American editor for Americans. Now even if you do not find yourself drifting back to Europe you will want to have your books welcomed there; and it is therefore important that you should not write about European men of letters in such a way as to infuriate them. And the very surest way to infuriate them is to say, whether truly or romantically only matters to the extent that truth will offend more than romance, that you discovered them and rescued them from obscurity and poverty. Already you have implied that you are the uncle Pumblechook of Wells, Conrad, and Kipling. To give you a more vivid notion of how they are likely to feel about it, I will now write you an account of

—HOW I DISCOVERED FRANK HARRIS—

In the early nineties I was beyond all competition the champion feuilletonist of the London weekly press. At the end of the previous decade I had made a meteorically rapid reputation on the then newly founded Star. A couple of years later Edmund Yates, who had made a remarkable success with his paper The World, which he founded and indeed invented, discovered that his musical feuilletonist was in trouble, through an affair of gallantry that made the Continent more desirable as a residence than London. I was already Yates's "art critic"; and William Archer assured Yates that I was the only possible successor to the fugitive. The transfer from the Star was promptly effected; and from that time my weekly two pages of The World, with those of Theodore Childs on Parisian Life, Archer on the theatre, and the impudently amusing Woman's Walks of the late Lady Colin Campbell (who used to get me to put "the feminine touch" into her letters to Yates) formed a constellation against which no other paper in London could compete.

When Yates died, I resigned. I knew that I must have a real editor: one with some fight in him, not afraid of shadows, and master of the paper and not the slave of somebody playing for a peerage or a seat in the next cabinet. Griffiths, Yates's successor, was no use to me; and though at his earnest request I went on long enough to conceal from the public the real reason of my resignation, I dropped off at the end of the season, and began looking round for a new editor capable of appreciating and standing up to my work.

One cold winter day I was walking on the embankment: the benches of which are the only furniture of the homeless, frozen, penniless outcasts of London. At one of the outcasts I looked a second time, struck by his fine eyes and something familiar in his expression. Suddenly I recognized him as Frank Harris, who had edited an obscure rag called The Fortnightly Review for a miserable pittance. In a flash it came to me that Frank was the man I needed. I spoke to him; told him to wait on his bench for my return; pressed a shilling into his frozen fingers; and left the poor wretch, who was unable to speak and could only sob with gratitude. At that moment the once famous Saturday Review was on the brink of the abyss. I jumped into a hansom and drove to the office. I wasted no time in preliminaries. I said bluntly, "Nothing can save you but a feuilleton by G.B.S., and you know it. Well, I will fill two pages of any paper that is edited by Frank Harris." Ten minutes later I returned to the embankment, and said "Frank: you are the editor of the Saturday Review." He tried to say "Thank God!"; but his mouth was full of the sausage roll he had purchased with my shilling. His heart was full too.

The rest is history. I did not write about music; but I taught poor J.F. Runciman to write about it. Harris taught him to drink, unfortunately; and he died in the valley of humiliation. Cunninghame Graham and D.S. MacColl came in when Harris asked them to join *me*. I encouraged Harris to write his remarkable articles on Shakespear and to develop his talent for the short story, then made classical by the genius of De Maupassant, whom nobody in England before Frank had even approached in distinction.

When I abandoned journalism for playwriting, the paper of course fell to pieces at once, and Frank returned to the embankment until he emigrated. I have never regretted the patronage and encouragement I extended to him &c,&c,&c,&c.

There! What do you think of that? Now what I want you to note specially is that being false, it causes you nothing worse than an impulse of indignation drowned almost at once in contempt. *But if it were true, it would be far more unpleasant.* Moral: in your reminiscences of men of letters, dont dwell too much on what you did for them: they would much rather hear about what they did for you, if they ever did anything.

Here endeth the first lesson.

What has become of all your plays? What was the matter with them? Stage sailors, eh? You must have got very near the right thing. What was wrong?

Ever

G. Bernard Shaw.

HARRIS to SHAW [H/4]

[By early 1917 Shaw was no longer persona non grata, *and had been invited to visit the British armies in France as a guest of Sir Douglas Haig. Shaw's story of his trip to the front in Flanders would appear in the* Daily Chronicle *on 5, 7 and 8 March 1917. Kipling's patriotism had been loud and jingoistic since the beginning of the war, while Shaw had been anti-war (although anti-Junker) and sought a negotiated peace.*

Leopold von Ranke, a professor at the University of Berlin in the mid-1800s, was the leading historian of sixteenth- and seventeenth-century Europe. His claim, quoted approvingly by Harris, is, "But as educator of the people there has never been a royal line like the Hohenzollerns." Harris's postscript reference to "Mrs. B. B." is to Elizabeth Barrett Browning. Albert Ballin, head of the Hamburg-American Line, would commit suicide on hearing of the Kaiser's abdication in 1918.]

3 Washington Square, New York
February 1, 1917

My dear Shaw:—

Thanks for your letter and your account of discovering me which did not make me indignant but made me howl with laughter. All this discovering of the sun at noon day whether done by you or by me is of course pure absurdity, or, if true, only a sign of the moment when we got over our puppy blindness and managed to see out of our own eyes.

I could never have discovered Conrad or Wells or Kipling. I do not see them now, not even as lesser lights ruling the night. Carlyle and Meredith and Browning and Swinburne were such light to me, but the Wellses and Chestertons and Conrads and Kiplings are only Chinese lanterns swaying about under the trees and throwing fantastic colored gleams here and there on the shadow shapes that come and go; one after the other they flare out, Death being the master of that ceremony.

But you are in another sort of category and one thing in your letter touched me profoundly. I am always conscious of a tartness in you and it made me roar to see that you feel conscious of something like this in me for you advise me to put some vinegar in my salad and not bitter; no vitriol. I do not think this is quite fair to me. I have often been called bitter by the Kiplings and Wellses and others because I do not see their value. Unless a man is called to write great things he should never use a pen except to write letters or keep his books, but what seems strange to me is that I always get a sarcastic vein out of you even when I ask for the serious.

Now you are going to the trenches probably to see more than they let me see in the first six weeks of the war which taught me enough of the madness not to want to see anything more of it. I would give anything to know how it really affects you, but I am sure that the insanity of it all, the murderous stupidity, will strike you first, last, and all the time.

Still, tell me about it, will you? It would be kind of you.

I wish you could see the Germans as I see them. I am no more in love with the Hohenzollern than with Guelphs; but I remember being struck as a young man by a great sentence from Ranke. He said:

> Aber als Erzieher des Volkes ist keine königliche Race je da gewesen wie die Hohenzollern.

They have really tried to be "educators" of their people. "Windy Bill" as I christened the present Emperor with that reverence which is peculiar to me, is just an average specimen of the race. Everything he has done has been a half-product—half bad, I mean, half good. He has backed up his merchants. He made Ballin; he made the German mercantile marine *and* the German navy which excited England's envy and brought about this war. If he had only given back Metz and the French part of Lorraine to France twenty years ago instead of establishing a navy he would have completed Bismarck's work instead of endangering it.

But you do not want me to talk to you about these things only. I would like you to see the German soldier as I see him, patient, strong, obedient, decent; and his officer, burning with patriotism, feeling in some dumb way that Prussia has done great things in the world and that he is a part of the great work & willing to die at any time for that consciousness and its fulfilment.

True, there are noble Englishmen too in the war and noble Frenchmen—I simply ache for them. It was intolerable to me even to live in France, impossible to work or think, feeling choking thought, choking life itself.

What will your feelings be? I would give anything for just a page from you of what the real Shaw feels from Calais to the trenches and home again some night.

Well, well, you have done brave great things. Far away from you I lift my hat and cheer. All good be with you and may you do greater things still and so confound complacency.

Yours ever,
Frank Harris

P.S. I am sending you a few pages—a pen-portrait of poor Ernest Dowson—the poet whom you may have known & a page or two of a plea for peace—this last rendered nugatory, I'm afraid by the dreadful challenge of the Allies & the appalling answer of Germany in favor of the submarine was *à outrance*:

Now it is up to Wilson to play the man & keep this people at least out of the fight. Yours ever. F.H.

P.S.[2] You tell me I'm not & can't be an American: You are mistaken: I am more typically American than you imagine. Here I am succeeding: my democratic sympathies help me on this side as they lamed me in London. I'm going to try to write a play: write when you can. Your letters are the wine of life-time, as Mrs. B. B. said, "the wine that's meant for souls." I've just been contrasting your patriotism with Kipling's to your advantage. I send you the paper soon. Yours ever, F.H.

SHAW to HARRIS [H/4]

[Shaw's language in referring Hesketh Pearson's article to Harris was taking into account the likelihood of the letter being read by the postal censor. The news from Russia was the overthrow of the Czar in the Kerensky revolution. By November the world was further surprised by the overthrow of Kerensky by Lenin and Trotsky.]

10 Adelphi Terrace
30th March 1917

My dear Frank Harris,

This, in great haste.

Hesketh Pearson has gone out with his regiment to Mesopotamia. His wife tells me that he attempted to send you the enclosed article without knowing the regulations. It was of course sent back to him, and arrived after his departure. Mrs Pearson has therefore appealed to me to get it through to you in proper form. As it has no reference to politics I take the responsibility for it and send it as from myself.

Good news from Russia, eh? Not quite what any of the belligerents intended, any more than Bismarck intended to make France a republic in 1870; but the Lord fulfils himself in many ways. It is probably not the last surprise he has up his sleeve for us.

Yours ever
G. Bernard Shaw

SHAW to HARRIS [C/4]

[Harris in Pearson's *had attacked the inequities and real horrors of the women's night court in New York, and his exposé of police and judicial brutality toward prostitutes was too explicit for the sensibilities of John Sumner, executive secretary of the Society for the Suppression of Vice. He urged that a warrant be issued for Harris's arrest and that copies of the May 1917 number be seized. Although Harris managed to ward off imprisonment he had to pay a $300 fine. Having always held a low opinion of American justice, Shaw was not surprised.*

An Irish Home Rule convention to which Shaw unsuccessfully aspired to be a delegate accomplished nothing, and the Stockholm conference to develop a peace formula along Socialist lines foundered when both Britain and Germany refused to give passports to prospective delegates.

The Shavian postcard had no salutation.]

10 Adelphi Terrace
31st July 1917

That sort of thing is always going on in America. What is the use of writing at the angry ape? If he wont listen to Shakespear he wont listen to me. I have no illusions about the Golden West: probably, however, it only seems the worst place in the world politically and juridically because there is less hushing up: that is, less solidarity among the governing class than in England or Russia.

I have tried without success to get nominated to the Irish Convention. I am delegated to the Allied Socialist Conference in London next week, and to Stockholm; but I cannot see what Socialism has to do with the war. War is not a Socialist game; and it is one at which the loser must pay. If there be a loser, he will have to pawn his shirt. Only a draw can make the sort of pious peace the Russians are dreaming of possible. So we must await the event.

GBS

HARRIS to SHAW [H/4]

97 Central Park West, New York
November 23rd, 1917

My dear Shaw:—

Herewith I send you a copy of your superb "Memories of Oscar Wilde." I think it a most excellent piece of work and have said so. I do not think our estimates differ very widely and the points of difference seem to me extremely interesting. I have treated them in a couple of pages of introduction in which I speak gratefully of your kindness to me.

This stay in America has taught me that I have no country and no kin and I feel more completely an exile here among my own people than I ever felt even in England. There is no art here, no storied past, no seductive memories. I find the life bare and common to a frightful degree. The people are all intelligent, all bright, but there are no intellectuals; the heights are uninhabited and the dead level of the commonplace afflicts me with an appalling sense of human stupidity. I suffer as if I had been skinned; all the nerves laid bare; and I long for peace, long to resume my life in France with a sort of maniacal intensity.

But they have whipped the ape here to anger as you said and they are going on whipping him with appeals to patriotism and pluck in the most disgraceful way. Meanwhile papers that criticise the government are ruthlessly suppressed, and the capitalistic mobs encouraged to deal out their own justice resulting in outrages and assaults upon individuals which would be incredible in any other country.

I have no business to inflict all this on you for I imagine you must suffer a good deal from the same sort of thing in London. Perhaps you would tell me about this. It would interest me for I want to make my pen portrait of you a complete one. I intend to put you as the first figure in my second volume of these "Contemporary Portraits."

By the by I wish you could send me McCabe's book on you which I do not seem able to get here, or anything else that will throw light upon you.

The popular edition of my Life of Oscar with your memories will be out in a few weeks now; I am only waiting indeed to hear from you: it must wait now till spring!

If you have a photograph you like and would write a word or two on it I would add it to these memories or preface them with it.

Once again thanking you for your kindness to me, I am,

Ever Sincerely Yours,
Frank Harris

SHAW to HARRIS [H/4]

[The "a few literary men made hysterical exhibitions of themselves" refers not only to the general outcry over his "Common Sense About the War" from jingoistic writers but to the campaign, led by playwright Henry Arthur Jones, to expel Shaw— the organization's ornament—from the Dramatists' Club in 1915. The hysteria would crumble as the war turned into a bloody stalemate, and by 1918 Shaw had been transformed into sage and prophet. For details about this period in Shaw's life see the editor's Journey to Heartbreak *(1971, 1973).*

Shaw's "solution of the Irish question" was his long essay, How to Settle the Irish Question, *which appeared in the London* Daily Express *on November 27–29, 1917, in the New York* American *on December 23 and 30, 1917, and January 6 and 13, 1918, as well as in other papers and in Dublin and London as a pamphlet.*

Holy Willie is the narrator of Robert Burns's bawdy and satiric "Holy Willie's Prayer," a lusty Presbyterian elder whose liquorishly fervent and remorseful devotion becomes more stern and violent as he tipples. Julia Frankau wrote under the name "Frank Danby." Emery Walker was an artistic and publishing associate of William Morris.]

10 Adelphi Terrace
4th January 1918

My dear Frank Harris

I have already sent you back the Wilde letter corrected for publication. If it has not reached you you had better send me another, as it must have been torpedoed. It is better nowadays to send things in duplicate, as their arrival is so uncertain.

In your letter of the 23rd, you would surprise me, if you had not surprised me in the same way so often before, by the indignant amazement with which you discover every twenty four hours that the night is dark and the day occasionally wet and cold or hot and oppressive. America is America: what did you expect? It is true that the choir of Beauvais and the stained glass of Chartres are not in Fifth Avenue; but who, except yourself, ever supposed they were? Even less reasonable was your wild notion that America is the land of freedom. I am supposed by simple folk to be a sort of apostle of freedom, with magical powers of agitation. When any outrage, from a blasphemy prosecution, or the raiding by the police of an art school because drawings of naked statues have been shewn at the annual prize show, to a birth control prosecution or the enforcement of one of the laws existing in several American states that anyone who says or does or wears anything calculated to excite sexual emotion shall be sent to penal servitude, particulars are sent to me with an appeal for the assistance of my powerful pen. I dont think a year has passed during the present century that some monstrous case of the kind has not occurred. I have repeatedly refused invitations to visit America except on condition of receiving a safe-conduct from the President. In South Carolina they not only have all the horrors of factory child slavery as they existed at the beginning of the XIX century in Lancashire, but also a law of absolutely indissoluble marriage, outdoing the Roman Catholic Church, which at least admits of dispensations. America has the morals and the outlook of a XVII century village with a development of capitalism which only a very highly organised Socialism and an ultra-modern freedom of thought could control. I once told the Americans so in a much discussed article entitled "A Nation of Villagers." There was some protest but no defence: all the sensible people who alluded to it laughed and owned up. The others sulked, but had not the gumption to point out that the same thing is true all over the world: nowhere has there been any real revision of religion, morals and political science since the Reformation: indeed in parts of Italy there has been none since the Etruscans painted their caves near Orvieto. But there are depths even in the abyss: Ulster and the Scotland of Holy Wil-

lie are worse than Weimar and Bayreuth, or, let us admit,
Boston. There has always been a corner of London where Dr
Johnson and Keats and George Meredith could breathe, even
though Shelley and Byron were driven out; and the Intellectuals, the Benthamites, the Positivists, and the Fabians have
run no risk of lynching. There may be such a corner in Chicago;
and there are Greenwich Villages and places of communities of
one kind or another where cranks have a fairly good time. But
I think it is impossible for anyone who knows American lynching, American Inquisition legislation, and American graft, to
deny that America is illiberal, superstitious, crude, violent, anarchic and arbitrary to a degree that makes a man like you feel
much nearer the Pilgrim Fathers, and much further from Bergson, than in the culture centers of Western Europe. Therefore I
am inclined to laugh when you tell me you feel more an exile in
America than you ever felt in England. I could have told you
you would. You add "Here, among my own people." But do you
suppose that a naturalisation paper can make an American out
of a Galway Welshman? And, frankly, are you at home anywhere except in the lovely Alsatia which is politely called the
Riviera? Do you suppose that your blasting scorns and raging
pities, your culture of which you are so conscious and your
ruffianism of which you are so amusingly unconscious, are domestic virtues anywhere? Unless your wife tames you, you will
always be a combination of the Wandering Jew and Colonel
Blood, incongruously endowed with literary genius. And even
the endowment is a crotchety one; for you have a taste for
Literature (a thing I care no more for than Michael Angelo
cared for plaster and red lead) like Gosse and Sidney Colvin,
along with a Maupassantique imagination and a critical *flair*
for genius that is seldom associated with literary Pococuran-
tism. The late Julia Frankau once remonstrated with me for not
being sufficiently considerate of your literary sensitiveness: she
said that to a man like you, my jumping your Shakespear claim
was like stealing your last farthing. That was an exaggeration,
of course; but literature, merely as literature, has a romantic
charm for you: that is why you paint pen portraits of literary
men as Raphael painted Madonnas. I like doing thumb nail
sketches of them myself occasionally; but I have no romantic
veneration for them; and I believe you have. But then I have no
veneration in me. A phrenologist told me so in a vegetarian

restaurant nearly forty years ago. "How do you know?" I said. "Havnt I the bump?" "Bump!" he exclaimed. "It's a hole." Henry Irving once complained to Emery Walker that I seemed lacking in that agreeable quality.

McCabe's book is quite useless except for the purpose of writing a portrait of McCabe. Some of his work, dealing with facts, is very good. But just as the cucullus does not make the monk, the throwing of it away does not rub off the apostolic succession. McCabe is still Father McCabe, believing that if a man does not believe in transubstantiation, he will steal spoons. He is so saturated with the conception of virtues and vices, sins and graces, as occurring in sets: for example, the seven deadly sins, the three last things to be remembered &c, that he is incapable of critical analysis, and unhesitatingly infers from any single belief or quality or defect a whole group of beliefs, qualities, defects, or all three together, with which the single one is associated in his imagination. He has carried this to such extravagant lengths in his book about me that it is hardly too much to say that the book contains nothing about me. Having become aware that I do not share his crude secularist materialism, and that I think he would have remained in the Church if he had had a little more sense (though he would have come out of it if he had had a little more again) he devotes page after page to shewing what a fool I am to believe in Noah's Ark, Jonah and the Great Fish, the infallibility of the Pope, Calvin's Institutes, Swedenborg's Revelations, Blake's prophetic books &c, &c; going to church every Sunday in a tall hat and frock coat; opposing all Liberal measures; denying that the earth moves round the sun; applauding the burning of Giordano Bruno and so on and so forth. It is pure waste of time to read it: his confusion is so gross that it is not even funny. G.K. Chesterton's book is far better, because, though G.K.C. apparently never read a word of mine, or saw more than one play (which he does not remember) he makes me a peg on which to hang a very readable essay on things in general. Archibald Henderson's biography, and the private memoranda in the possession of O'Bolger of Philadelphia are the only documents from which you would learn anything about my circumstances. The death of my mother set me free to tell O.B. more than I could allow Henderson to publish in her lifetime. But why not read my works? It is a heavy job, I know, and one which must be dropped and relieved from time to time; for my stuff in very large doses would drive you mad; but it is really the only way.

I cannot send you a photograph. Pictures are not allowed by the censorship.

Considering the sensation my Common Sense About the War made in November 1914, when it was treason to write otherwise than as a raving madman, and French and Kitchener, Asquith and Grey were magnified beyond Alexander and Hannibal, Lincoln and Richelieu, I have not much to complain of in the way of incivility. A few literary men made hysterical exhibitions of themselves; but every attempt to have me mobbed, in the theatre or on the platform, failed completely: I spoke in public throughout the month in which Common Sense appeared to crowded audiences without a word of remonstrance or opposition, challenging questions on the war or any other subject the audience liked. In the autumn of 1915 I returned to the platform and delivered a harangue of such length that it nearly killed me, in the course of which I recalled the terrible scene in the Bacchae of Euripides, where the Bacchante who thinks she has torn a stag to pieces in the Dionysian frenzy finds that the dripping head she carries in triumph is that of her own son; and I said that many an English mother would wake from her patriotic delirium to the same horror. That was the plane on which I spoke; and I carried everything before me. The press was the biggest I ever saw at a meeting; but the censorship stopped all the reports, only the Manchester Guardian defying it.

Therefore I cannot reasonably complain; but you must remember that I am not a Pacifist or a pro-Hohenzollern, and that last January I was officially invited to the front, and my articles passed by the censor without the deletion of a single word. Still, my repudiation of the official position about Belgium, and my determination not, if I can help it, to allow the Foreign Office to gain prestige by the war, has roused more fury in several quarters than the utterances of the out-and-out pacifists. The paper which raged most furiously against me, the London Daily Express, came to me the other day for my solution of the Irish Question. Possibly you have seen the articles in the New York American.

Perhaps I should add, however, that I did not intend to get

mobbed, and that I have never yet met a tactician clever enough to manoeuvre me into a completely disadvantageous position. Others who have not gone half as far as I have, with less luck and less adroitness, have had some very unpleasant experiences.

Ever
G. Bernard Shaw

HARRIS to SHAW [H/4]

[David Graham Phillips (1867–1911) satirized the newspaper publisher, the political boss, the industrial magnate, the fortune-hunter, etc., in a series of novels of which the best-known remains Susan Lennox, Her Fall and Rise, *a Sister Carrie sort of novel written in 1908 but only published in 1915 (serially). When it was first released in book form in 1917 the Society for the Suppression of Vice objected, forcing the deletion of some passages.*

Robert W. Chambers (1865–1933) had published Athalie *in 1915. Among his other novels were* The Conspirators, The Cambric Mask *and* The Business of Life. *"Whartons" probably refers to novels by Edith Wharton.*

The Matamoros affair concerned Mexican commercial rights along its Rio Grande border with the United States.]

29 Waverly Place, New York
February 6th, 1918

My dear Shaw:—

I have just received your letter of the 4th of January and read it with infinite amusement and some profit.

What you take from the Bacchae is one of the finest things I ever read. I wish to goodness I had thought of it but I didn't and must congratulate you. It makes me want to print your letter here in spite of your sneering at my "ruffianism." I do not for the life of me understand what you mean; I never played ruffian in my life, but you seem still to believe that the lies people tell about one must have some germ of truth in them; or are you judging me by what you call my "lurid language?"

You can't write to me or about me without calling me names; I have never felt this inclination towards any one and so cannot understand it in you. It puzzles me whenever I meet it. Lope da Vega calls Saavedra-Cervantes every name he can put his tongue to and Cervantes replies by praising his "most excellent, ingenious and amusing comedies." You talk of my being over-conscious of whatever little scholarship or culture I have and you evidently think I plume myself on it. You are completely mistaken in this. No memory-wallet however well-filled can add to a man's stature or increase his insight. I am always marvelling for example at Wells's shortsightedness in regard to this war. He predicted at the beginning that the Germans would be beaten in three months. I cannot believe myself so much wiser than he is for his Time-Machine and some other things make me rate him as a good mind and so I say continually, "What a pity Wells didn't learn German." Of course I know that if he had learned any other language but his own or any other people he could not mis-see the German as he does, but I prefer out of a sort of courtesy to explain my superiority by this seemingly adventitious advantage. As a matter of fact I am always shamefacedly conscious of my want of scientific knowledge; I spent a year or so in chemistry and wish I had given another to physics and still another to biology, but I didn't and so shall go maimed of these antennae and without their vivifying influence to my grave. Is this regret due to the pirate in me or the Captain Blood you always talk of?

Our points of likeness and unlikeness are so extraordinary that it seems I am continually surprising you while you just as continually surprise me.

I had a false idea of America because I had an ideal of it taken from my life in the west as a boy forty odd years ago when there was a great deal of freedom and a great deal of humanity in spite of occasional lynchings or other atrocities. There was no child slavery then in the southern cotton mills or even in the mills of Lowell, Massachusetts, and it was easy for anyone who had health and strength to earn a good living just as it was extremely difficult for anyone to make a fortune, as it probably is to-day in a farming community.

I found in Kansas and Colorado a highly developed respect for law and the Supreme Court of the United States had again and again set a very high example as in the famous Matamoros judgment when international rights were held to be more important than the self-interest of the United States. There was a good deal of prudery and an occasional lynching that shocked me but as a young man I did not feel them intolerable. In the long interval from 1875 to 1914 the two worst faults of American civilization increased rather than diminished. The prudery has become even more marked than in Great Britain and the capitalistic tyranny has reached heights undreamed of anywhere in Europe.

Strikers are shot down by capitalistic thugs as if they were wild beasts and state powers and even federal powers used ruthlessly to suppress strikes.

All you say about America is true. My view was formed from Kansas, Colorado, Nebraska, Wyoming and Texas in the early seventies; you have evidently considered the later manifestations of capitalism in the eastern states.

What you call my "ruffianism" is revolt against convention which you incarnated almost as strongly in London as I did. You carried it into dress and on to the stage, whereas I suppose I put it in papers and showed it in my books; but you are quite as much a ruffian as I am or ever was, and you seem even more unconscious of it in yourself than I am.

You laugh at my weakness for literature and literary ideals, but you were much nearer the conventional standard and more in sympathy with it than I was. I had books returned to me that the printer would not print; these very "portraits" you speak of had to have a great deal of realism taken out of them before I could get them published. I believed, and believe, that the sex business is extremely important; that you cannot know a man without knowing his faith and practice in this respect, and I wanted to state them about the men I knew, but I was not allowed to in England and I am not allowed to in America. You, on the other hand, seem to have no difficulty in this matter.

Our likenesses and unlikenesses are best seen perhaps in our books about the war.

You see England and English faults from the Irish angle much in the same way that I do. Your "Common Sense About the War" I have no doubt is excellent, but you please English prejudice at the same time by attacking the Germans, whereas I wrote and spoke in favor of the German people. You said that the Allies would win in the war and cheered them on so to speak to the winning. I told them in so many words that they could not win, and in spite of all her Hohenzollerns and feudal government I declared that Germany had done so much for humanity that she could not be beaten by all Europe in arms.

My "ruffianism" here seems to have been right; but why should you gird at it? I do not believe in your heart you would take exception to anything I state in that book of mine "England or Germany," just as I am sure without having read it that I would swallow whole your "Common Sense About the War."

But my praise of the Germans and my belief in their efficiency are not the chief reasons why I am more hated in England than you are. You have a sense of humor and the mediocrities thereby avoid the necessity of taking you seriously. They say, "Shaw is making fun of us; it is only 'pretty Fanny's way'."

But I have no such gift of humor and consequently they want to murder me and men like Arnold Bennett, Wells, Conrad and Harrison are not ashamed of shouting pro-German at me just as they shouted pro-Boer at both of us twenty years ago.

You have put your finger on one difference between us. You have no reverence for greatness and great men and I have a good deal, particularly for the great artist whether in literature or in art. He seems to me the worthiest thing I have found on this earthly pilgrimage; he has to taste of all the fruits and yet never eat too much of any of them; he has to understand all the faults and all the stupidities and yet not be governed by any of them; he has to stand against all the devilish tyrannies and loathsome hypocrisies and the vile acts of the yahoos, and yet never forget that he too is of the unfeathered biped race. I have a mitigated admiration for Carlyle and Meredith and Shaw, and even perhaps Frank Harris, but I certainly do not feel any for the Lloyd Georges and Curzons, the Kaisers and Clemenceaus. I prefer Lenin to Lansdowne and Trotzky and Henderson and Liebknecht to Hertling and Hoffmann and Hindenburg; and I believe you do too.

One thing I find I have passed over in your letter and that is the stained glass of Chartres not to be found on Fifth Avenue—the want of artistic feeling in America.

This was typified to me at an exhibition the other day of some of the early water colors of Cezanne. Three or four of them were hung upside down. I turned one right side up and pointed out to the proprietor that he could see the line of roof.

"Oh yes," he said; "it does look like a roof."

"I suppose," I added, "you took it for a drainpipe."

"Well," he said, "to tell you the truth, I did not pay much attention to it; I do not expect to sell many of them; no money in them you know."

Whereas I should be as proud of a Cezanne, or almost as proud, as I am of a Shaw letter.

In your last paragraph you take exactly the same position as I have taken here as editor of Pearson's.

When I published the "Candid Friend" in London I protested against the atrocities of the Boer war and I found out how dangerous it was to go against English public opinion, so that when we entered the war here I had already had my lesson; I could subscribe to every word of this last paragraph of yours; "I did not intend to get suppressed," etc., and while forty socialist papers have been ruthlessly slaughtered I am still allowed to say something of what I wish to say. [*In margin*: "The 'Ruffian' lost £20,000 on this Quixotism!"]

Now I have finished except that what I wanted to get from you was seemingly what you have told O'Bolger and will not tell me. I have read your works at least as carefully as you have read mine so that your advice to me on that point is superfluous. It is the incidents of your life from four to thirty that I am ignorant about and must possess before I can write about you at all properly. What were you about in the formative time say from 16 to 22 or 25. The earlier stages are the most important. When and how did you get rid of the Religious Rack? Had it infected you deeply? What books or men helped you to your freeing? And to forming your new belief? What is that really? I mean do you believe in a personal life after death? Or the gradual amelioration of mankind?

Then the economic difficulty? Did that press you, deprive you of anything?

If you imagined that I was going to paint you in the spirit that Raphael painted his Madonnas I wonder why you asked God to save you from me in your previous epistle.

Yours ever,

Frank Harris

P.S. I am attending to the copyright business in your name and everything as carefully as possible, but I hope you won't limit my use of these "Memories" of yours to this edition, for it is this book of Oscar Wilde which has kept me above water since

I have been here and which promises to give me the small amount of money I shall need after the war to return for a year or so to that blessed Riviera or to the Latin Quarter of Paris which I regard as the Paradise of men of letters and which you speak of very aptly as our Alsatia.

By the way please let me have your opinion of O. Henry. It would do good here; serve to point Americans to a real writer instead of to the Chambers and Whartons that they idolize.

There is one other American whom you ought to know besides O. Henry and this is David Graham Phillips. Have you read any of his books? If not I would send them to you; some of them were published by Harmsworth in a shilling or sixpenny library. He is nearer Balzac's stature in my opinion than anyone who has written in English fiction, and I wish I could get him taken seriously here. I would rather have him than a dozen Dickens. Please tell me whether you have read him or not and whether you would care to make his acquaintance.

Yours
F. Harris

SHAW to HARRIS [H/2]

[Félicien Rops (1833–1898) was a technically brilliant Belgian etcher and lithographer famous for his book illustrations, often satirical, sometimes licentious, always controversial. Adolphe Adam (1803–1856), whom Shaw charges with complaining that he only liked music which soothed him, was a Parisian composer of popular operas and ballets.

Paul Verlaine (1844–1896), the French Symbolist poet, probably appears in a negative context because he was also a drug addict and a cadger of money. H. W. Massingham was Shaw's friend and editor of The Nation; *Horatio Bottomley was a Shavian enemy and editor of the jingoistic and irresponsible* John Bull. *Mrs. Humphry Ward wrote novels of religious uplift; Lady Jessica Sykes apparently had helped Harris years before to fill* The Candid Friend *with her gossip and photographs of aristocratic friends, but Harris would deny the allegation. Douglas is very likely Oscar Wilde's friend Lord Alfred Douglas, who had become notorious for his litigiousness in the wake of allegations made later about him and Wilde; Cronwright-Schreiner (who took his wife's name to hyphenate onto his own) was novelist Olive Schreiner's husband.*

Fanny's First Play was Shaw's feminist spoof, which played for 622 performances in its first London run (1911–1912). Misalliance (1910), which ran only for eleven performances, is a farce about parents and children which has become of the sure-fire staples of the Shavian repertory.

Shaw's discussion of the Boer War and the European war then in progress are largely self-explanatory. Balfour and Hertling were, respectively, the British and German foreign ministers at the time of writing.

Robert Bontine Cunninghame Graham (1852–1936), a widely traveled Scottish writer and one-time Socialist M. P., was a Sha-vian model for Sergius *in* Arms and the Man *and* Hector *in* Heartbreak House.*]

10 Adelphi Terrace, London W.C.
5th March 1918

My dear Frank Harris:

You must not take my comments on your personal characteristics as sneers and disparagements. If you do you will find me an impossible man to have any relations with. I tell you you are a ruffian exactly as an oculist might tell you that you are astigmatic. I will tell you now more precisely what I mean—if I have done so already you have brought the reputation on yourself.

Somebody in London society who likes interesting people meets you and invites you to dinner. He asks you to take in a bishop's wife. You entertain her with deep-voiced outpourings of your scorn for the hypocrisy and snobbery of the Church, finishing up with a touch of poetry about Mary Magdalene and her relations with Jesus. When the poor lady escapes to the drawing-room and you find yourself between the bishop and Edmund Gosse, you turn the conversation on to the genius of Rops, and probably produce a specimen of his work, broadening your language at the same time into that of the forecastle of a pirate sloop.

And if you observe the least sign of restiveness or discomfort on the part of the twain, you redouble your energy of expression and barb it with open and angry scorn. When they escape upstairs in their turn, they condole with one another. Gosse says, "My God, what a man!" The bishop says, "Oh, impossible; quite impossible!"

Now though this particular picture is a fancy one, it is not founded on any lies that people have told me. I have seen and heard you do such things; I have been condoled with, and have had to admit that you are a monster, and that clever as you are, it is impossible to ask anyone to meet you unless they are prepared to stand anything that the uttermost freemasonry of the very freest thought and expression in the boldest circles can venture on. I have met men who have been so shocked and wounded by you that they have been unable to talk about you. I have seen a man of the world with no prejudices to be shocked, nevertheless screw himself up into the most rigid correctness to force you to keep on correct ground. Poor old Adolphe Adam used to run away from Beethoven's symphonies crying "J'aime la musique qui me berce!" You would have run after him with a trombone blaring Beethoven's most challenging themes into his ears.

Now intensely disagreeable as this was to our Adams and snobs and conventional people in general, it was not at all disagreeable to me. It was quite genuine and natural, like Beethoven walking truculently through the court group with his hat thrust down on his eyebrows when Goethe stood aside politely hat in hand like a good Geheimrath. When Beethoven's brother put "Land-besitzer" (Landed Proprietor) on his visiting card, Beethoven put "Hirnbesitzer" (Brain Owner) on his. All that was ruffianism on Beethoven's part; but it was an assertion of real values; and the man who asserts real values cannot be passed over by nobodies, or disliked by somebodies, merely because he asserts them in a ruffianly way. And your ruffianism was on the whole of this description. If it had been aristocratic insolence and impatience of self-restraint like that of Randolph Churchill or Douglas, it would have been intolerable. As it was, I liked it.

BUT—and here is the point of insisting on it as I do, it damaged you socially. It must have agonized Wilde, not merely because he was a snob and could hear Shakespear saying, "Harris, with his teeth ever in the plump calf of prosperity," but because he shrank from seeing nice and innocent people wounded and scorned merely because they were not geniuses. But Wilde did not greatly matter socially; what did matter, was that though one could ask you to meet Julia Frankau and Lady Jessica Sykes, one could not ask you to meet Mrs. Humphry Ward. You may say: "God be praised for that! I never wanted to meet Mrs. Humphry Ward." All the same, you cannot have a career in London as a journalist and politician unless you can be trusted to take Mrs. Humphry Ward in to dinner and leave her under the impression that you are either a very respectable or a very charming man.

You may say that this may be true, but why rub it into you now that you are out of London? Well, you are out of London; but you have left a reputation there, part of which consists of a vague impression that in some way or other you made yourself impossible and had to go off to Monte Carlo and then to America, where you publicly shook the dust of London from your feet. People whose curiosity is roused by your writings ask, "What was wrong with Frank Harris?" Wasn't he a Jew, or a financial blackmailer-journalist, or another Verlaine, or a German spy, or something? It is necessary to reply. "No, he was simply the most impossible ruffian on the face of the earth," and explain in the sense in which I have explained above.

There are points on which you cannot be defended. The failure of The Candid Friend was the failure of a paper which you gave your name to and did not edit. If you had worked at it as Massingham works at The Nation, or even as Bottomley works at John Bull, you would have become a power in the land. After the first two numbers you left it to a lady-drunkard, who kept it going very cleverly with her old letters and photographs of royal personages, but could not save it. But at least you did not let her put your name to things that you did not write. You reached that stage with Vanity Fair, in which coarse and illiterate attacks on your own ideals and friends appeared with the initials F.H. I dont suppose you ever saw them, or ever went near the place to read the wretched rag (you simply *couldnt*); and when the Press Cutting people sent them to me, I knew before I had read three lines that you had not written them. But other people were not so discriminating. When it came to Modern Society, God forsook you in righteous indignation and delivered you into the hands of your enemies by the hands of a scribbler too silly to know how to steer clear of the law. You got two weeks where Wilde had got two years. You deserved hanging. What had a man like you to do with the dregs of bucket-shop finance and journalism?

What I reproach you with is an extraordinary stupidity which is too serious in its results to be excused as innocence; and yet it is a sort of innocence. When Mrs. Frankau said to me "You dont know what a sensitive and simple soul he is," I knew what she meant, though I replied, "I know what a damned fool he is." Because your natural point of honor was in high literature and not in journalism, you thought that there was no point of honor in journalism. You were like the incorruptible lady who wouldnt take money, but took diamonds. In Fanny's First Play, Mrs. Knox, speaking of her husband's aunt, says "She used to pick up handkerchiefs if she saw them lying about; but you might trust her with untold silver." You could be trusted with Shakespear, but not with a newspaper. Now put your hand on your heart if you can, and deny that all this is true. I rub it ruthlessly into you because I am afraid that you will do just the same thing with Pearson's and reduce yourself to actual destitution. You are a dangerous man—to yourself; and when I see you once more walking along the edge of a precipice over which you have fallen three times, breaking more bones every time, I shove myself between you and the gulf at the risk of your quarrelling violently with me.

And now to change the subject gradually, I cannot remember what I said about your "pluming yourself on your culture." But I now say "Go on doing it." The time has come when the value of culture should be insisted on as never before. Illiterate blackguards are trying to ride the whirlwind and direct the storm, and the result that Europe is having its hat blown off, and seems likely to have its head blown off.

As to myself, of course I am a ruffian. Set a ruffian to catch a ruffian. But I am only ruffianly nor-nor-west. Though it be ruffianism, yet there's method in't.

In the South African business I was not a pro-Boer. I never got over Olive Schreiner's "Story of an African Farm." Some few years before the war Cronwright Schreiner came to London. I asked him why he and Joubert and the rest put up with Kruger and his obsolete theocracy. He said they knew all about it and deplored it, but that the old man would die presently and then Krugerism would be quietly dropped and a liberal regime introduced. I suggested that it might be dangerous to wait; but it was evident that Oom Paul was too strong for them. During the war a curious thing happened in Norway. There, as in Germany, everyone took it for granted that the right side was the anti-English side. Suddenly Ibsen asked, in his grim manner, "Are we really on the side of Mr. Kruger and his Old Testament?" The effect was electrical. Norway shut up. I felt like Ibsen. I was of course not in the least taken in by the Times campaign, though I defended The Times against the accusation of bribery on the ground that it was not necessary to pay The Times to do what it was only too ready to do for nothing. But I saw that Kruger meant the XVII century, and the Scottish XVII at that; and so, to my great embarrassment, I found myself on the side of the mob when you and Chesterton and John Burns and Lloyd George were facing the music. It is astonishing what bad company advanced views may get one into.

Today something of the same kind is happening. I stand with Balfour and against Hertling in contending that the Balance of Power is not obsolete. This is a Balance of Power war between Democracy and Plutocracy; and also an experimental test as to whether modern war can settle anything except the hash of the combatants. It must be fought out, either to a stalemate, which means the defeat of war as an institution or to a result sufficiently decisive for either Wilson or the Kaiser to impose their terms. I do not believe in the least in the efficiency of the German governing class. If the German army had been efficient and ready it would have gone straight to Paris. It missed its rush, and practically lost the war, because it came to Liege without siege guns and had to turn tail almost at the gates of Paris because Von Cluck dashed on without food. The first year of the war proved abundantly that old Liebknecht was right when he so implacably ridiculed the legend of German education and efficiency. The Prussian system delivered Germany into the hand of the Lieutenants and the Generals who made themselves agreeable to Wilhelm; and the result was that even Kitchener and French were able to bluff them and stall them off until we improvised an army. You cannot take me in with modern education. Secondary schools, like prisons, forcibly prevent young people from hearing music, reading books, and travelling. I am an educated man because I escaped from school at 14, and before that was only a day-boy who never wasted the free half of my life in learning lessons or reading school-books. Read my preface on parents and children to the play Misalliance; and then you wont have to ask me what I think about the common notion of the immortality of the soul.

O'Bolger is an Irishman: a professor of literature at an American university. He got Shaw-struck, and extracted a great deal of autobiographical information from me by sending me questionnaires which he could not have drawn up without a very minute and inquisitive study of Henderson's biography (as I write this, a letter from Henderson proposes a new edition) and other documents. Under this provocation, and with the job thus made easy for me, I went into the details of my early family life, with its queer and quite innocent *ménage à trois* (the young man with three fathers in Misalliance is a fiction founded on my own experience). O'Bolger got this solely through his diligence in study and his persistence in cross-examination. But I cursed the day when I began answering him. The autobiographer is the dog returning to his vomit. Have you noticed how Goethe gets away from the subject of himself to give long sketches of the forgotten and now quite uninteresting young men who were his acquaintances in his youth? Or how Wagner leaves you with a more vivid notion of Spontini as a conductor at Dresden than of himself? Rousseau fades out of his confessions when he grows up: in the end you know all about Madame de Warens and much less about the adult man Rousseau than you get from his other writings. Well, I find I cant go over my autobiographical stuff again, not only from lack of time, but from loathing. I believe I kept copies of some of the notes I sent to Henderson and O'Bolger and it occurred to me once or twice to rake it out and publish a recast of it as my own, on a plan of my own. But for the moment the effort is beyond me.

I can only say generally in reply to your questions that almost all the guessing that goes on about my antecedents is just like Macaulay's guess that Bunyan was an old soldier of the parliamentary army, whereas he was really in the King's army. The mischief begins with my coming of a Protestant family of trueblue garrison snobs. The moment you begin to make inferences from that, you are lost. I become a boy Puritan, a royalist, a rebel against my family, and all manner of nonsense unspeakably remote from the truth. Before I was ten years of age I got into an atmosphere of freedom of thought, of anarchic revolt against conventional assumptions of all kinds, utterly incompatible with the generalized concept of an Irish Protestant family. I was forbidden nothing and spared nothing. My maternal uncle, clever and literate, was an abyss of blasphemy and obscenity. My mother, brought up with merciless strictness by a rich hunchbacked aunt to be a perfect lady, and disinherited furiously by her for being (consequently) ignorant enough of the world to marry my father, had such a horror of her own training that she left her children without any training at all. My humorous father, a sort of mute inglorious Charles Lamb, who disgusted my mother by his joyless furtive drinking and his poverty and general failure, could no more control me than he could avoid being thrust into the background by an energetic man of genius (an orchestral conductor and teacher of singing) into whose public work my mother threw herself when he taught her to sing, and who made life possible for her by coming to live with us. This man's hand was against every man and every man's hand against him. He had his own method of singing; and everyone else's was murderously wrong. He would not hear of doctors: when my mother had a dangerous illness he took the case in hand; and when he at last allowed my father to call in an eminent physician, the e.p. looked at my mother and said "My work has already been done." He was equally contemptuous of the Church, though he could conduct Beethoven's Mass in C better than his pious rivals. He had no time to read anything, and took Tyndall on Sound to bed with him every night for years (he slept badly) without ever getting to the end of it. There was no sex in the atmosphere: it was never discussed or even thought about as far as I could see: You had only to hear my mother sing Mendelssohn's "Hear my Prayer" or even listen to the note of her voice to understand that she might have been the centre of a *ménage à mille et trois* without an atom of scandal sticking to her, no matter how hard it was thrown. You will see that my circumstances were quite unusual, and that nobody could possibly deduce them from general data.

Someday I shall write an essay on the *ménage à trois* as distinct from "The Eternal Triangle" on the stage. There are plenty of instances. If writers could get away from their obsession with the sexual cuckoo to the much more common intellectual or character cuckoo, a most interesting chapter would lie open. Coleridge and the Gillmans, Ruskin and the Severns, Wagner and the Wesendoncks, Herbert Spencer and the Potters, are all like Lee and the Shaws. You might try your hand at it; but unfortunately you and a certain actress who is supposed to be the very incarnation of sex are the two most naive prudes of my acquaintance; and you would miss the whole point of the thing by not only assuming that the woman was the cuckoo's mistress, and that this was the interesting part of it, but by being as shocked at it as a nun. I have always been impatient of the continual attempt to make the reading of books and poems a substitute for sexual experience. Such books are not records of experience: they are mostly the delusions of impotence described for the consolation of inexperience. Archer once complained that my plays reeked with sex; and I have certainly gone further than any author I know in the legitimate handling of it as a human motive, my little play called Overruled being the final possible limit in the presentment of its incidents. The people who read Man and Superman, not only the comedy, but the confessions of Don Juan in Hell, without seeing that I know a great deal more about sex than, for example, Swinburne, and quite as much as Tolstoy or De Maupassant, may be put aside as hopelessly deficient on that side, missing the colors only because they are blind. But it is this very knowledge that has made me again and again insist that adultery is the dullest of themes in fiction, and has occasionally moved me to tell people that if they want a brothel they had better go to a brothel and not come to me for a book. I have published three plays as "Plays for Puritans" to shew how independent the drama is of mere love affairs; and I have again and again challenged a comparison of the novels of Dickens, and his contemporaries of the sex-barred period, with the comparatively morbid, limited, and miserable later sex-obsessed literature, of Don Quixote with the love stories so stupidly interpolated in it, of Macbeth and Hamlet with Antony and Cleopatra and Romeo and Juliet, to shew what a curse this miserable preoccupation of literature with sexual infatuation is. The greatest sex literature we have, that of Strindberg, is really a fierce protest against this tyranny, which is only a reaction from the sexual and emotional starvation of the respectable middle class.

The great difficulty of dealing with my education lies in the fact that my culture was so largely musical. It will be admitted that no one without as much familiarity with the masterpieces of music as with those of literature could write adequately about Wagner. But the same thing is true of me. You cannot account for me by saying that I was steeped in Dickens, or even later in Moliere. I was steeped in Mozart too; it was from him that I learned how art work could reach the highest degree of strength, refinement, beauty and seriousness without being heavy and portentous. Shelley made a great impression on me: I read him from beginning to end, prose and verse, and held him quite sacred in my adolescence. But Beethoven and early Wagner were at work alongside him. Then there was science, in which I have never lost my interest. I even claim to have made certain little contributions to the theory of Creative Evolution (which is my creed: you can compare the third Act of Man and Superman with Bergson's treatise). Socialism sent me to economics, which I worked at for four years until I mastered it completely, only to find, of course, that none of the other Socialists had taken that trouble. I do not read any foreign language easily without the dictionary except French. I have a sort of acquaintance with Italian, mostly operatic; and you could not put a German document into my hands without some risk of my being able to understand it; but what you call knowing a language: that is, something more than being able to ask the way to the Bahnhof or the Duomo, puts me out of court as a linguist. As to Latin, on which all my schooling was supposed to be spent, I cannot read an epitaph or a tag from Horace without stumbling. Naturally I make use of translations and musical settings. I know Faust and the Niblung's Ring as well as the Germans know Shakespear. I am very unteachable, and could not pass the fourth standard examination in an elementary school—not that anybody else could; but still, you know what I mean.

O. Henry has been a godsend to me. A few weeks ago I got poisoned by the phosphorus in a compound supposed to be synthetic egg, of which a lady gave me an overdose. In the subsequent intoxication and colic and horror, I fell down a steep flight of stairs on my head, and had to lie up for some days in consequence. That was where O. Henry came in. He would be a miracle if he were not standing on the shoulders of Kipling and

Cunninghame Graham, whom he has assimilated so wonderfully that he may be regarded as the summit of that kind of story telling. He has an immense receptivity and range of observation, producing the impression of unlimitedness which marks the first class in these matters.

Phillips I never read and never heard of.

Mark Twain is a classic. He is also a shocking Philistine; but then he belonged to a period in which even so great a man as Dickens was a Philistine. His Yankee at the Court of King Arthur is a mere *gaffe*; but Huckleberry Finn and such Philippics as that against Funston are great. The quality is very unequal; there are things in A Tramp Abroad and other books of his that would barely pass from the funny man of a cyclist's club; but in letters the strength of the chain is its strongest link. I like writers of the Dickens-Twain sort: you dont. I am too susceptible to their fun. Dickens and Mark Twain were very honest, whereas in Balzac there is a great deal of sheer imposture: bogus learning, bogus profundity worst of all, bogus character and heroism. Lytton, Disraeli, and Victor Hugo all had a taste for humbug. I dislike that in them, and like the Dickens-Twain dislike of it.

I hope this letter is long enough to console your exile.

Ever
G. Bernard Shaw

HARRIS to SHAW [H/4]

[The copyright registration was to protect Shaw's interests in his Oscar Wilde letter-memoir Harris was publishing. The "tract on Socialism" in Harris's Fortnightly Review *was "On Mr. Mallock's Proposed Trumpet Performance" (April 1894), which was later reprinted as a booklet,* Socialism and Superior Brains *(1909). Miss Goldman was American Socialist activist Emma Goldman (see Harris's letter of August 30, 1924).]*

29 Waverly Place, New York
March 14th, 1918

My dear Bernard Shaw:—

Herewith your copyright card under the seal of Congress, and so that matter is I hope, settled to your satisfaction.

I have written you three or four long letters and received none from you lately except the great one about the Bacchae of Euripides. You would be put in prison for two years and fined ten thousand dollars for saying half as much here, if they did not give you twenty years. I am warned that it is not well even to mention Miss Goldman's name.

I asked you in one letter for your opinion of O. Henry and I had his books sent to you; I don't know whether you have looked at them or not; in any case that would take you a little time. I also asked you if you had read the books of David Graham Phillips whom I esteem still more highly—a sort of American Balzac.

I wish I had some life of you and that tract on Socialism which you contributed in '93 I think, to the *Fortnightly*. Fancy it is twenty-five years ago! How life passes. And the only thing that fills me with awe unspeakable is the sense of infinite space, uncreated, uncaused, unconditioned, in comparison with which God and man are mere accidents.

Ever yours,
Frank Harris

HARRIS to SHAW [H/4]

[Harris's proposed magazine of short fiction never got off the ground.]

29 Waverly Place, New York
April 1st, 1918

My dear Shaw:—

I do not know how to thank you for your superb letter.

You must not think that I could possibly be offended at your calling me a ruffian or anything else. I knew that you meant something when you said it; I only wanted to find out exactly what the something was. Now I have found out, and can see a good deal of justification for your criticism.

I knew society in France and Germany and Russia before I knew it in England; consequently I got used to much freer speech than is cutomary in either England or America, particularly on matters of sex; but I found English prudishness far stronger in the middle-classes than in the Smart Set, and so, after finding out what the Smart Set was like I made up my mind to have nothing to do with the middle-class which I disliked for a hundred reasons and did not mind whether I offended or not. I dare say at times as you say, I did offend them purposely; their prudery was mixed up with a general woolliness of thought which annoyed me intensely; and their contempt of art and all ideal things with their submissive subservience to the actual used to exasperate me.

Curiously enough, though this is the same people I feel much more in sympathy with [the] Americans except when they try to exercise petty despotisms; then they become almost as ridiculous and offensive as the English; but they do not belard their despotism with hypocrisies as the English do. The English imprisoned Bertrand Russell for "his good," but here they do not pretend to be moral reformers; they send you to prison or suppress you because they want to punish you and they say so; it is the gloss of hypocrisy over everything in England that I dislike as I dislike the coagulated grease of bad cooking.

I enclose herewith the first review of our book because it may interest you. It appeared in the New Republic and is written by a man called Francis Hackett, a young Irishman who has very distinct ability. He wrote the best criticism of my "The Man Shakespeare," that appeared in America, but this criticism of Oscar Wilde is not so good.

I am going to get three or four books of David Graham Phillips and send them to you. You really ought to know him; he is a more important novelist it seems to me than any we have produced in England, but I should like to have your judgment of him. You have got O. Henry right in the main but I think he deserves more credit than you give him for his originality.

In haste,
Yours ever
Frank Harris

P.S. I use things from every letter you send me because I think it does you good and I know it does the people here good to have your incisive judgments. I reproduce your postcard about the angry ape as you will see.

I reopen this letter to ask you why you have never written a short story of any sort? Short-story writers have now and then tried to write plays, but you, so far as I know, have not yet written a short story. I wish I could persuade you to write one because I am starting a new fiction magazine to be called "Camouflage." I think we shall make a success of it at once, but if I could begin with a story of yours needless to say it would give me such a start as nothing else could. What do you say to the idea?

By the way tell me the stories of O. Henry that you like best. I should like to know how nearly our tastes agree.

Yours,
F. H.

SHAW to HARRIS [H/4]

[Shaw's stories were later put together in Short Stories, Scraps and Shavings *(1931), in the collected edition of his works. The music piece was "The Serenade" and the Irish graveyard tale was "The Miraculous Revenge."]*

10 Adelphi Terrace
7th May 1918

Dear Frank Harris

Short stories? In your sense of the word, none at all. Of late years I have produced two short scraps of fiction. One of them, a war story supposed to be written for children, is called The Emperor and the Little Girl. It was written for the Vestiaire Marie José, some Belgian War Charity, and has been published in American, English, and some foreign magazines. It is an imaginary scene between the Kaiser and a little girl at night on the battle field.

The other, written some years before the war, was called, I think, Aerial Football. It is a story of a drunken charwoman who gets run over by a motor bus in the Grays Inn Road. A bishop is driving past; and his carriage pulls up so suddenly to avoid the skidding bus that the jerk breaks the bishop's neck. They both go up to the Celestial City and find at the gate St Peter and other Heavenly personages. This story appeared in Colliers. They gave me, in addition to the price, a prize of $1,000 for the best story of the year or something of the kind. I flung this back with great indignation; and they made the most of the advertisement for both of us.

I can remember nothing else in the way of short stories except a few that I wrote in my nonage. One, which got published in some musical magazine, was about a man who fell in love with a lady who was music mad. His rival cut him out by singing, and promised to serenade her some night with Schubert's "Standchen." My hero had no voice, but he went to a military bandmaster; learnt to play the serenade on the French horn; and perpetrated it at night beneath her window. Deceived by the unearthly sounds of the instrument, she thought what she heard was the rival singing. She turned him down at once and married my hero, who had the sense not to undeceive her, though his vanity was naturally a little hurt.

Another story was about one of those legendary graveyards in Ireland of which they tell you that it used to be at the other side of the river, but that when they burned some wicked person in it, it was miraculously carried across by angels and the wicked one left alone. I always felt, as an economist, that it was a monstrous waste of divine power to shift all the dead saints instead of simply shifting the dead sinner. In my story the hero, a neurotic aesthete, falls in love with the niece of a priest who has become famous through this miracle occuring to a burial ground in his parish. The priest kicks the aesthete out of the house, and the aesthete goes that night to a sinner's grave, digs him up and buries him again with the saints, with the result of course that there is a countermiracle, the saints being promptly transported back again by the angels to their original resting place and the unfortunate priest convicted of imposture and ruined. This story was printed many years after it was written in a magazine called Time, which had come into the hands of Sonnenschein the publisher.

Two other stories of the same period were lost before they got into print. One was based on the fact that a photograph will sometimes show marks on the skin that are invisible to the eye: for instance, smallpox pustules before the eruption becomes visible. A woman has murdered her husband, and in the struggle he has struck her in the face with a brand which he has heated to stamp his monogram on some amateur work of his—I forget what. She manages to obliterate the mark, which would have convicted her; but as a widow she fascinates a photographer, who makes her sit to him. In the dark room he finds an unaccountable mark on the negative, which is, of course, the brand. I sent this tale to some magazine and never heard anything more about it. The other derelict was a description of a nightmare in which the sleeper was chased fantastically in and out and up and down through all sorts of strange mad places. This sort of fun evidently did not appeal to the editor who threw it away; but of late years it has been exploited in the cinema, where a delirious flight and pursuit of this kind is *de rigueur*.

There you have the whole history of G.B.S. as a short story writer. I wrote such things very easily and with some enjoyment, and might easily have been ruined by success in that department if the editors of the early eighties had been more intelligent than those who left you to publish Montes the Matador at your own expense.

It was an unlucky time for artistic literature. Publishers' capital had turned to providing for the newly literate products of the board schools. They could not stand fine art or tradition in literature: the only effect it made on them was that of being sneered at. Zola got them by writing newspaper reports instead of novels. Poe, Dumas pére and Sir Walter Scott had to be replaced by quite illiterate rehandlings of their themes. If you and I had never read anything, and dipped our pens in the ink in exactly the same spirit as we poked the fire, we should have been much more popular in our generation. I have never regretted this: if the people who used to go to dog-fights now go to crude melodramas, I dont object to the melodramas crowding my plays off the stage: the movement is a social gain; and my turn will come when the melodramas are left as far behind as the dog-fights; but while the grass grows—

Since I wrote to you about O. Henry I have been trying to find out why what I said about him was so unsatisfying, and I am rather pleased to see that it did not quite satisfy you either. I think the omission was a very simple one: I said nothing about his charm. It is not enough to say that he has all the qualities: that he has this quality of Kipling's and that quality of Cunninghame Graham's and the other quality of De Maupassant or yourself, or even that he can play riotously with them all. The combination is not additional but chemical: it produces something to which the others are merely ingredient. I can only call it charm, meaning the particular attraction that the others have not got, though their state may be the more gracious. I cannot name my favorite story. No violent preference has yet arisen. Besides, I havent yet read them all. I have heard of certain private adventures of Phillips, culminating in his being sandbagged, on very imaginative authority; but I know nothing of his books. Hackett's review of the great Life of Wilde gives a very favorable impression of his critical ability. His remark that Wilde was less concerned to reform the world than to alter it so that it would keep him in countenance is what I call good reviewing. But he should have followed it up; for the truth is that all the reformers are striving to make the world congenial to themselves. There is, at bottom, no other method of evolution than that of backing your own tastes. When Oscar heard the child crying in prison, his pity was certainly not for himself. There is a story that Jesus Christ once began to notice that some very shady people were getting into Heaven. At last he could stand it no longer, and went to the gate and accused Peter of neglecting his duties. Peter immediately became very sulky, and would neither deny nor explain. Jesus would not be put off; and at last Peter took him round outside the wall to one of the bastions, where they peeped round the corner and saw the Virgin Mary letting down her girdle from the parapet and helping up the poor devils whom Peter had turned away. Wilde might have half a chance there because he not only felt for the children but stuck to it and wrote about it when he got out.

Ever

G. Bernard Shaw

HARRIS to SHAW [H/4]

[Arnold Bennett had attacked both Harris and Shaw for alleged pro-Germanism early in the war, Harris with far more cause; however much of the abuse heaped upon those who called for negotiation was hysterical. Adela Schuster had been a friend to Oscar Wilde in the dark days when most of his friends had deserted him.

The postscripted quotation from Shakespeare, from Timon of Athens, actually is "tis honor with most lands to be at odds."]

29 Waverly Place, New York
July 14th, 1918

My dear Bernard Shaw:

You tell me you get Pearson's which I am sending you regularly, and therefore you will see that I am doing my best to spread the true gospel about Bernard Shaw. The idea that because a man has a sense of humor he has no serious convictions, is rooted I find in the Anglo-American consciousness. They pretend here not to believe it, but they do. However, I think I am killing it—gradually.

Something you wrote to me in March has been much in my mind. You tell me in one of your letters with a frankness which honors you, that "there were things in my career which could not be defended," and you go on to tell me what they were. You assert that the failure of the *Candid Friend* was a "personal failure" due to laziness seemingly, that in *Vanity Fair* I sank still lower, and that in *Modern Society* I reached the limit; and you ask—"what had a man like you to do with the dregs of bucketshop finance and journalism."

You misread the whole thing I think and do me injustice. I will give you my view of it in a few words which you can accept or reject as seems good to you.

So long as I was in favor of English imperialism; so long as I dreamt of a confederation of English states with an imperial senate, so long everything was forgiven me in England. The moment I came to understand or to believe if you will, that England was unfit to be the heart of such a commonwealth; too sordid, too selfish, too witless to achieve such a destiny, I lost caste in England and gradually everyone turned against me. The turning point was quite apparent to me on the *Saturday Review* when I attacked the British oligarchy and defended the Boers. You were converted to the true faith you think by Ibsen, but I still think that I was right and that the moral downfall of England was made plain to everyone by that vile attack upon the Boer Republic whose integrity England had again and again promised to respect. In starting the *Candid Friend* I knew I was going against public opinion. I was told that I should be prosecuted if I kept on writing; an intrigue in the office got me out of power, but I struggled on and lost all the money I had made on the *Saturday Review*.

You say that articles appeared in *Vanity Fair* with my initials attacking my ideals and my friends. If you will point me out one I will cry *"peccavi."* I am absolutely unconscious of any such article, and as for there being continually articles of that sort I must beg you to correct or verify that misstatement. I have one volume of *Vanity Fair* here with me. There is not one article in it that I consider unworthy. I would sign any of them to-morrow.

Before getting *Modern Society* I tried to buy the "World" and succeeded indeed, but a stupid solicitor while promising me to pay money which I had drawn and given him, omitted to do so for a couple of days though he told me it had been done, and so the sale was vitiated because it leaked out that I was the purchaser and the Harmsworths did not want any more of me in journalism. I took *Modern Society* as I took *Hearth & Home*, as I would have taken anything to try and get a living. It cost me my last pennies and you say it served me right.

Now you found you could write plays and I will venture to say that you have made more out of your worst play than I have made out of all my books put together. I have written a volume or two of short stories that are good; my work on Shakespeare too is going to stand. "Contemporary Portraits" you yourself have said are the best kind of that work you have seen; this Life of Oscar Wilde you have praised, but did you know that my books up to the time I wrote this Oscar Wilde, have never even paid for their printing. I did the Shakespeare book on my knees. I am four hundred pounds out on it at this moment. All of my work cost me money from thirty to fifty-five, and to all of it—I am speaking of my books—I gave the best in me; and to most of my journalism too. Had my talents been a playwright's and yours a storyteller's it might have been that you would have needed the indulgence or sympathetic understanding you deny me.

But I am sure you meant your whole moral condemnation to be for my good and to make me do better on "Pearson's." Well, I have done [my best with] Pearson's: Every number of it socialistic and for peace and therefore unpopular. I have written one third or one half of it nearly every month in order to make a living. I have done it as well as I knew how to do it yet I am hardly one thousand dollars ahead for 2 year's work; but after all that is not my fault.

Some of your attempts at reading me are very curious. You

say—"because your natural point of honor was in high literature and not in journalism you thought there was no point of
honor in journalism." That is an admirable defence if I needed
it, but I do not think it is true or needed.

I remember one day after I had got back from South Africa in
June or July, 1896, the Jameson raid having taken place in
January, Rhodes sending for me. He had been a friend of mine
since '87 and I was attacking him bitterly. I saw him by appointment in Beit's house in Park Lane. He told me I had been
his first friend in England. He begged me to come on his side.
"At any rate stop attacking," he said. He told me that Beit who
was also present, would make me rich if I would consent. I
should have a directorship on his (Rhodes's) best companies; he
would get me any place in South Africa I could hope for.

I said I wanted money but I could not take it.

"What will the Boers ever do for you?" he went on. "You are
mad, man. Sheer crazy."

And now you reproach me for an "extraordinary stupidity."
Rhodes and Shaw agreeing with twenty odd years between
them.

When I read such surface criticism as this of yours I say to
myself with Browning's Andrea del Sarto:

> "Let some good son paint my two hundred pictures;
>   Let him try."

It may be that the future will judge me differently. In all my
life I have never yet been on the popular side. That is something that consoles me now when other things are growing
dim. Wells it seems foams at the mouth when my name is
mentioned. Arnold Bennett I had to sit on here for silly lies he
told about me in the *New York Times*. Conrad returned a book
declaring he did not want to read anything by me. Yet I have
done something to help all these people to the positions they
now occupy; not that that matters much. But at least I have
never attacked them till they vilified me. More sinned against
than sinning—by men perhaps but I cannot urge the same plea
in regard to woman. So balance, I daresay is even enough. I
don't whimper. I have fought for unpopular causes; & yet have
had a great life on the whole.

I agree with all you say about the German oligarchy and

Junkerthum; but you should not attack German education. True they often develop memory instead of mind but they do think of mind and when they meet it, are reverential of it and not contemptuous like the English. Think of Hauptmann's position in Germany and Nietzsche's or even Heine's. Think of the way Heine & Nietzsche attacked German ideals and German pride and German patriotism again and again and again and yet they had thousands of readers. When I attacked English idols I found few readers and no helpers. Is the fault really mine? Let us leave it to the future.

One of these days I hope you will read David Graham Phillips. I am sending you and Miss Schuster a couple of his books. To me he is a sort of American Franz Hals, but the book he meant to be his masterpiece, "Susan Lennox," is a poor book— alack and alas. He was shot down here in the street by a vain fool who thought that Phillips had libelled his family in one of his books, and Phillips, it was found, did not even know them, had never heard of them; but he was foully murdered and everybody was quite careless of it because none of them had any idea that Phillips was the greatest novelist that America has produced; greater in my opinion than any English novelist except perhaps Fielding and Thackeray when he wrote "Vanity Fair."

Your admiration of Dickens is comprehensible to me; I cannot put it higher than that; I do not share it at all; but "The Tale of Two Cities," and "Barnaby Rudge," and "Nicholas Nickleby" I read as a boy with some interest. Twain has written "Tom Sawyer" and "Huckleberry Finn," good enough boys' books but both the same boy and I cannot rate him even as high as I rate Kipling who, after all, is the representative genius forever of the fourth-form. Twain's "Joan of Arc," is I think the worst book I have ever seen or tried to read, and who could fail with such a subject, but a puritanic ass!

You [and] I are somehow at opposite poles; that is probably a good thing for both of us.

I cannot close this letter without thanking you for the splendid thing you wrote about the Declaration of Independence. I have put it aside to be used in my autobiography.

I have read Henderson on you but he has written a dreadful book. I wish you would send me your book of musical criticism. I do not mean only that one, Wagner, but the other one which I have not got.

I am going to bring out my new volume of "Contemporary Portraits" I hope in October next, and as you will be the first figure in it I wish you would send me the portrait you prefer, or if possible a pencil sketch that you like.

Sincerely ever,
Frank Harris

P.S. When you spoke of my attacks on England as coming from a "wounded feeling for England's greatness" you got to the very heart of the matter. I left America and went back to England because I thought more could be done there but the shameless theft of Egypt and the shameless attack on the Boers cured me of any lingering patriotic fervour I may have cherished. The Bard says: "It's noble with most lands to be at odds."

Yours ever
Frank Harris

P.S. A superb use you made of the image in the Bacchae. Enclosed is a little story I want you to read. More power to you.

SHAW to HARRIS [H/4]

[Shaw's Fabian Society crony Hubert Bland was a successful journalist, when he was not womanizing, until his sight failed. Shaw's treatises on education include the long prefaces to Major Barbara *and* Misalliance. *Harris constantly hoped to make money out of libel actions, but generally the findings were the reverse of expectations. The first, in 1896, came when Sir Alexander Mackenzie sued the* Saturday Review *because of an unsigned article by John Runciman which charged Mackenzie— then principal of the Royal Academy of Music—of manipulating scholarships and conducting his office in such a low manner as to be "at the cesspool of academical musical life." Harris tried to evade responsibility by pleading illness at the time and citing other causes of office confusion but the court awarded Mackenzie damages of £400. Ernest Hooley was a* fin de siècle *millionaire who, with Harris's pen behind him, promoted Bovril as universal panacea, entertained lavishly, and went into bankruptcy in 1898 with Harris rushing to the Public Receiver to claim large indebtednesses. Harris probably mis-recollected James Huneker's 1906 collection of Shaw criticism,* Dramatic Opinions and Essays *(culled from Harris's own* Saturday Review*) as a volume of music criticism.]*

10 Adelphi Terrace
[27th Sept. 1918—posted from Kerry on the 30th]
Dear Frank Harris

Your letter of the 14th July is still unanswered; so here goes.

I may be quite wrong in this or that detail as to your career in London journalism after the Saturday Review passed out of your hands. For instance, your letter is the first intimation of the screaming joke which you mention so seriously: to wit, that you were once the editor of Hearth and Home. I feel that I may see you editing The Leisure Hour and Good Words before I die.

But I read The Candid Friend, because you sent it to me from the office, and because Lady Jessica [Sykes], who knew my wife, tried to get hold of me when she was editing it for you. After the first two numbers I dont believe you wrote fifty lines in it all told until it expired.

Vanity Fair never came my way except when the Press Cutting people sent me its invariably scurrilous references to me. I did not suspect you for a moment of writing them, not on sentimental grounds, but because you could not have written so badly if you had tried for a year. At last there came a surpassingly bad article, apparently written by the office boy, signed F.H. I was not surprised at your leaving the editing to the office boy; but when he actually used your signature (which you seldom used yourself) I concluded that you had become utterly reckless. That article has long since been collected by the dustman: I cannot tell you the date of it, and it may very well be that the paper had passed out of your hands, and that some Freddy Hicks or Frank Hodges was airing himself in it. But there the article was, anyhow; and it was quite in the style of the things that had been coming to me during the time when you were the reputed editor.

Then came that ridiculous action you took against some candidate for whom you had written speeches, and who, I suppose, irritated you by some *gaucherie* or other. Finally there was the Modern Society affair, in which at last someone to whom you had abandoned your functions let you in for a criminal prosecution.

All this time you talked freely about Ernest Terah Hooley in a manner which shewed that you were more interested in him than in literature and it was current gossip in journalistic circles that it was a common practice with financial journals to write articles exposing shady promotion, and make them buy off the insertion: blackmail, in short. You were suspected of this method of making papers pay: on what grounds I do not know; but it was clear that Vanity Fair was no more like The Saturday Review than The Mystery of a Hansom Cab was like Hamlet, and that you were living mostly in Monte Carlo. The conclusion was that either you were leaving your newspapers to be edited by anybody who happened to be on the spot, and not even troubling to keep the standard up to Lady Jessica or Blanchamp, or else you had fallen off as a literary hand to an extent that could only be accounted for by utter demoralization, and that your character had collapsed with your talent. As I came across you a few times, and saw that the latter was not the right explanation, I fell back on the former.

But you suffered also from your personal style. Like everyone else, I took you to be much more a man of the world than you really were. As I told you, it was Julia Frankau who first opened my eyes to the fact that the buccaneer of Monte Carlo, the pal of Lord Randolph, the impressive editor of The Fortnightly and the Saturday, the financier who gave tips to Hooley, and the scorner of the transparent and trivial West End, was a romantic boy and even a sensitive child without the ghost of a notion of the sort of society he was living in and the people he was up against. You were so surprised and indignant at finding that England was England, and human nature human nature, and so hurt by the knocks that seasoned adventurers in London soon cease to feel, and, what was worse for you so absurdly unconscious of the shock and jar of your Anschauung against that of Eton and Oxford, and of the Savile Club's resentment of your scale of literary values, which reduced most of its members to pigmies, and piffling pigmies at that, that you never really knew where you were, or what you might say or do with impunity. You often seemed to be brutally and truculently outraging susceptibilities which no doubt would not have existed in a community of Napoleons and De Maupassants, but which are the whole life of the London you had to steer through. Instead of teaching that poor devil Runciman manners, which were really all that he lacked to make him a first rate critic, you taught him to drink; and he died prematurely and miserably in consequence. I dont pretend that you were responsible for his ruin: men have to save themselves: the point is that you did not know what was the matter with him. When he was stupid enough to be insolent to Hubert Bland, Bland knocked him down, to his great astonishment; for he had no idea that insolence was not the normal thing in intercourse with people whom he happened to dislike. But when he was insolent in your paper to Mackenzie, and let you in for damages, thereby getting *you* knocked down for his bad behaviour, you agreed with him on the fundamental point that people who are not geniuses of the first order have no right to common civility. Your theory of manners was the same as his: the practice varied only as the climate of South Shields (or whatever the barbarous place was in which Runciman was allowed to tumble up an unlicked cub) differs from the climate of Ireland. I have an eye for these things because I had to learn manners myself: I, too, in my nonage, was occasionally wanting in respect to people of cruder tastes and blunter wits than myself.

Now it is hard enough on either people to know that you think you know more than they do! It is not possible for the most vigilantly considerate man of high talent to go through the world without moving those who feel at a disadvantage with him to quite furious moments of hatred and envy; but when you openly scorn these victims, and wipe your boots on them publicly, you sow dragon's teeth in all directions. You certainly saved a great many in London: but you did it naively and unconsciously to a much greater extent than anyone could have guessed from your style, which was that of a man who knew every corner of society and human nature, and did nothing without knowing it. Whereas, as I say, I believe that Julia was right, and that half the time you had not the least idea of the pain you were causing or the fierce animosity you were rousing.

Publishing your books at your own expense, as I have now done for many years in England, is the price you had to pay for your independence.

Pearson's proves my case as regards the papers you didnt edit. Pearson's is quite obviously edited by Frank Harris. Whenever you really edit a paper, there is no mistake about it. And when you dont edit it there is no mistake about that either.

What you say about [Cecil] Rhodes is very interesting. Why did you not sell yourself to Rhodes? If I had been Rhodes I should have said "Why not sell yourself? You have the reputation of being a man without conscience, a city article black-mailer, a reckless libeller, a pirate in finance and journalism. You have no right to a reputation you have not earned. Come and earn it. If you refuse, nobody will give you the least credit: they will only say 'He couldnt get on even with Rhodes.'"

Your quotation from Andrea del Sarto is apt; but it was not by stealing the King of France's money to spend on his worthless slut of a wife that Andrea learnt how to take a bit of chalk and correct the arm that Raphael misdrew. Raphael might with more force have said

> "Let some perfect draughtsman make my two hundred friends: Let him try."

And could Andrea have put a mother's protecting hand on a child's back as Raphael put it in that pencil study for The Incendio which is in the print room at the British Museum? He could found the *plein air* school in his frescoes 300 years before it became the ambition of all the Paris studios; and Raphael never did anything half so clever. All the same Raphael was the divine Raphael, a prince among painters; whilst Andrea, with an opportunity from Francis I as great as the pope could offer Raphael, used it to become a thief.

You are quite right about the German respect for Art and intellect; as distinguished from the English contempt for it and respect for money and acres and push. But what is called education!—however, I have said my say about that in two immortal prefaces. Let it suffice.

Your ignorance of Dickens is a frightful gap in your literary education. He was by far the greatest man since Shakespear that England has ever produced in that line. Read Little Dorrit, Our Mutual Friend, and Great Expectations. Until you do you will not have the very faintest notion of what the name of Dickens means. Barnaby Rudge is mere boy's work in comparison. He did not come of age until Ruskin and Carlyle probed his social conscience to the depth, and he made a beginning of his great period with Hard Times. But when it came, it *was* great.

I dont know what you mean by my book of musical criticism. I have never reprinted my musical articles. There is nothing but The Perfect Wagnerite.

I cannot send you a portrait, because pictures have been so ingeniously used for enemy communications that they are now barred by the censorship. What have you done with the Rothenstein drawing you had? There is a book of sayings from my works compiled by my wife, with a photogravure picture of Rodin's bust of me which I might perhaps get through. I believe the publisher can send it if he is prepared to guarantee that he picked it at random out of a thousand copies, and can certify that it has not been tampered with. I will have a try, anyhow.

I got the story about the madman safely. Why have you always been so curiously shy of publishing your stories in your own papers and writing your name well across them? I believe you suffer from the sort of neurosis that prevents certain actors from ever becoming anything more than "character actors." They are adepts at disguise, and can act very effectively in a disguise; but if you ask them to "play straight," as one must do in the grand school or in "leading business," they are paralyzed with stage fright immediately, and simply cannot do it. There are journalists, too, and even authors, who can write with the greatest impudence as "we" without a signature or over a *nom de plume*, but can hardly be persuaded to write a letter for publication because it involves the first person and the name and address. Thus Brodribb makes a great reputation as Henry Irving, Miss Evans as George Eliot, Duval (or whatever it was) as Victor Hugo, Arouet as Voltaire, though as Brodribb, Evans &c&c they would have been as awkward as an actor making a speech before the curtain. Even Oscar shrank from Fingal O'Flahertie and hankered after Sebastian Melmoth. I wonder whether you would have made yourself more widely known as Ferdinand Hohenstaufen. You are, like most of us, a mass of contradictions. You sail the Spanish Main with the blackest of flags, the reddest of sashes, the hugest of cutlasses, and the thinnest of skins.

I am writing all this drivel on the coast of Kerry with nothing visible in the grey but the white horses on the waves and a blanket of incessant rain zenith high and horizon far. However, you deserve it. You seem to extract what Ibsen calls a salutary self-torture from making me hold up the distorting mirror of London before you. What an amusement!

Ever
G. Bernard Shaw

29/9/18

P.S. Fifield the publisher says he has sent you not only the Selected Passages with the Rodin portrait, but the booklet called Socialism and Superior Brains, which is mostly a reprint of the reply to [W.H.] Mallock which I wrote for you when you edited the Fortnightly, and which contains a photograph of me taken by myself.

HARRIS to SHAW [H/4]

29 Waverly Place, New York.
October 22, 1918

My dear Shaw:

I have this morning received your interesting letter posted from Kerry on the 30th.

I want to deal with your view of myself here and settle it once [and] for all. There is much that is true and of real insight in what you say and much that is completely mistaken.

I have got a *Vanity Fair* before me now for all the time of my editorship. There is not a single scurrilous reference to you and no article good or bad on you signed F.H. so all that must have been at some time when I was not editing it.

You seem to think I ought to have put myself in all my journalism. Whenever I did it hurt the journal (I mean financially) and all I wanted journalism for was to make money out of it; but you can take it from me that I made it decently and never from blackmailing; in fact I do not believe there is any blackmailing by journalists in London to speak of. The blackmailing is all done by the great houses; by the Rothschilds and others, who lend their names to enterprises on condition that they are financially rewarded for so doing.

The whole truth about me came out when Hooley went bankrupt. He had given my name to the referee as one of the journalists like Harry Marks who had had large sums of money out of him, ten thousand pounds on one occasion. When I claimed that he owed me four thousand pounds I got rather an unpleasant letter from the referee asking me to please establish my claim.

I went down and told him that I had put seven thousand five

hundred pounds in Schweppes [notes,] I think it was, on condition that I got twelve thousand five hundred or fifteen thousand pounds, I forget the amount, cash or shares as Hooley received the same if and when he succeeded.

"Yes" said the referee to me, "Mr. Marks put ten thousand in and received his twenty thousand, but he never put a penny in. Can you prove that you gave any money to Mr. Hooley; in other words that it was an honest transaction?"

I produced my check with Hooley's endorsement. The referee immediately apologized to me and declared that I was the only journalist who had acted fairly. He allowed my claim just as he cut out Marks's and the claim of the man on the "Daily Mail."

You are right, however, in saying that my view of life and of writers was utterly different from that of Eton and Oxford and the Savile Club. I remember an amusing meeting with Andrew Lang once at the very beginning of my career when he told me that I would not make a success with the *Fortnightly* unless I got Rider Haggard and Stevenson to write for me, and I shocked him by asking who Stevenson was and who Rider Haggard [was]. You call this ruffianism, but it is absolutely Emerson's answer to Landor who kept talking to the great American about Southey. Emerson ends his chapter with "but who was Southey?"

It is a good thing in a mealy-mouthed silly society like that of London to have someone standing for real values. They hated me for doing it and I didn't care a damn for their hatreds though they revenged themselves by telling lies about me.

But do you think they talked no lies about you? I would not dream of bringing them up to you but they were talked.

You tell me that I should have taught Runciman manners and instead of that I taught him to drink. That is utterly untrue. Blanchamp and he learned to drink together. Long before I saw Runciman I had established the rule that I would only take one glass of whiskey and soda in the whole day. I never drank except at my meals and then moderately. I never when alone ordered a bottle of wine; always a half bottle. If I took a liqueur with my coffee at my one meal which was always lunch, I did not then take the glass of whiskey and soda later in the day. Where you got the idea from that I taught Runciman to drink I don't know. I remember giving both Blanchamp and him a long lecture about it once.

You make it a crime on my part that I allowed Runciman to insult Mackenzie in my paper and that Mackenzie got damages against me, but it only shows the state of things in England when perfectly fair art criticism is not allowed. Why don't you reproach Whistler for bringing his action against Ruskin and getting a farthing damages and being laughed at in open court and scorned by barristers and judge alike? It was Whistler's protest against an idiot society. I made a protest too in my way and did not whine any more than Whistler whined when he got beaten.

Another point. I am not ignorant of Dickens. I read him as a little boy and disliked him heartily. I should like to read "Little Dorrit" and "Our Mutual Friend" and "Great Expectations" again but I am afraid I could not wade through them.

I wish you had said what you think of Pearson's because I have managed at length to buy it and I am doing it as well as I can because now I have nothing else to rely on than my own work and strange to say I find that people want to hear me speak here whereas in England nobody wanted me and the less I spoke the better the journal used to go.

This is surely enough about myself for all time; now for more interesting stuff.

You say your publisher Fifield has not only sent me "Selected Passages" with the Rodin portrait but the booklet "Socialism and Superior Brains." I have not received them yet and I think they are the first books that have gone astray. I wish you would ask him to send me the photograph of yourself taken by yourself. I have dug up the reply to Mallock and your "Truth About the War."

A curious thing about my pen portrait of you is, that although I could do you quite short, and I am certain I could do a readable book on you, I seem to be unable to do fifteen thousand words or so on you. I have never had such difficulty in my life. I have spent weeks and weeks on it and have held up this new book of "Contemporary Portraits" because of it for I am determined that your portrait shall be my best, or at least a good one. I am afraid now that I shall not be able to bring out the book this side of Christmas, but I will do it or die doing it so one of these days you may expect my picture of you.

The idea of your thinking that I could write a scurrilous

article on you. I cannot bear even to write about Wells because he has fallen so low over this war. I looked upon him as a man of genius and now he shames me with his drivel about the Bishop and God and the rest of it. A man with two eyes who prefers to use only one. I know enough about him to almost kill him here and yet I prefer not to write about him at all; and that has always been my attitude to men of any genuine insight. There are so few of them in the world and the prophets are so badly treated that I never wanted to increase their sufferings. If I cannot help them honestly I remain silent. But you, thank God, I could always talk about with hearty admiration and I think I always shall.

I am dreadfully afraid that this manful German answer will make Wilson cry for unconditional surrender and a dreadful prolongation of the war. Could you not write a moderate word upon "justice tempered with mercy." You will see I have used Wilson's inaugural address in the last issue in order to try and recall him to his best self. I wonder could you help the good cause with a few words. Fancy we have lost four years in this dreadful dog fight. Your letters are almost the only thing that keep me alive; they help me enormously here. If you cannot write about conditions of peace could you not write about the spirit of England and the way she is shaping towards peace. I think she is getting more moderate which is a good sign. Send me your best book "Caesar and Cleopatra" with autograph and your "Devil's Disciple." I have all the rest now I think.

Sincerely ever,
Frank Harris

P.S. "The Candid Friend" would need an acre of explanations and I do not think it worth talking about. I have just got "Socialism and Superior Brains" so suppose the other book will follow immediately.

SHAW to HARRIS [H/SY]

[Looking over a copy of the letter twelve years later, Shaw added the parenthetical identification of playwright Henry Arthur Jones as the author who complained that Shaw's wartime statements were akin to kicking one's mother on her deathbed. He

*also changed "People" to "People of his kidney" in the paragraph
about Arthur Balfour.*

*Shaw was digging deep into American history for his "George
Washington colonel" reference at the end of his letter, referring
to a quashed officers' coup against General Washington which
led to the arrest of the conspirators. The Debs-Liebknecht comparison was to the imprisonment of pacifist Socialist Eugene V.
Debs in America for sedition; while Communist (and pacifist)
agitator Karl Liebknecht in Germany was released in October
1918, before the war was over, Debs still languished in jail
under Wilson.]*

March 10, 1919

My Dear Harris:

Your article on "How The British Lion Crowns Himself with
American Laurels" does not really affect the truth of my general statement of the position. The British Empire has smashed
the German Empire: that is the point to be seized. That she did
it with French troops, with Russian troops, with Italian troops,
with Portuguese troops, with Irish and Indian troops, and finally with American troops, only enhances the demonstration of
her amazing instinctive war craft. If it could be shown that the
British navy did not exist, and that not a single English soldier
had been under fire, the demonstration would be all the more
imposing: indeed, it would be miraculous.

The question of personal prowess is for schoolboys. For grown
men the interest of the actual fighting lies in the absurd vicis-
situdes of the campaign. All the armies won glorious victories
and incurred crushing defeats; but none of them seemed to
matter. Napoleon at Waterloo and Pompey at Pharsalia suffered only trifling reverses in comparison with Gough in the
rout of the Fifth Army and Cadorna at Caporetto. Yet these
were the preludes to victory. The French ought to call it the
war of the *à peu près*; Paris nearly taken, Verdun all but cap-
tured, the channel ports only just not reached, St. Quentin and
Cambrai on the verge of falling, Rheims morally if not militar-
ily stormed, Jutland "a damned near thing" (Jellicoe's book
implies your verdict on it), and the decision, after every one
had given up all hope of a decision, achieved with appalling
completeness by Famine. There were moments when all seemed
lost; yet nothing happened. At the first gas attack four miles of

our line vanished in strangulated terror and left the way to the sea open; and the result was no worse than if it had been held by fifty million troops. When we suddenly changed from taking less than our share of the line to more than we had men for, and the collapse of Gough was followed by a warning from Haig that the Germans were through, the panic here was so utter and shameless that the Government frantically abandoned the harvest and conscribed Ireland (on paper); yet the upshot was more triumphant for us than when Haig exploded nineteen volcanoes simultaneously on the Messines Ridge, and seemed in full flood towards Berlin. The Turks drove us into the sea at Gallipoli; sent our fleet flying from the Straits; and gathered Kut and General Townshend like daisies. They might just as well have made us a present of Constantinople and Baghdad without striking a blow.

The American Army was so farcically inexperienced at first that it had to be brigaded with the French Army; and the moment it was cut loose and left to itself its lines of communication jammed and it was left without food and munitions for two days, during which it was at the mercy of the Germans (if they had only known); yet the American Army wiped out the St. Mihiel salient and saved Colonel House from having to send General Pershing home to be run for the Presidency as a consolation prize.

I asked a British war correspondent what his grounds were for saying that the British Army could knock the American Army into a cocked hat. He said that the British Army could knock any of the other Allied Armies into a cocked hat. "But why?" said I. "Well," said he, "it is like this: In your communication lines, on which the whole thing depends, you order the men to drive to the right. The English soldier drives within a foot of the right. The French soldier drives within two feet of it. The Belgian soldier drives within three feet of it. The American soldier asks who in hell you suppose you are talking to, and makes up his mind that no bloody staff car is going to pass his lorry if he can help it. And that is why the sheeplike Englishman can beat the brave American bully boy every time when it comes to scientific soldiering." I daresay there is enough truth in this picturesque summing-up to be worth repeating. The way in which the American boys slaughtered and defeated themselves by rushing on machine guns without tanks while Haig's men, who had learned their lesson, got off with a tenth of the American casualties, was heartrending to hear about.

Do not encourage the Americans to underrate the British as warriors. Like all the Allies, they have had plenty of staggering reverses. They have been beaten by the Turks and by the Germans in engagements which will fill glorious pages of Turkish and German history, and not be mentioned in English history at all. They have been stampeded on occasion with a comic completeness that would not let down a Chaplin film at its wildest. But, as they say themselves, what of it? At the battle of Waterloo the British artillery ran away so flagrantly that the Iron Duke would never allow an official history of the battle to be written. But the British came out on top. In 1914 the French Army, as Joffre told it bluntly in the face of Europe, disgraced itself by its headlong retreat from Namur. The Portuguese Army, after holding a frightful position for several days, apparently with unquenchable valor, achieved a record skedaddle. But for the resulting intervention of the British General, Lord Cavan, the Italians who surrendered at Caporetto would have been starved to death after the armistice by their own commanders. I will assume, as I am writing this to America, that no American ever blenched, ever ran, ever sat down and cried like a child, ever ceased posing for his picture in the next number of "Life." But the American soldier's heart knows its own bitterness; and it is for him to tell his countrymen the truth when he hears them explaining how the American Army won the war when all the Europeans were whipped to a frazzle.

When everyone has owned up, England remains the most formidable single fighting Power in the world. I have insisted on that of set purpose; and I insist on it still, not as a mere Jingo brag of how Von Kluck has pleaded in his own defense that in the retreat from Mons the British soldier, even when the British Army was running away at a speed which sometimes worked out at eight miles an hour, had an incredible and impossible quantity of fight left in him (perhaps from lack of imagination), but because the most dangerous mistake that could be made in the world now is the mistake of America underrating England as a fighting power.

I do not think there is much danger of the converse mistake being made. England knows fairly well that she could not have won without America. The supplies from America before the

States came formally into the war and the staggering demonstration of their ability to send men by the million across the Atlantic at a time-rate which nobody had believed possible, had an effect far beyond that of their actual feats in the field; for the American Army had not had time to learn its business in that department, and its exploits can give no measure of what it would be capable of in full training. It took the British and German armies years to shape with any sort of efficiency: indeed, the French Army, in spite of its initial collapse, was probably the best trained at the start, though perhaps I am influenced in saying this by my own observation and comparison of the passing glimpses I got before the war at Treves and Toul, of the daily work of the German and French soldiers.

Of course, the Germans fought splendidly; but then, so did everybody. Heroes and Thermopylaes were six a penny in Europe before the war had lasted three months.

I rejected your Paris information as to the British having promised an army of a quarter of a million to the French, because Haldane's figures are precise, and are confirmed by the Brussels documents, whereas the size of the old British Army, which was known to the French, made an offer of 250,000 men impossible. French gossip, which always assumes that other countries have conscription and millions of men to play with because France has them, might easily invent such a story; but it could not have come from a military expert.

As to the panic in which Mr. Balfour appealed for American help, it prevailed all through the war. There were moments during the submarine campaign when it was excusable; but much of the funk was chronic and contemptible. Civilian and parliamentary England often reminded me of a certain prize fighter who flourished when I was a boy. His skill and power were such that he was always victorious at his weight; but he was so nervous that they had to keep a mirror in the ring to show him his face between every round to disprove his piteous pleas that his features were obliterated and that they must throw up the sponge for him, as he would surely be killed if he went on. People of his kidney, with howls of rage and terror, denounced as "pro-German" all who ventured to express the slightest doubt that the Germans were irresistible and that England was at her last gasp. One well-known author (Henry Arthur Jones) at a moment when England was playing the very devil with the enemy, told me that England was his mother, and that I had "kicked his dying mother on her death-bed," because I told him that Germany had not a dog's chance of winning, and the British Lion was never going stronger. On the other hand, the retreat from Mons was bragged about as if it were a masterpiece of victorious strategy. We were, it was said, luring the Germans into a trap. Nothing that you can say of the demoralization wrought by the war among the civilians can be too severe; but is any one in a position to cast the first stone?

You can tell the Americans from me that they have seriously compromised the credit of republicanism throughout the world by their outrageous repudiation, at the first shot, of all the liberties the Declaration of Independence proclaimed. When they began by sentencing a George Washington colonel to imprisonment for life, and followed that up by a series of persecutions which culminated in the ridiculous sentence on Debs, they disgraced their country, disgraced Wilson, and gave Germany, which had tolerated an avowed traitor like Liebknecht for an incredible time before at last sentencing him to only four years' imprisonment, the right to claim that even under the Kaiser she was much freer than the United States under its boasted democracy. As a republican I am ashamed of the American patriots; and you may tell them so with my compliments. I have had to stand up for Wilson, not as an American, but as a great man of whom his country is apparently utterly unworthy. Heaven knows we did abominable things here when we could not go to bed without fearing that we should be wakened by a bomb coming through the roof; but at least we raised our War Loans without the help of highwaymen.

That is all I have to say about the Laurels. Let the British and American Jingoes scramble for the leaves to their hearts' content; I take it that your business and mine is to uproot the tree and cast it into the bottomless pit. Ever,

G. Bernard Shaw.

HARRIS to SHAW [H/4]

[The new Shaw play which Harris saw in New York on March 15 in its first professional run was the wartime spoof, Augustus Does His Bit *(1916), performed as part of a double-bill. Ada Tyrrell was a Shaw friend from Dublin days. She had sent*

Harris a snapshot of Shaw as a boy in Dublin, writing Harris,
"My first memory of George is a little boy in a Holland overall
sitting at a table constructing a toy theatre. 'Sonny' the other
Shaws called him, then. . . . Even at that early age—George was
about ten—he had a superior manner to his sisters and me, a
sort of dignity withal, and I remember feeling rather flattered
when he condescended to explain anything I asked him, though
we girls were a year or two older." Harris used her entire de-
scription of Shaw in his portrait.

The first line of the letter refers to an article Shaw had writ-
ten for William Randolph Hearst's New York American. *Shaw*
liked to write for Hearst, for whom money was no object if he
wanted the contributor badly enough.]

29 Waverly Place, New York,
March 15, 1919

My dear Shaw:

I am sending you this article criticizing your first paper in
the "American" because you seem to me altogether wrong. Germany had whipped the world till America came in and how you
could have fallen into this error God only knows.

I have got a little account of you as a boy from Mrs. Ada
Tyrrell which is most interesting. I shall send you soon my
full-length portrait of you which I have completed and which I
think you will like. All I can say is, if you don't like it, your
taste for sugar must be excessive for I have written it con
amore.

Now I want you to stand and deliver about this fulsome praise
of England of yours. Even Wells admitted that the French were
better officered and had a better army. Our returning soldiers
here say there was no comparison and that up to the very last
the Germans were better at the game than the Allies; yet you
say that England out-generaled and out-fought the Germans
though I hear that they were chiefly distinguished for training
their artillery in one battle on their own men when they were
advancing. You will be writing next in praise of the English
navy for keeping its port in safety and leaving the whole of the
Baltic to the Germans. You could not have got Nelson to do
that.

Now do take off those rose-colored glasses of yours and let us
see the real Shaw. I am going to see your new play to-night.

Please tell me whether you get Pearson's regularly: strange to say, it's succeeding.

Yours ever,
Frank Harris

HARRIS to SHAW [H/4]

[Harris enclosed his profile of Shaw with this letter, hoping for some reaction which would add spice to his prose. His description of how wartime dissent was treated in America is strained but not without basis. Eugene Debs, American socialist spellbinder, was imprisoned for wartime pacifist speeches. Harris's description of mob behavior in the American South does not differ from press accounts.]

29 Waverley Place, New York
April 24th, 1919

My dear Shaw:

Here is the pen-portrait of you which I promised and which is to head my new volume of "Contemporary Portraits."

I think that in the main it will seem to you true and fair, but I have still a paragraph to put in explaining that any bodily weakness in you has not had its usual consequence in meekness of mind. In fact I have to go over this sketch again but in the main I think it may stand as the best I can do of you and I send it to you for any corrections or emendations you may care to make in it. Even frank disagreement or hint of doubt may set me thinking on the point and result in a better sketch.

Please give yourself the trouble to read it carefully but I assure you it has cost me more pains in the writing than anything I have done in years.

I have not published your splendid letter yet, for which I thank you a thousand times, but of course I shall publish it in the June number I hope, or at any rate in the first number after peace is declared. Your criticism of the way Americans raised the money is so true and so terrible that I am certain they would suppress any paper that published it; but as soon as peace is signed I intend to publish it with what you previously wrote to me about American liberty.

What you say about the imprisonment of Debs is true but have you heard the truth about how conscientious objectors have been tortured and done to death in American prisons? England has treated these noble men badly enough God knows, but England has not tortured them and murdered them as Americans have done.

I am sending you an article of mine on the subject. I wish you would write a few words on it. I am sending you too an article on the lynching of negroes and the torturing of negro women. My soul sickens over these things, but if we do not speak and speak strongly they will go on outraging our very conscience and degrading the soul of humanity.

I am endeavoring to make you more and more listened to in America as the highest voice in England. For God's sake give me deathless words about these vile torturings and lynchings of a race whose only crime is that it is weak.

I know I am taking up your time but you have done a great deal of good here already and believe me a couple of pages from your heart about these things will make a great difference.

I think you altogether over-rate Wilson. To me he is another Gladstone with the cant of idealism in his mouth cloaking selfish motives. I would rather trust Clemenceau who in '71–'75 fought for the amnesty of the communards against his own popularity than a hundred Wilsons. Think of giving the Saar Valley to France and crippling Germany, and Dantzig to the Poles who are nothing but Hausknechte in the port, hewers of wood and drawers of water—a small minority of the worst.

Perhaps you do not agree with me in these things, but in the lynchings and torturings I am sure I have you with me. Please write me a page about them. I want to make the first number after peace is declared the most tremendous protest against American evils that has ever been written.

The other day we read of how a tortured negro's eyes were burnt out and when he screamed with pain a woman thrust a red-hot poker into his mouth. Shaw we should surely find some word to stop it.

I hope to be back in Paris at the beginning of the year and to be able to write my autobiography and get away from this journalism forever. I haven't much time left!

Sincerely ever,
Frank Harris

HARRIS on SHAW [X/CP]

[Unable to find a commercial publisher for his second volume of biographical sketches, Harris privately published Contemporary Portraits. Second Series *from his 57 Fifth Avenue address in 1919. Shaw was his first subject, complete to portrait photograph frontispiece, and the later pages of the forty-four page "portrait" cribbed so thoroughly from Shaw's letters that the entire text would be redundant here. Nevertheless, enough follows to represent Harris's method and perspectives. Shaw would respond in his own way, to Harris's delight—and reward.]*

Contemporary Portraits: George Bernard Shaw

Don Quixote lived in an imaginary past; he cherished the beliefs and tried to realize the ideal, of an earlier age. Our modern Don Quixotes all live in the future and hug a belief of their own making, an ideal corresponding to their own personality.

Both the lovers of the past and the future, however, start by despising the present; they are profoundly dissatisfied with what is and in love with what has been or may be. . . .

But Shaw is more than an iconoclast.

His work as a dramatist is at least as important as his critical energy. In this respect I always think of him as a British Moliere gifted with as fine a wit as the great Frenchman and at least as wide a reach of thought. . . .

More than once Shaw has played true prophet and guide and stood against the selfish policies and hypocrisies of his nation with high disregard of personal consequences. That he has not been imprisoned or banned or even persecuted is due to the fact that he is very English in many things and that his humor has saved him from being taken too seriously. Yet he deserves to be taken seriously, and I have put forth my high appreciation of him at the outset to induce my readers to reconsider this superficial impression of him.

It was in September, 1894, that I bought *The Saturday Review* and set myself to get the ablest men to write for it, careless what their opinions might be.

Most newspaper men in London had heard of G. B. S.: his initials stuck in the mind because they were the same, or very like, those given to a famous pipe and advertised till they had become a household word. George Bernard Shaw profited by the coincidence. He made himself known as a journalist by his papers on music in *The Star*, a cheap Radical evening paper, and preached socialism to boot wherever he could get a hearing.

In 1892 he began writing for *The World*, a paper of some importance so long as its founder and editor, Edmund Yates, was alive. But Yates died six months or so before I bought *The Saturday Review*, and I knew that Shaw would resent the change. The idea of connecting Shaw the Socialist orator with the high Tory *Saturday Review* pleased me; the very incongruity tempted and his ability was beyond question. Now and again I had read his weekly articles on music and while admiring the keen insight of them and the satiric light he threw on pompous pretences and unrealities, I noticed that he had begun to repeat himself, as if he had said all he had to say on that theme.

What should I ask him to write about? What was his true vein? He had as much humor as Wilde—the name at once crystalized my feeling—that was what Shaw should do, I said to myself, write on the theatre; in essence his talent, like Wilde's, was theatrical, almost to caricature, certain, therefore, to carry across the footlights and have an immediate effect.

I wrote to him at once, telling him my opinion of his true talent and asking him to write a weekly article for *The Saturday Review*.

He answered immediately; a letter somewhat after this fashion:

"How the Dickens you knew that my thoughts had been turning to the theater of late and that I'd willingly occupy myself with it exclusively for some time to come, I can't imagine. But you've hit the clout, as the Elizabethans used to say, and, if you can afford to pay me regularly, I'm your man so long as the job suits me and I suit the job. What can you afford to give?"

My answer was equally prompt and to the point:

"I can afford to give you so much a week, more, I believe, than you are now getting. If that appeals to you, start in at once; bring me your first article by next Wednesday and we'll have a final pow-wow."

On the Wednesday Shaw turned up with the article, and I had a good look at him and a long talk with him. Shaw at this time was nearing forty; very tall, over six feet in height and thin to angularity; a long bony face, corresponding, I thought, to a tendency to get to bedrock everywhere; rufous fair hair and long, untrimmed reddish beard; gray-blue English eyes with straight eyebrows tending a little upwards from the nose and thus adding a touch of Mephistophelian sarcasm to the alert, keen expression. He was dressed carelessly in tweeds with a Jaeger flannel shirt and negligent tie; contempt of frills written all over him; his hands clean and well-kept, but not manicured. His complexion, singularly fair even for a man with reddish hair, seemed too bloodless to me, reminded me of his vegetarianism which had puzzled me more than a little for some time. His entrance into the room, his abrupt movements—as jerky as the ever-changing mind—his perfect unconstraint—all showed an able man, very conscious of his ability, very direct, very sincere, sharply decisive.

"I liked your letter," Shaw began, "as I told you; the price, too, suits me for the moment; but—you won't alter my articles, will you?"

"Not a word," I said. "If I should want anything changed, which is most unlikely, I'd send you a proof and ask you to alter it; but that is not going to occur often. I like original opinions even though I don't agree with them."

After some further talk, he said:

"Very well then. If the money appears regularly you can count on me for a weekly outpouring. You don't limit me in any way?"

"Not in any way," I answered.

"Well, it seems to me that the new *Saturday Review* should make a stir."

"After we're all dead, not much before, but that doesn't matter," I replied. "I've asked all the reviewers only to review those books they admire and can praise: starfinders they should be, not fault-finders."

"What'll the master of 'flouts and jeers' think?" asked Shaw. (Lord Salisbury, the bitter-tongued Prime Minister, had been a constant contributor to *The Saturday Review* twenty years before, and was understood still to take an interest in his old journal.)

"I don't know and I don't care," I replied; and our talk came to an end.

Shaw was a most admirable contributor, always punctual unless there was some good reason for being late; always scrupulous, correcting his proofs heavily, with rare conscientiousness, and always doing his very best.

I soon realized that the drama of the day had never been so pungently criticized; I began to compare Shaw's articles with the *Dramaturgie* of Lessing, and it was Shaw who gained by the comparison.

His critical writing was exactly like his speaking and indeed like his creative dramatic work; very simple, direct and lucid, clarity and sincerity his characteristics. No pose, no trace of affectation; a man of one piece, out to convince not to persuade; a bare logical argument lit up by gleams of sardonic humor; humor of the head as a rule and not of the heart. His writing seemed artless, but there is a good deal of art in his plays and art too, can be discovered both in his speaking and in his critical work, but whether there is enough art to serve as a prophylactic against time, remains to be seen.

His seriousness, sincerity and brains soon brought the actor-managers out in arms against him. Naturally they did not condemn his writing, but his dress and behaviour. Two or three of them told me at various times that Shaw was impossible.

"He often comes to the theatre in ordinary dress," said one, "and looks awful."

"You ought to thank your stars that he goes to your theatre at all," I replied. "I certainly shall not instruct him how to clothe himself."

"What I object to," said another, "is that he laughs in the wrong place. It is dreadful when a favorite actor is saying something very pathetic or sentimental to see a great figure in gray stretch himself out in the front stalls and roar with laughter."

"I know," I replied grinning, "and the worst of it is that all the world laughs with Shaw when he shows it the unconscious humor of your performance."

An amusing incident closed this controversy. One night a manager told Shaw he could not go into the stalls in that dress. Shaw immediately began to take off his coat.

"No, no," cried the actor-manager; "I mean you must dress like other people."

Shaw glanced at the rows of half-dressed women: "I'm not going to take off my shirt," he exclaimed, "in order to be like your clients," and forthwith left the house.

The dispute had one good result. Shaw asked me to buy his tickets. "I hate the whole practice of complimentary tickets," he said. "It is intended to bind one to praise and I resent the implied obligation."

Of course, I did as he wished and there the trouble ended.

At rare intervals I had to tell Shaw his article was too long and beg him to shorten it. For months together I had nothing to do except congratulate myself on having got him as a contributor; though at first he was strenuously objected to by many of my readers who wrote begging me to cancel their subscriptions or at least to cease from befouling their houses with "Shaw's socialistic rant and theatric twaddle."

An incident or two in the four years' companionship may be cited, for they show, I think, the real Shaw. William Morris, the poet and decorator-craftsman, died suddenly. Shaw called just to tell me he'd like to write a special article on Morris, as a socialist and prose-writer and speaker. I said I'd be delighted, for Arthur Symons was going to write on his poetry and Cunninghame Graham on his funeral. I hoped to have three good articles. When they arrived, I found that Symons was very good indeed and so was Shaw; but Cunninghame Graham had written a little masterpiece, a gem of restrained yet passionate feeling: absolute realistic description lifted to poetry by profound emotion.

Shaw came blown in on the Monday full of unaffected admiration.

"What a story that was of Graham's!" he cried, "a great writer, isn't he?"

I nodded: "An amateur of genius: it's a pity he hasn't to earn his living by his pen."

"A good thing for us," cried Shaw, "he'd wipe the floor with us all if he often wrote like that."

I only relate the happening to show Shaw's unaffected sincerity and outspoken admiration of good work in another man.

I came to regard him as a realist by nature, who, living in the modern realistic current, was resolved to be taken simply for what he was and what he could do, and equally resolved to judge all other men and women by the same relentless positive standard. This love of truth for its own sake, truth beyond vanity or self-praise, is a product of the modern scientific spirit and appears to me to embody one of the loftiest ideals yet recorded among men.

It marks, indeed, the coming of age of the race and is a sign that we have done with childish make-believes. From this time on we shall turn our daily job into the great adventure and make of its perfecting our life's romance. Shaw's realism, his insistence on recognizing only real values was so intense that it called forth one of Oscar Wilde's finest epigrams:

"Shaw," he said, "hasn't an enemy in the world and none of his friends like him."

. . . .

One day in *The Saturday Review* office I got a letter from a friend of very considerable ability, begging me not to let Shaw go on "writing drivel about Shakespeare; on his own job he's good, but why let him talk rot?" I had noticed Shaw's divagations; but he used Shakespeare like the British use the ten commandments as a shillelagh, and as Shaw took the great dramatist generally to point unconventional morals, I didn't wish to restrain him. But one day his weekly paper was chiefly about Shakespeare, and he fell into two or three of the gross common blunders on the subject: notably, in one passage, he assumed that Shakespeare had been a good husband—the usual English misconception.

I wrote to him at once:

"You are writing so brilliantly on the weekly theater-happenings, why on earth drag in Shakespeare always like King Charles's head, as you know nothing about him." I got an answer by return:

"What in thunder do you mean by saying I know nothing of Shakespeare? I know more about the immortal Will than any living man," and so forth and so on.

I replied:

"Come to lunch one day at the Cafe Royal and I'll give you the weeds and the water your soul desires and prove into the bargain that you know nothing whatever about Shakespeare."

When we had ordered our lunch Shaw began:

"Who's going to be the judge between us, Frank Harris, on this Shakespeare matter?"

"You, Shaw, only you," I replied, "I am to convince you of your complete and incredible ignorance."

He snorted: "Then you have your work cut out; we can't sleep here, can we?"

"The time it will take," I retorted, "depends on your intelligence—that's what I'm reckoning on."

"Humph!" he grunted disdainfully. We had our meal and then went at it hammer and tongs.

"You believe," I began, "that because Shakespeare left Stratford after being married a couple of years and did not return for eleven years, he loved his wife?"

"No, no," replied Shaw, "I said in my article that in his will he left his wife 'the second-best bed' as a pledge of his affection. I remember reading once something that convinced me of this; I don't recall the argument now; but at the time it convinced me and I can look it up for you if you like."

"You needn't," I replied, "I'll give it you; it's probably the old professorial explanation: the best bed in those days was in the guest room; therefore the second-best bed was the one Shakespeare slept in with his wife."

"That's it," cried Shaw, "that's it, and it is convincing. How do you meet it?"

"Aren't you ashamed of yourself?" I replied. "Here's Shakespeare, the most articulate creature that ever lived, the greatest lord of language in recorded time, unable in his will to express a passionate emotion so as to be understood. Why, had he even written 'our bed, dear,' as the common grocer would have done, we'd all have known what he meant. Shakespeare could never write 'the second-best bed' without realizing the sneer in the words and intending us to realize it as well. Besides——"

"Good God," interrupted Shaw, throwing up his hand to his forehead impatiently, "of course not; how stupid of me! Confound the mandarins and their idiot explanations!"—and after a pause: "I'll give you the second-best bed; I'm prepared to believe that Shakespeare did not love his wife. Go ahead with your other proofs of my ignorance."

At five that afternoon we left the table, Shaw declaring he would never write again about Shakespeare if I'd write about him.

On that, I began my articles on Shakespeare, which afterwards grew into books; but Shaw has not kept his vow. He has written again and again on the subject and always with a bias, being more minded to realize Shaw than Shakespeare. But ever since that talk he has shown cordial appreciation of my work on the subject.

Towards the end of my tenure of *The Saturday Review*, Shaw was making a great deal of money by his plays, thanks mainly I believe to their extraordinary vogue in the United States.

Casually he told me one day that every article he wrote for me cost him much more than he got for it.

"I mean," he said, "the same time spent on a comedy would pay me ten times as much. I'm losing $500 a week at least through writing for you."

"You must stop writing for me then," I said, ruefully. "But I'm about to sell the paper, and if you could have kept on for a couple of months, say till September (it was then July or August if I remember rightly), I'd be greatly obliged."

"Say no more," he exclaimed. "I'll go on till your reign comes to an end."

"It's very good of you," I replied; "but I hardly like to accept such a sacrifice from you."

"I look upon it as only fair," he replied. "Your bringing me to *The Saturday Review* to write on the theatre did me a great deal of good in many ways. You not only made me better known, but forced me to concentrate on the theatre and playwriting, and so helped me to success. It's only fair I should pay you back a part of what you helped me to earn."

"If you look at it like that," I replied, "I have no objection. You are making a lot of money then by your plays?"

"Not in England," he said, "but in America more than I can spend. My banker smiles now when he sees me, and is in a perpetual state of wonderment, for miracle on miracle, a writer is not only making money, but saving it."

Some time before this Shaw had married and had taken to wife, as he said himself, a lady who was "more than self-supporting." Consequently he found himself in 1898 much better than well off, freed from all sordid care. The first part of his life, the struggle of it, came thus to an end.

Shaw's apprenticeship as Goethe calls it, was now over and done with. He had reached the point where he began to produce as a master and show his true being. There will be nothing novel in his growth, nothing that should surprise us; he develops normally, naturally, and his life's history is to be found in his works.

Without dissecting his plays—*The Devil's Disciple, Caesar and Cleopatra,* and best of all, I think, *Candida,* I have to notice a certain limitation in Shaw, peculiarly British, which discovered itself in *Mrs. Warren's Profession.* There is no excuse for founding a play on this subject unless you are minded to amend or overthrow the conventional standpoint. If you only mean to affirm and defend it, why touch the scabrous subject at all? The conventions of this world are surely strong enough without being buttressed by the Bernard Shaws. As soon as the hero and heroine of *Mrs. Warren's Profession* get a hint of the truth, they don't even verify it, but both drop all thought of marriage and bow before the conventional ideal, whereas one expects the hero at least to struggle and revolt. But the conventional reading of the matter is peculiarly British, and Shaw's tame conformity here shows that his interest in sex-questions is very slight, to say the best for it.

It is a peculiar dominance of mind over heart and over body, a rooted preference in Shaw for reflections and ideas with a contempt of sensations and even emotions that gives the Mephistophilian cast to his personality. His excessive preoccupation with the play of mind often hurts his dramatic writing. For instance, in *The Devil's Disciple,* after *Arms and the Man* probably his most popular play, Dick Dudgeon and Parson Anderson and even General Burgoyne are not differentiated in character; they are all Shaw. In the second act Parson Anderson exclaims "Minister be faugh!" as if he were the Devil's Disciple, and Burgoyne sneers at the marksmanship of the British army and talks about "our enemies in London—Jobbery and Snobbery, incompetence and Red Tape," exactly as Shaw talks, in and out of season.

This onesidedness or predominance of intellect over heart and body, leads directly to the root-fact of Shaw's nature.

Very early in our acquaintance I had been surprised by one thing in him. The hero of one of his first books had been a prizefighter; Shaw made him very strong whereas most prizefighters are like Fitzsimmons, ape-armed, but not muscular. Shaw's extravagant ill-placed admiration of strength had stuck in my mind. I soon found out that he was never physically strong; he told me one day that his work often exhausted him so that he was fain to go into a dark room and lie flat on his back on the bare floor, every muscle relaxed, for hours, just to rest. The confession surprised me, for in the prime of life the ordinary man does not get tired out in this way.

A certain weakness of body in Shaw was sufficient to explain his undue admiration of the prizefighter's strength and his own vegetarianism and other idiosyncracies. But if asked why he abjures meat Shaw retorts that flesh-eating is an unhealthy practice and that the strongest animals such as the bull and the elephant are strict vegetarians; but that hardly satisfies one. The truth, I think, is that the physical delicacy in Shaw detaches him from the common run of men whose appetites are gross and insistent. This comparative weakness of the body, too, allows his brain to act undisturbed and thus his appeal strikes one as peculiarly intellectual; as thin, so to speak, or at least thin-blooded.

. . . .

And now what is the sum total of the whole story? My readers must see that I regard Shaw the iconoclast, Shaw the railer at British conventions and British hypocrisies, Shaw who has been wise enough or lucky enough to mount himself on a stout bank-balance instead of an aged Rosinante, and from that vantage to attack British conceit and complacent materialism; Shaw the scoffer and sceptic and socialist, as assuredly the most powerful and highest moral influence in the Britain of this time. He has taken the place left vacant by Carlyle and has given proof of as fine a courage and as high a devotion to Truth as the Scot. He has scoffed at the idea of a personal immortality as contemptuously as at the idea of a state where the few suffer from too great wealth almost as much as the many suffer from an unmerited destitution.

Shaw's religion, his view that is of the true meaning of life deserves to be stated:

"This is the true joy in life," he says, "the being used for a purpose recognized by yourself as a mighty one; the being thoroughly worn out before you are thrown on the scrap-heap; the being a force of nature instead of a feverish selfish little clod of ailments and grievances complaining that the world will not devote itself to making you happy."

In the main this is the creed of Carlyle too and of Goethe though the great German brings joy into it by making the individual himself work consciously for the highest purpose.

Everyone, I think, who treats of this period in history will have to consider Bernard Shaw as far and away the most important figure in Great Britain for nearly a quarter of a century. True, he has no new word in religion for us, no glimpse even of new and vital truth; but he walks honestly by such gleams of light as come to him in the present.

And some of Shaw's plays are at least equal in worth to his critical work and will hold the stage for generations to come. He is among the greatest of English humorists. Everyone can see now that Shakespeare's humor was adventitious and fortunate rather than characteristic. Take Falstaff out of his work and all the other clowns, including even Dogberry, would hardly furnish forth one evening's entertainment. And Falstaff and Dogberry belong to the earliest part of Shakespeare's life; after thirty he became increasingly serious. But Shaw's humor is richer to-day at sixty odd than when he began; the flashes of it illumine every part of his work. The British stage knows no comedies superior to *John Bull's Other Island, Candida,* and *Caesar and Cleopatra.*

And this is the Shaw that will hold an unique place in English literature; the humorist, iconoclast and prophet; the laughing philosopher, whom no one to-day can afford to ignore.

. . . .

This is the highest merit of the man, that while mocking sentimentality he is always true to the best in him as needle to the pole. He has shown us all that a Briton can rise above secular British prejudices and that ingrained English habit of excusing oafish stupidity by the conceit of moral superiority, as if dullness and goodness were Siamese twins.

He has pictured Caesar standing before the Sphinx and admitting that he, too, is "half brute, half woman and half God, and no part of man." The confession though doubtless personal, does not do Shaw justice. I have always thought of him as of Greatheart in Bunyan's allegory, a man so high-minded and courageous he will take the kingdom of heaven by storm and yet so full of the milk of human kindness that he suffers with all the disadvantages of the weak and all the disabilities of the dumb. He is the only man since William Blake who has enlarged our conception of English character; thanks to the Irish strain in him he encourages us to hope that English genius may yet become as free of insular taint as the vagrant air and as beneficent as sunshine.

SHAW to HARRIS [H/ML]

[Shaw's commentary on Harris's biographical method was meant of course to serve a dual purpose, and Harris accepted the gift of "How Frank Ought to Have Done It" gratefully. It would become the appendix to the second volume of Contemporary Portraits *(1919). Harris prefaced what he retitled "Shaw's Portrait by Shaw, or How Frank Ought to Have Done It," with an explanation:*

> After finishing my pen-portrait of Shaw I sent him a copy asking him to correct any errors in it. He replied by telling me that I was incorrigible and sending me the following portrait of himself as an example of how I should have written about him. Just as I published Shaw's views of Oscar Wilde in my book on Wilde so now I publish Shaw's self-portrait so that my readers can compare it with my view of him.—FRANK HARRIS.

Harris had possibly sent more copy from his book to Shaw than the G.B.S. portion, for the Shavian reference to Woodrow Wilson may refer not only to Harris's letter of April 24 but to passages in Harris's portrait of Arthur Balfour, in which Balfour's Old World experience and sophistication are contrasted to President Wilson's innocence: "Mr. Wilson is of his own sort, a scholar and amateur of life with the deficiencies of the bookish."]

10 Adelphi Terrace, London W.C.2.
24th May 1919

Dear Frank Harris,

Your portrait is not a bit of use. No wonder you found it a stiff job. You were working under a double handicap. First, you dont know me: you have not met me often enough, nor worked in my cliques. Second, you have been scrupulously anxious to do me justice and be loyal to me. That is noble, but unreadable.

The only way I can help you out is by doing the job myself as you must do it. It is much shorter than arguing with you from point to point. I can say things about myself that nobody but an enemy could say; and he probably wouldnt have wit enough. I can give you a lot of little significant facts, of which you are frightfully short. And I can save you the time—which you cant afford—that it would take to read carefully through several million words of mine and get up the whole history of the last quarter of the nineteenth century and the first quarter of the twentieth.

It has been a queer job, and would have been impossible if I had not [had] the dramatic faculty that enables me to see the stage effect I am producing, and to exploit it histrionically for the inner purpose that drives me on without any real complicity in its artificiality. The inner life has no place in individual portraits because it is not an individual thing: it drives me as it drives everyone else. The portrait must give the accidents of the surface, the idiosyncrasies of the vehicle: that is why I am able to give them away with so much detachment. They amuse me as much as they amuse anyone else: more, perhaps, for I naturally exaggerate their importance.

Be careful about Wilson. There is a case against Wilson; but it is the case of Tom Paine against Washington; and I think you will admit, in the perspective of history, that Paine got his values wrong. Wilson has had an impossible task; and years will elapse before his success or failure can be estimated. Even those who are behind the scene, who alone know the secret understandings by which the parties have squared each other, cannot place him as we can now place Washington or Lincoln. What is certain is that he succeeded in making himself the spokesman of the right side when he entered the field; and I backed him accordingly, and shall continue to do so until I find a better man to back. Dont raise an alarm of damp sheets when there is a fire to be put out.

Ever,

G. Bernard Shaw

SHAW to HARRIS [X/CP]

How Frank Ought to Have Done It

Before attempting to add Bernard Shaw to my collection of Contemporary Portraits, I find it necessary to secure myself in advance by the fullest admission of his extraordinary virtues. Without any cavilling over trifles I declare at once that Shaw is the just man made perfect. I admit that in all his controversies, with me or anyone else, Shaw is, always has been, and always will be, right. I perceive that the common habit of abusing him is an ignorant and silly habit, and that the pretence of not taking him seriously is the ridiculous cover for an ignominious retreat from an encounter with him. If there is any other admission I can make, any other testimonial I can give, I am ready to give it and apologize for having omitted it. If it will help matters to say that Shaw is the greatest man that ever lived, I shall not hesitate for a moment. All the cases against him break down when they are probed to the bottom. All his prophecies come true. All his fantastic creations come to life within a generation. I have an uneasy sense that even now I am not doing him justice: that I am ungrateful, disloyal, disparaging. I can only repeat that if there is anything I have left out, all that is necessary is to call my attention to the oversight and it shall be remedied. If I cannot say that Shaw touches nothing that he does not adorn, I can at least testify that he touches nothing that he does not dust and polish and put back in its place much more carefully than the last man who handled it.

I will tell some anecdotes of Shaw. Oscar Wilde said of him "He has not an enemy in the world; and none of his friends like him."

Once, at a public dinner given by the Stage Society, Shaw had to propose the health of the dramatic critics; and Max Beerbohm had to reply. Before the speaking began Max came to Shaw and said "You are going to say, aren't you, that you are a critic yourself?" "I dont know what I am going to say" said Shaw; "but I daresay I could bring that in." "Promise me that you will" said Max: "I want to make a point about it." "Anything to oblige you" said Shaw; and he did. Max began his speech thus: "I was once at a school where the master used always to say 'Remember, boys, I am one of yourselves.'" A roar of laughter saved Max the trouble of pointing the moral.

Robert Lynd said of Shaw's Common Sense About the War that though nobody could take any reasonable exception to it, yet, from the moment it appeared, the war was spoken of and written about as a war between the Allies on the one hand, and, on the other, Germany, Austria, Turkey, and Bernard Shaw.

When Shaw contested a seat at the London County Council

election as a Progressive, after six years' hard Progressive drudgery on a Borough Council, with the advantage of being one of the inventors of municipal Progressivism, not only was he defeated by the defection of all but the irreducible minimum of Liberals and temperance reformers (Shaw is a teetotaller), but the leading Progressive papers openly exulted in his defeat as a most blessed deliverance. The only other people who voted for him were those who had never voted before. This was proved by an increase in the poll at the next election, when the adored actor George Alexander was the victorious candidate.

These are the things that happen to him in his most popular moments, when he is in no way breasting and opposing the current of public opinion. When, as often happens, he has to take his chance of being lynched for telling some unpalatable truth, numbers of persons who have never before dared to betray any hostility to him believe that they have him "on the run" at last, and vent on him a bitterness and violence which must have been rankling in them for years.

The result is that hardly anyone who has not met Shaw thinks of him otherwise than as a man of disagreeable appearance, harsh manners, and insufferable personality. He knows this, and says "I always astonish strangers by my amiability, because, as no human being could possibly be so disagreeable as they expect me to be, I have only to be commonly civil to seem quite charming."

No truthful contemporary portrait can ignore either this extraordinary power of exciting furious hostility, or the entire absence of any obvious ground for it. It has been said that Shaw irritates people by always standing on his head, and calling black white and white black. But only simpletons either offer or accept this account. Men do not win a reputation like Shaw's by perversity and tomfoolery. What is really puzzling is that Shaw irritates us intensely by standing on his feet and telling us that black is black and white white, whilst we please ourselves by professing what everyone knows to be false.

There is something maddening in being forced to agree with a man against whom your whole soul protests. It is not that he expresses your own view more accurately than you yourself could. But you cannot bear your inmost convictions to be shared by a man whose nature you hold to be monstrous and subversive. It is as if a man had offered to walk a bit of the way with you because you were going in the direction of his home, and you knew that home to be the bottomless pit.

As a matter of fact there is nothing in Shaw's political and social program, not even his insistence on basic equality of income and its dissociation from every kind of personal industry or virtue, at which a thinker of adequate modern equipment need turn a hair. He is a perfectly safe man on a committee of any sort: a man of tact and circumspection who kept the Fabian Society, of which he was a leader for twenty-seven years, free from the quarrels that broke up all the other Socialist organizations.

Yet the monstrosity is there; for Shaw works at politics in the spirit of one helping a lame dog over a stile which he believes to be insurmountable. "Every man over forty is a scoundrel!" he proclaimed when he was himself over forty. He makes no secret of his conviction that the problems raised by modern multitudinous civilization are beyond our political capacity and may never be solved by us. He attaches little value to mere experience, holding that it is expectation of life and not recollection of it that determines conduct. He reminds us repeatedly that as Evolution is still creative Man may have to be scrapped as a Yahoo, and replaced by some new and higher creation, just as man himself was created to supply the deficiencies of the lower animals.

It is impossible to take offence at this, because Shaw is as merciless to himself as to us. He does not kick us overboard and remain proudly on the quarter deck himself. With the utmost good-humor he clasps us affectionately round the waist and jumps overboard with us, and that too, not into a majestic Atlantic where we might perish tragically, but into a sea of ridicule amid shrieks of derisive laughter. And this intolerable trick is played on us at the most unexpected and inopportune moments. "No man" said Sir Henry Norman "knows how to butter a moral slide better than Shaw." Shaw's championship thus becomes more dreaded than the most spiteful attacks of others. During the first Ibsen boom in London he proposed to help an American actress in an Ibsen enterprise by interviewing her. To his astonishment the lady told him with passionate earnestness that if he wrote a word about her she would shoot him. "You may not believe here in England that such things are possible" she said; "but in America we think differently;

and I will do it: I have the pistol ready." "General Gabler's pistol" was Shaw's unruffled comment; but he saw how intensely the lady shrank from being handled by him in print; and the interview was not written. Some of his best friends confess that until they were used to him quite friendly letters from him would sometimes move them to furious outbursts of profanity at his expense. He tells a story of a phrenologist with whom he got into conversation at a vegetarian restaurant in his early days. This man presently accused Shaw of being "a septic," meaning a sceptic. "Why?" said Shaw. "Have I no bump of veneration?" "Bump!" shouted the phrenologist: "It's a hole." If Shaw's manners were offensive one could at least punch his head; but his pity for your inadequacy and his own is so kindly, so covered by an unexceptionable observance of the perfect republican respect to which you are entitled, that you are utterly helpless: there is nothing to complain of, nothing to lay hold of, no excuse for snatching up the carving knife and driving it into his vitals.

I, Frank Harris, was editing The Fortnightly Review when I first met Shaw about an article. He had an engaging air of being more interested in me than in the article. Not to be mock modest, I suppose I *was* more interesting than the article; and I was naturally not disposed to quarrel with Shaw for thinking so, and shewing it. He has the art of getting on intimate and easy terms very quickly; and at the end of five minutes I found myself explaining to him how I had upset my health by boyishly allowing myself to be spurred into a burst of speed on the river in an outrigger, and overstraining myself. He gave his mind to my misfortune as sympathetically as my doctor, and asked me some questions as to how much care I was taking of myself. One of the questions was "Do you drink?" I was equal to the occasion, and did not turn a hair as I assured him that a diagnosis of delirium tremens could not be sustained; but I could not help becoming suddenly conscious that I expected from men an assumption that I am not a drunkard, and that I was face to face with a man who made no such assumption. His question was too like one of those asked in Butler's Erewhon to be entirely agreeable to human frailty. In Shaw's play Captain Brassbound's Conversion, the captain introduces his lieutenant with the words (or to this effect) "This is the greatest scoundrel, liar, thief, and rapscallion on the west coast." On which the lieutenant says "Look here, Captain: if you want to be modest, be modest on your own account, not on mine." The fact that Shaw *is* modest on his own account, and gives himself away much more freely than his good manners allow him to give away his friends, does not really make the transaction any more agreeable to its victims: it only robs them of their revenge, and compels them to pay tribute to his amiability when they are furiously annoyed with him.

It is difficult to class a man who gives himself away even to the point of making himself ridiculous as vain. But all Shaw's friends agree that he is laughably vain. Yet here again he confuses our judgment by playing up to it with the most hyperbolical swank about his intellect. He declares that he does so because people like it. He says, quite truly, that they love Cyrano, and hate "the modest cough of the minor poet." Those who praise his books to his face are dumbfounded by the enthusiasm with which he joins in his own praise, and need all their presence of mind to avoid being provoked into withdrawing some seventy-five per cent. or so of their eulogies. Such playacting makes it difficult to say how much real vanity or modesty underlies it all. He himself denies that he is conceited. "No man can be" he says "if, like me, he has spent his life trying to play the piano accurately, and never succeeded for a single bar." I ask him to give me a list of his virtues, his excellences, his achievements, so that I may not do him the injustice of omitting any. He replies "It is unnecessary: they are all in the shop window."

Shaw plays the part of the modest man only in his relations with the arts which are the great rivals of literature. He has never claimed to be "better than Shakespear," though he does claim to be his successor. The much quoted heading to one of his prefaces has a note of interrogation after it; and the question is dismissed by himself with the remark that as Shakespear in drama, like Mozart in opera, and Michael Angelo in fresco, reached the summit of his art, nobody can be better than Shakespear, though anybody may now have things to say that Shakespear did not say, and outlooks on life and character which were not open to him.

Nevertheless I am convinced that Shaw is as willing to have his plays compared with Shakespear's as Turner was to have his pictures hung beside Claude's. Yet when he was invited to a dinner in Paris in honor of Rodin, he wrote that he had the honor of being one of Rodin's models, and was sure of a place in the biographical dictionaries a thousand years hence as "Shaw, Bernard: subject of a bust by Rodin: otherwise unknown." He struck the same note when, finding that Rodin, though an infallible connoisseur in sculpture, had no books in his collection except the commonest kind of commercial presentation volumes, he presented him with a Kelmscott Chaucer, and wrote in it

> I have seen two masters at work: Morris who made this book:
> The other Rodin the Great, who fashioned my head in clay.
> I give the book to Rodin, scrawling my name in a nook
> Of the shrine their works shall hallow when mine are dust by
> the way.

In the same vein is the inscription he proposed for a pedestal to Lady Kennet's statue of him, now in the Bournemouth Municipal Gallery.

> WEEP NOT FOR OLD GEORGE BERNARD: HE IS DEAD
> AND ALL HIS FRIENDS EXCLAIM "A DAMNED GOOD JOB!"
> THOUGH RANKING GEORGE'S CELEBRATED HEAD
> HIGH IN THE MORE UNCOMMON SORTS OF NOB
>
> LONG AT ITS IMAGE KATHLEEN'S HAND HAD PLIED
> WHEN THE LORD SAID "NOT THUS GREAT WORK BEGAT IS.
> COPY NO MORE: YOUR SPIRIT BE YOUR GUIDE:
> CARVE HIM SUB SPECIE AETERNITATIS
>
> SO WHEN HIS WORKS SHALL ALL FORGOTTEN BE
> YET SHALL HE SHARE YOUR IMMORTALITY"

Later on The Evening News asked him to write his own epitaph. In response he drew a weed-overgrown tombstone, and on it the lines

HIC JACET
BERNARD SHAW
Who the devil was he?

Now I confess I am not convinced by this evidence of modesty. I am not sure that it is not rather the final artistic touch to

Shaw's swank. For what was the origin of the Rodin bust? Rodin knew nothing about Shaw, and at first refused to undertake the commission. Mrs Shaw thereupon wrote to Rodin pleading that she wished to have a memorial of her husband, and that her husband declared that any man, who, being a contemporary of Rodin, would have his bust made by anyone else, would pillory himself to all posterity as an ignoramus. Rodin, finding that he had to deal with a man who knew his value, weakened in his refusal. Mrs Shaw then ascertained from Rilke, the Austrian poet, then acting as Rodin's secretary, what his usual fee was for a bust. The money (£1,000) was immediately lodged to Rodin's credit on the understanding that he was to be under no obligation whatever in respect of it, and might make the bust or not make it, begin it or leave it off at his pleasure: in short, treat the payment as a contribution to the endowment of his work in general and remain completely master of the situation. The result, of course, was that Rodin sent for Shaw to come to Paris at once; installed him and his wife as daily guests at his Meudon villa; worked steadily at the bust every day for a month until it was finished; and went beyond his bargain in giving the sitter casts of it.

Here we have the diplomatic Shaw, the master of blarney, and the penetrating art critic; and not for a moment do I suggest that there was the slightest insincerity in his proceedings. Had there been, Rodin would not have been taken in. But was there no vanity in it? Would so busy a man as Shaw have left his work and gone to Paris to pose like a professional model for a whole month if he had not thought his bust as important as the busts of Plato which are now treasures of the museums which possess them?

Shaw is an incorrigible and continuous actor, using his skill as deliberately in his social life as in his professional work in the production of his own plays. He does not deny this. "G.B.S." he says "is not a real person: he is a legend created by myself: a pose, a reputation. The real Shaw is not a bit like him." Now this is exactly what all his acquaintances say of the Rodin bust, that it is not a bit like him. But Shaw maintains that it is the only portrait that tells the truth about him. When Rodin was beginning the work in his studio, Mrs Shaw complained to him that all the artists and caricaturists, and even the photographers, aimed at producing the sort of suburban Mephistopheles they imagined Shaw to be, without ever taking the trouble to look at him. Rodin replied "I know nothing about Mr Shaw's reputation; but what is there I will give you." Shaw declares that he was as good as his word. When Paul Troubetskoy saw the bust he declared that there was no life in the eyes; and in three hours frenzied work he produced his first bust of Shaw, now in America. As a *tour de force* it is magnificent; but it is Mephistopheles, not suburban, but aristocratic. Shaw liked the bust, and liked Troubetskoy; but his wife would have none of it, nor of the curious portrait by Neville Lytton, suggested by Granville-Barker's remark that Velasquez's portrait of Pope Innocent was an excellent portrait of Shaw. Lytton accordingly painted Shaw in the costume and attitude of Innocent; but though the picture shews what Shaw would be like in the papal chair, Pope Bernard will never be identified by any antiquary with the subject of the Rodin bust.

Augustus John's three portraits of Shaw are even less reconcilable with the Rodin. John has projected all Shaw's public strength and assurance at their fullest intensity, indeed at more than lifesize. "There is the great Shaw" says the sitter when he shews his friends the picture. But when he points to the Rodin, he says "Just as I am, without one plea." De Smet's portrait is that of a quiet delicate elderly gentleman: Shaw likes its resemblance to his father. The statuette by Lady Scott is friendly and literal: the half length statue by Lady Kennet of the Dene (the same lady) is a companion to that of Shakespear in Stratford church. Sigmund Strobl's bust ranks with those by Rodin and Troubetskoy. Troubetskoy finally modelled Shaw at full length, lifesize, in his platform pose as an orator. This fine bronze has come to rest in the National Gallery of Ireland, which possesses also his portrait by John Collier, prosaic, but lifelike enough to have been mistaken by Mrs Shaw for Shaw himself in Collier's studio. Mrs Shaw was fastidious about portraits of her husband. Of Laura Knight's she said to G.B.S. "Laura has given you her own singleminded sincerity; but you are always acting." On seeing a photograph of Epstein's famous bust (the last) she said "If that thing enters this house I leave it"; and it never did. Shaw admired its workmanship but acknowledged it only as representing some aboriginal ancestor of his. Davidson's bust is a spirited but hasty sketch.

No wonder H. G. Wells complained that he could not move a

step without being outfaced by an effigy of Shaw. Modest Shaw may be; but he has sat for memorials of himself by the greatest masters of his time. Can such modesty be justified until he has been dead for at least five hundred years?

Shaw is the greatest pedant alive. Dickens's man who ate crumpets on principle could not hold a candle to him in this respect. Descriptive reporters have said that Shaw wears a flannel shirt. He never wore a flannel shirt in his life. He does not wear a shirt at all, because it is wrong to swaddle one's middle with a double thickness of material: therefore he wears some head-to-foot under-garment unknown to shirt-makers. The flannel fable arose because, at a time when it was socially impossible for a professional man to appear in public in London without a white starched collar, he maintained that no educated eye could endure the color contrast of ironed starch against European flesh tones, and that only a very black and brilliant negro should wear such a collar. He therefore obtained and wore grey collars. Now that the fashion is changed, he wears collars of various colors; but the dye is always chosen to carry out a theory that the best color effect is that of two shades of the same color. His jacket is of the smartest West End tailoring; but it is unlined, on principle. He formerly addressed his letters high up in the left hand corner of the envelope. A mere affectation of singularity, you say. Not at all: he would talk to you for an hour on the beauty of the system of page margins established by the medieval scribes and adopted by William Morris, and on its leaving space for the postman's thumb. When the postman complained that the postmark obliterated the address Shaw returned to the normal practice.

He justifies his refusal to use apostrophes and inverted commas in printing his books on the ground that they spoil the appearance of the page, declaring that the Bible would never have attained its supreme position in literature if it had been disfigured with such unsightly signs. He is interested in phonetics and systems of shorthand; and it is to his pedantic articulation that he owes his popularity as a public speaker in the largest halls, as every word is heard with exasperating distinctness. He advocates a combination of the metric system with the duodecimal by inserting two new digits into our numeration, thus: eight, nine, dec, elf, ten, and eighteen, nineteen, decteen, elfteen, twenty, and so forth. He likes machines as a child likes toys, and once very nearly bought a cash register without having the slightest use for it. When he was on the verge of sixty he yielded to the fascination of a motor bicycle, and rode it away from the factory for seventyseven miles, at the end of which, just outside his own door, he took a corner too fast and was left sprawling. He has been accused of being one of the band of devoted lunatics who bathe in the Serpentine throughout the year, rain or shine; but this is an invention, founded on his practice of swimming in the bathing pool of the Royal Automobile Club every morning before breakfast, winter and summer, his alleged reason being that as an Irishman he dislikes washing himself, but cannot do without the stimulus of a plunge into cold water. He is, as all the world knows, a vegetarian, valuing health highly but declaring that men who are any good trade on their stocks of health to the utmost limit, and therefore live on the verge of a breakdown. All really busy men, he holds, should go to bed for eighteen months every forty years to recuperate. I could easily fill another page with his fads; but I forbear.

Shaw's gallantries are for the most part non-existent. He says, with some truth, that no man who has any real work in the world has time or money for a pursuit so long and expensive as the pursuit of women. He may possibly have started the protest against the expensiveness and the exactions of beautiful women which is the main theme of Harley Granville-Barker's Waste and The Madras House. Nobody knows his history in this respect, as he is far too correct a person to kiss and tell. To all appearances he is a model husband; and in the various political movements in which his youth was passed there was no scandal about him. Yet a popular anecdote describes a well known actor manager as saying one day at rehearsal to an actress of distinguished beauty "Let us give Shaw a beefsteak and put some red blood into him." "For heaven's sake dont" exclaimed the actress: "he is bad enough as it is; but if you give him meat no woman in London will be safe."

Anyhow, Shaw's teaching is much more interesting than his personal adventures, if he ever had any. That teaching is unquestionably in very strong reaction against what he has called Nineteenth Century Amorism. He is not one of your suburban Love is Enough fanatics. He maintains that chastity is so powerful an instinct that its denial and starvation on the scale on which the opposite impulse has been starved and denied would wreck any civilization. He insists that intellect is a passion, and that the modern notion that passion means only sex is as crude and barbarous as the ploughman's idea that art is simply bawdiness. He points out that art can flourish splendidly when sex is absolutely barred, as it was, for example, in the Victorian literature which produced Dickens. He compares Giulio Romano, a shameless pornographer, pupil of Raphael and brilliant draughtsman, with Raphael himself, who was so sensitive that though he never painted a draped figure without first drawing it in the nude, he always paid the Blessed Virgin the quaint tribute of a *caleçon* in his studies of her, and contrived to decorate the villa of a voluptuary with the story of Cupid and Psyche without either shrinking from the uttermost frankness or losing his dignity and innocence. Shaw contends that when art passed from Raphael to Giulio it fell into an abyss, and became not only disgusting but dull.

The eternal triangle of the Paris stage he rejects as proving adultery to be the dryest of subjects. He wrote Plays for Puritans to shew how independent he was of it. He demands scornfully whether genuine virility can be satisfied with stories and pictures, and declares that the fleshly school in art is the consolation of the impotent.

Yet there are passages in his plays which urge that imaginary love plays an important part in civilized life. A handsome hero says to a man who is jealous of him "Do not waste your jealousy on me: the imaginary rival is the dangerous one." In Getting Married, the lady who refuses to marry because she cannot endure masculine untidiness and the smell of tobacco, hints that her imagination provides her with a series of adventures which beggar reality. Shaw says that the thousand and three conquests of Don Juan consist of two or three squalid intrigues and a thousand imaginative fictions. He says that every attempt to realize such fictions is a failure; and it may be added that nobody but a man who had tried could have written the third act of Man and Superman. In the final act of that play, too, the scene in which the hero revolts from marriage and struggles against it without any hope of escape, is a poignantly sincere utterance which must have come from personal experience. Shakespear in treating the same theme through the character of Benedick might conceivably have been making fun of somebody else; but Tanner, with all his extravagances, is first hand: Shaw would probably not deny it and would not be believed if he did.

Shaw's anti-Shakespear campaign under my Saturday Review editorship was all the more unexpected because I was one of the few London editors to whom Shakespear was more than a name. I was saturated with Shakespear. That I should be the editor of an attack on Shakespear of unheard-of ferocity was the one thing I should have declared confidently could never possibly occur to me. What made the adventure odder was, first, that Shaw, who delivered the attack, was as full of Shakespear as I: second, that though we were both scandalized by the sacrilege we were committing, neither of us could honestly alter a word in one of the articles. They were outrageous; but there was nothing to withdraw, nothing to soften, nothing that could be modified without bringing down the whole critical edifice.

The explanation is simple enough. Shaw's first shot at Shakespear was fired in 1894. Ibsen's first broadside on England caught the London theatre between wind and water in 1889. Shaw had written his Quintessence of Ibsenism in the meantime, and was judging everything on and off the stage by the standard set up by the terrible Norwegian. Many lesser men fell short of that standard; but Shakespear was the most conspicuous victim. "It is useless to talk of Shakespear's depth now" said Shaw: "there is nothing left but his music. Even the famous delineation of character by Molière-Shakespear-Scott-Dumas-*père* is only a trick of mimicry. Our Bard is knocked out of time: there is not a feature left on his face. Hamlet is a spineless effigy beside Peer Gynt, Imogen a doll beside Nora Helmer, Othello a convention of Italian opera beside Julian." And it was quite true. Only in the Sonnets could we find Shakespear getting to the depth at which Ibsen worked.

Shaw was full not only of Ibsen, but of Wagner, of Beethoven, of Goethe, and, curiously, of John Bunyan. The English way of being great by flashes: Shakespear's way, Ruskin's way, Chesterton's way, without ever following the inspiration up on which William Morris put his finger when he said that Ruskin could say the most splendid things and forget them five minutes after, could not disguise its incoherence from an Irishman. "The Irish" he says "with all their detestable characteristics, are at least grown up. They think systematically: they dont stop in the middle of a game of golf to admire a grandeur of thought as if it were a sunset, and then turn back to their game as the really serious business of their life." His native pride in being Irish persists in spite of his whole adult career in England and his preference for English and Scottish friends.

It will be noticed that my portrait of Shaw is both more and less intimate than any other I have penned. More, because Shaw tells the whole world all that there is to be told about himself. Less, because I have never sat on a committee with him; and that is the only way to see much of him. Shaw is not really a social man. He never goes anywhere unless he has business there. He pays no calls. Once he was induced by Maurice Baring to go to a bachelor's party of the usual British type, with grown men throwing lumps of bread at one another, telling smutty stories, and conscientiously striving to behave like rowdy undergraduates. "Gentlemen," said Shaw, with deadly contempt for their efforts, "we shall enjoy ourselves very much if only you will not try to be convivial." On their persisting he got up and left. He complains that only in the presence of women will men behave decently.

After lunching at the Savile Club on his arrival in London he resolved that he would never be a literary man nor consort with such. "I might have spent my life sitting watching these fellows taking in each other's washing and learning no more of the world than a tic in a typewriter if I had been fool enough" he says. I tried to cure him of this by inviting him to my Saturday Review lunches at the Café Royal; but it was no use. He came a few times, being sincerely interested in the Café, in the waiters, in the prices, in the cookery: in short, in the economics of the place; but he concluded that Harold Frederic and I ate too many steaks, and that it was a waste of money to pay Café Royal prices for his own plateful of macaroni, which he could obtain elsewhere for tenpence. The fact that I paid for it made no difference: he objected to a waste of my money just as much as of his.

I have sometimes wished that other people were equally considerate; but Shaw's consideration amounts to an interference with one's private affairs that is all the more infuriating because its benevolence and sagacity makes it impossible to resent it. All attempts to draw him into disinterested social intercourse are futile. To see as much of Shaw as I could easily see of any other man of letters in London, I should have had to join his endless committees. Our relations as contributor and editor were useless for social purposes: he came to the office only when we were in some legal difficulty, mostly to demonstrate with admirable lucidity that we had not a leg to stand on. He is accessible to everybody; but the net result is that nobody really knows him.

There is a cutting edge to Shaw that everybody dreads. He has in an extreme degree the mercurial mind that recognizes the inevitable instantly and faces it and adapts itself to it accordingly. Now there is hardly anything in the world so unbearable as a man who will not cry at least a little over spilt milk, nor allow us a few moments murmuring before we admit that it is spilt and done for. Few of us realize how much we soften our losses by veiling them in an atmosphere of sympathies, regrets, condolences, and caressing little pretences that are none the less sweet because they are only anesthetics. Shaw neither gives nor takes such quarter. An Indian prince's favorite wife, when banqueting with him, caught fire and was burnt to ashes before she could be extinguished. The prince took in the situation at once and faced it. "Sweep up your missus" he said to his weeping staff "and bring in the roast pheasant." That prince was an oriental Shaw.

Once at Westminster Bridge underground station, Shaw slipped at the top of the stairs, and shot down the whole fight on his back, to the concern of the bystanders. But when he rose without the least surprise and walked on as if that were his usual way of descending a flight of steps they burst into an irresistible laugh. Whether it is a missed train, or a death among his nearest and dearest, he shews this inhuman self-possession. No one has accused him of being a bad son: his relations with his mother were apparently as perfect as anything of the kind could be; but when she was cremated, Granville-Barker, whom he had chosen to accompany him as the sole other mourner, could say nothing to him but "Shaw: you certainly are a merry soul." Shaw fancied that his mother was looking over his shoulder and sharing the fun of watching two men dressed like cooks picking scraps of metal from her ashes. He is fond of saying that what bereaved people need is a little comic relief, and that this is why funerals are so farcical.

In many ways this mercurial gift serves Shaw's turn very

well. He knows much sooner and better than most people when he is in danger and when out of it; and this gives him an appearance of courage when he is really running no risk. He has the same advantage in his sense of the value of money, knowing when it is worth spending and when it is worth keeping; and here again he often appears generous when he is driving a very good bargain. When we stand amazed at his boldness and liberality, it is doubtful how far he is capable of facing a real danger or making a real sacrifice. He is genuinely free from envy; but how can he be envious when he can pity every other man for not being George Bernard Shaw? The late Cecil Chesterton has left it on record that when he, as a young nobody, met the already famous Shaw, he was received on terms of the frankest boyish equality. This shews only that Shaw makes no mistakes about men and manners. All that can be predicted of him is unexpectedness.

And so, with all his engaging manners and social adroitness, Shaw often seems one who does not care what he says, nor what others feel. It explains why "he has not an enemy in the world; and none of his friends like him." His Caesar's "He who has never hoped can never despair" is imposing; but who can feel sure that its inspiration is not infernal rather than divine? Compare it with the piously hackneyed "This is the true joy in life, the being used for a purpose recognized by yourself as a mighty one; the being thoroughly worn out before you are thrown on the scrap heap; the being a force of Nature instead of a feverish little selfish clod of ailments and grievances complaining that the world will not devote itself to making you happy." There is no smell of brimstone about this; but ask any of Shaw's fans which of the two quotations is the more Shavian.

I shall not attempt to carry the portrait any further. Shaw is almost a hopeless subject, because there is nothing interesting to be said about him that he has not already said about himself. All that he has left for me to deal with is something that has escaped not only his biographers but himself. Neither he nor they have ever attempted to explain Wilde's epigram. He is violently resented and hated as well as admired and liked. Pinero signed a friendly private letter to him "with admiration and detestation."

I have tried to depict a consistent character (and Shaw's character is almost mechanically consistent) that can produce such contrary effects. Nobody has yet tried to do this: his defenders have ignored the dislike: his assailants have denied his qualities and invented faults which do not exist. I have made no attempt to sit in judgment nor play the chivalrous friend. I have sketched the man's lines as they appear; and though the resultant figure is free from deformity, yet he can give us all a shudder by saying "Imagine a world inhabited exclusively by Bernard Shaws!" This is only a trick; for a world of anybody would be unbearable. But there is something in it for all that; and what that something is I leave you to discover, not understanding it myself.

HARRIS to SHAW [H/4]

[Louis Wilkinson was an Englishman who wrote as "Louis Marlow." Claude McKay did meet Shaw via Harris's introduction. He talks about his adventures, especially with Harris, in A Long Way from Home. *Shaw's sister Lucy suffered from depression during and after the war. She died on March 27, 1920.]*

40 Seventh Avenue, New York
November 13th, 1919.

My dear Shaw:

At last I am able to pass these "Contemporary Portraits" with your picture of yourself for press. I cannot thank you enough for it. It will help the sale of my book of course and in itself is a most amusing skit.

I wonder if I wrote such a thing about myself would it be read at all? I am afraid not. I have not humor enough to redeem it and I would have to confess such sins that hundreds of pages would be needed to make me even thinkable afterwards.

All this I am minded to do in my autobiography, but it will take three volumes to do it corresponding to my three voyages round the world at twenty, forty and sixty odd.

I envy you your supreme cleverness in being able to write such an amusing thing, but I still believe my portrait of you is the better one, and perhaps the best page in it the superb picture of you by Mrs. Tyrrell as a little boy laying down the law to your sisters and their girl playmates—all your elders.

I want you to do something for me. I was sold up in Paris and lost your three plays for Puritans which you had dedicated to me with these words: "To Frank Harris, half a dozen of whose like would have saved me the trouble and the English stage the shame of my preface." "George Bernard Shaw." It was dated 1900 I fancy. I want you to send me another copy with the old dedication in it, as I have some special shelves for these books.

I am getting out a collected edition of my works in fifteen or sixteen volumes which I hope will bring me in enough money to go back to Paris in 1920. I will send you a set as soon as it is ready, and of course I will send you the first copy of the Second Series of "Contemporary Portraits" off the press. By the way a Third Series is already written.

I want you to send me autographed copies of the three plays of yours I like best: "Candida" of course; "Caesar and Cleopatra" of course; and "Man and Superman."

"Candida" to me is as sweet as Goldsmith without a trace of mawkishness. Ever since I first read it I had no doubt of your place. And "Caesar and Cleopatra" is better still; your best so far, though I always hope for something still better from you; but you must hurry Shaw for your time is getting short; and with me too the sands are running out quickly. I have been plagued with pleurisy for two years now and this second dose has weakened me considerably. This is a climate for young folk: old trees can't stand transplanting.

I wrote long ago with greater truth than I then dreamed of, that we were like little apes clinging to the branch of Life's tree; nature keeps hitting our fingers till we gradually relax our grip; finally the pain becomes so great that we let go altogether and drop into the abyss. But if our work is all done that does not matter.

I have still this autobiography to do that will indeed be a "play for Puritans" for sometime to come.

I want to bespeak a kindly reception for my friend, Louis Wilkinson, whom I have instructed to call upon you. He has just written "Brute Gods," a fine book with a most memorable page or two in it.

I have also sent a colored man to see you called Claude McKay, with a letter of introduction. He is a genuine poet and deserves fair treatment at your hands. Perhaps you'll like to study him.

Forgive me for encroaching thus on your time. I wouldn't do it unless I thought the meetings would be interesting to you.

Don't forget to send me these books with a few words in your hand in each of them.

My greetings to Mrs. Shaw, and please tell me how your sister is getting on; her letters to me are desperately hopeless. Sincerely ever,

Yours,
Frank Harris.

HARRIS to SHAW [H/4]

40 Seventh Avenue, New York.
March 23, 1920

My dear Shaw:

I sent you two days ago a story on music. It was called "A Mad Love; or the Strange Story of a Musician."

I have often read you on music and have heard you talk on it once or twice. Now I sent you my contribution on the art.

Of course I know as well as you do that there is only one way to persuade a man that another is a great musician and that is to make him write great music. But I cannot do this and I am not in Paris where Balzac could get great poets to write poetry to put in the mouth of his Eugene de Rubempre. However, I think I have shown that my hero Hagedorn has thought a good deal about music, and is deeply interested in music, and is besides a man of quite extraordinary artistic endowment. His saying at the beginning that he wants to catch an everlasting cold may stand as an indication of this.

I have written half a dozen stories in America in the last six years, but my wife who is my supreme judge, has turned them all down; not one among my best she said till I wrote this story which she considers among my best.

I should like to dedicate it to you as the master of those who cannot sing, but I don't know whether you would like me to or not. You must let me know please and you must also let me know seriously what you think of the story. Does it make you think at all or was it all known to you before?

I want to put it as the first story of my new book "Undream'd of Shores," and I am going to write one on painting and one on literature. I also want to write about other arts that are not known yet and not practised, and one on the art of Life, the least known of all, the most difficult and the most important.

Of course what I want to do most is to get back to Paris and my life in Europe. In order to do this I am bringing out a set of my works—a complete set. If you would write half a page about me or a page you would help me to my ambition which is to get to Paris and live quietly for three years and write my autobiography. But you have been very kind to me and I hardly like to ask you for this last proof of kindness. Still, there it is.

I met Galsworthy when he was here and found him very pleasant and very intelligent within English limits. Really I am beginning to think that it needs a miracle of genius in an Englishman to grow straight.

Galsworthy lectured here and at the end of this lecture he told us that there was one man he was proud of having learnt about in America. Of course I began to wonder whether he was going to speak of me, but no, he meant George Washington of whom Carlyle you remember said—"He was a Cromwell with all the human juices expressed out of him."

I hope you get your Pearson's though you do not speak of it.

Sincerely ever,
Frank Harris

HARRIS to SHAW [H/4]

[Shaw had been very willing to send scraps and skits to Harris for publication but clearly was resisting writing anything which would suggest a Shavian imprimatur to any of Harris's writings.]

40 Seventh Avenue, New York
July 12th, 1920

My dear Shaw:

I have not had an answer to my letter of March 23rd which was accompanied by my little story "A Mad Love: the Strange Story of a Musician." (I'm afraid you never got that letter. So I send a copy of it)

I asked you to tell me what you thought of this story; it wouldn't take a quarter of an hour's reading, and I know you are interested in music and know more about it than most people, probably about ten times as much as I do.

I am not having a very good time here. The Postmaster-General holds the magazine up continually and in various ways my path is made difficult. A word of yours in answer to this letter of mine would have been a real kindness and as you have answered practically all my other letters I cannot make out why this one remains unanswered. If there is any reason please let me know it. I know there are people who continually circulate lies about me but you are not a man to believe foolish fiction.

One verse in "The Shropshire Lad" is always with me. I wonder do you know it:

"Now, and I muse for why and never find the reason,
    I pace the earth, and drink the air, and feel the sun.
Be still, be still, my soul; it is but for a season;
    Let us endure an hour and see injustice done."

Do you get the magazine regularly? How does it strike you?

I am out of touch with my generation and with my surroundings and am as lonely and forlorn as Lao-Tse who said you know that he resembled "one wave breaking on a desolate sea."

I should like to hear from you. Your letters mean a great deal to me.

Sincerely ever,
Frank Harris

HARRIS to SHAW [H/4]

[Jim Larkin, the Irish Socialist union organizer, was one of the leaders of the Dublin strike of 1913. Shaw spoke at an Albert Hall rally he arranged at the time. "Terence MacSwiney the Martyr," as Shaw would call the late Lord Mayor of Cork in an article, "The Irish Crisis" (New York American, December 25, 1921, and Manchester Guardian, December 27, 1921), would die in Brixton Prison late in 1921 after a hunger strike.]

40 Seventh Avenue, New York.
September 14th, 1920.

My dear Bernard Shaw:

It seems ages since I have heard from you though of course I saw your admirable letter on McSwiney, and as you will see from the current (October) number of Pearson's, praised it as it deserved.

I am sending you now my second volume of "Contemporary Portraits," or as you called them, "Characters," with yourself at the head of them and also bringing up the rear with your own self-estimate.

I think my sketch of you the worst of the lot though it certainly gave me more trouble than any of the others, just as the one on Dowson or Moore is probably the best. I can put in the black shadows in Moore, and I think I have vigorously, which makes the portrait life-like. I have a sneaking liking for the Dowson portrait because I loved the fellow whom I had always thought of as a weakling and who climbed Parnassus before any of us and holds his place in the Pantheon of Humanity unchallenged.

But you will tell me what you think of all the Portraits I hope and you will perhaps tell me, now that you have had the first book and the second, which of them you like best, and perhaps if you are in a kindly humor, which you consider the best done; that might help me in the future though I am beginning to be afraid that I am growing out of the stage of learner.

Your letters and contributions to the papers are almost delightful, but I confess I was frightened of you about this McSwiney thing and yet you hit the nail right on the head. I have always thought you a Yorkshireman, but there must be some Celt in you somewhere or else you profited by your Irish bringing-up. Is there any Irish blood in you? Do tell me; I should like to know.

And please write to me. If you only knew the pleasure I take in your letters you would write oftener.

I am producing all my books in a sort of definitive edition of fifteen or sixteen volumes and hope thereby to get enough money to go to Paris and write my autobiography which can only be written in France because it will treat of the senses as well as things of the spirit; and all with absolute frankness. I am going to see if a man can tell the truth naked and unashamed about himself and his amorous adventures in the world.

Write to me. And say a word if you please of the stupidity of keeping Debs in prison for stuff as good as "The Sermon on the Mount." Jim Larkin, too, and I am powerless though I've done all I know:—"Man's inhumanity to man!"

Yours ever,
Frank Harris.

SHAW to HARRIS [H/4]

[Despite the Adelphi Terrace address Shaw wrote most of the letter in Ireland, at his favorite Kerry hotel, on the edge of the sea at Parknasilla.

Leonid Krassin was Soviet Commissar for Trade and Industry and twice ambassador to London. Edward Elgar and Cyril Scott were contemporary English composers admired by Shaw. Lord Alfred Douglas was continuing his litigious ways. Shaw ignored the attacks and eventually made a friend of Douglas, who became a warm correspondent. Bruno was probably Guido Bruno, who had been arrested in New York in 1917 for publishing and selling a book containing a story, "Edna, A Girl of the Streets." Harris had appeared in his defense, which was bread cast upon the waters, as in 1919 Bruno would put together, from Harris's writings in Pearson's, The Wisdom of Frank Harris, *augmented by a "pen-portrait" of the great man by Shaw. It was, in effect, a benefit performance for Harris.*

A Nervenanstalt *was a mental institution, and the quotation from* As You Like It *which Shaw guessed at was actually "Men have died from time to time; and worms have eaten them. . . ." "Pepper and Houdin" were mid-nineteenth century show-business phenomena. French magician Jean-Eugène Robert-Houdin was the source of surname for American escape artist "Harry Houdini." Of the illusionist "Dr. Pepper" William Rossetti wrote in his diary from Paris in 1864, "In the evening to the Theatre Dejazet. . . . Here for the first time I saw Pepper's ghost trick."*

The Lines of Torres Vedras are a 28-mile series of fortifications which Wellington devised to protect Lisbon from the advancing French army. The French incurred heavy losses and were forced to retreat. In a disparaging reference to the United States, Shaw attacks Wilson's radical-baiting Attorney General,

*Mitchell Palmer, by attaching to his name that of Antoine Fou-
quier-Tinville, the Public Accuser before the French Revolutionary Tribunal whose instrumental role in the Reign of Terror
was rewarded with the guillotine after the fall of his mentor,
Robespierre.]*

10 Adelphi Terrace
September 15, 1920

Dear Frank Harris,

For months and months I have not had time to write any
letters longer than the unavoidable business ones.

I got the story about the musician, which you have spoilt by
your romantic habits. When are you going to drop these dreary
people who live for love and die for love, and who never, thank
God, exist outside a *Nervenanstalt*? "Men have died, and worms
have eaten them &c &c." This convention now dates so frightfully that your dropping into it stamps you as incorrigible. The
whole point of the story ought to be that this man with a
superhuman musical sense might easily be fallen in love with
by dozens of women with no senses at all: only appetites. How
could he take twopennorth of interest in them, except in the
way of Napoleonic relations? Catch Elgar or Cyril Scott killing
their musical genius for any woman!

I wrote the above beginning Heaven knows how many months
ago, apparently in a not very patient mood. I just recollected
enough about writing it to be convinced that I had written to
you. Now, on a hillside in the remotest part of Kerry, I open my
notebook at the wrong end, and discover the unfinished letter,
never sent.

I am now in a more easygoing mood; but still I hold to my
opinion. However, I must develop it by saying that the trail you
struck and lost in it is undoubtedly the right trail for you
to follow. We are both at the age of which Larouchefoucauld
said that people who have reached it, like very young persons,
should not talk about love if they wish to avoid being ridiculous. Your heroes henceforth must not be lovers, or martyrs,
or bullfighters, or café philosophers and Quartier Latin artis-
ticules; they must be mathematicians, men like Archimedes,
Descartes, Clerk Maxwell, or, if you must have a touch of art,
Leonardo da Vinci. Your damned mushy people must come up
against something hard, something utterly beyond them, some-

thing before which their selfpity becomes silly, their attempts at suicide unsuccessful stage gestures, and their concupiscence essentially impotence. You have been through the cabaret and perhaps found it agreeable, as you could without any effort be one of its heroes, and could also drink enough to take off the edge of your entire scorn for it; but you must not play down to it now with your confounded sham love affairs, which have obviously nothing to do with your actual experience and still less with those deductions from actual experience which enable a great writer to construct a tragedy from some externally squalid thing seen for the moment, or some overheard remark by a passing stranger. In this last story of yours it is quite plain to me that the musician with his faculty interests you, and that the love business does not interest you in the least: you are using it just as you use ink and paper as part of the business. Then, I say, drop the cabaret and the coroner and all the rest of that photographer's furniture, and put the worthless people in their proper place by shewing them up against something real.

I am the more moved to lecture you thus by a letter from Guido Bruno, with a booklet of erotic reveries, he not having got far enough in to know that there is nothing quite so boresome as other peoples' reveries in that kind. He wants to know whether he is right in saying that you are the greatest man that ever lived. Serve you right for not kicking him hard enough when he was working with you! Not that I demur to the appreciation he expresses in this clumsy way; for I should be greatly surprised to learn that he had ever struck your superior or even your equal in the section of the world that is the whole world for him. But you ought to point out to him, not that you are not quite as good a mathematician as Einstein or a composer as Strauss, but that young men of letters should begin— or all events *do* begin when they are worth their salt—with a stupendous contempt for contemporary celebrities, and that their admirations, when they have any, are always infatuations. However, now that I think of it, you probably *have* told him this and only set him drivelling the more.

Bruno resembles you in one respect. You are one of the very few men who combine an amateur's adoration of literature with a professional's skill in it. Shakespeare hadn't this adoration: Ben Jonson apparently had it. Stevenson hadn't it: Henley had it. Here, observe, its possession was correlated with a manifest inferiority on the professional side: Jonson was at bottom a poor playwright, and Henley, who could say things with a great air and a fine ear, had nothing to say. But Rodin, a very great man, had it: he filled houses and houses with heaps of stones that had half a square inch of surface on which a sculptor had worked: it was collecting gone mad. But he was an exception. Wellington, a more original soldier than Napoleon, avoided military society as I avoid literary society, and, like Shakespeare, retired to potter about mere pastimes for which he had no special aptitude as soon as circumstances set him free to do what he liked. I shall go on writing as long as there is a job for me and I can do it; but I shall never be an amateur or a collector: literary coteries will always loathe me and need never fear me intruding; and though I may potter at all sorts of things, from music and phonetics to motor bicycles and photography, I shall not potter at literature. But I believe that when your faculties are so decayed that you will be, like Ibsen at the last, unable to remember how to write, you will potter at literature, and endure the drunken reveries of minor poets and the shop of reviewers as an old jockey hangs about racing stables and clings to the acquaintance of bookmakers. This explains your success as an editor; but I can't reconcile it with your ability as a writer. It is as if Pepper were terrified by his ghost, or Houdin imposed on by his own sleight of hand. Bruno has the same qualification for editorship; but can he write anything original?

The time has come for you to get away from literature and from heroes and hero worship, and write your Gulliver's Travels or your Don Quixote. Don Quixote is most to the point, because Cervantes wasted his life in the pursuit of literature, and like Dickens in Pickwick, actually kept trying to give his masterpiece literary merit by interpolated stories of the conventional type before he felt his feet, strong as they were.

When they gave Rodin a banquet in Paris and asked me to go or send a message, I said that my immortality was assured, as a thousand years hence I should be in every biographical-dictionary as Bernard Shaw, *sujet de Rodin, d'ailleurs inconnu*. Now a Boswellian immortality is very little better; and I threaten you with that: you are always writing about other people, mostly literary people; and you don't unmask them: rather do you transfigure them with thick *maquillage*, very striking, skilfully laid on and romantically effective, but still *maquillage*. We know the Don in you; but what about Sancho: can you really not make him fit for publication?

The magazine reaches me safely, I think, though I do not keep count. I always read it, which is a proof that you are really editing it. By the way, Chesterton is not a Roman Catholic. His brother Cecil actually converted; but Gilbert is at the core not even Anglican, but a sound Protestant, as you will find if you ever get him into a corner. If you ask him does he believe in miracles, he will declare that he does of course, and will riddle the whole case against them superbly. But try my plan: admit that miracles occur every day and that there is just the same evidence for the miracles at Lourdes as for the Lines of Torres Vedras, and then ask him whether as a matter of simple fact he believes in the liquefaction of the blood of St. Januarius! You will soon feel the Belfast grit in him.

I do not see how you can better yourself by coming to London or Paris if you can keep Pearson's going. The French have lost their senses over the war: Krassin told me that the British statesmen are reasonable in comparison, and seem to know what they want and what possibilities there are of getting it, "it" being the Crimea. Anatole France cries out lamentably that France has not a friend in the world. I have said for a long time past that the feeling between France and England after Trafalgar and Austerlitz was friendly compared to the present *entente*. Even the land of Fouquier-Tinville-Mitchell-Palmer may be more congenial to you than the boulevards. In London the literary cliques are still unfriendly; whilst your disciples are young *frondeurs* without much power to help. Of course you will not be a pet of the cliques anywhere; but the difference between a going concern in America and beginning again (at our age!) elsewhere is enormous.

George Moore now publishes books through Werner Laurie by subscription: two guineas a volume. It seems to pay: at all events it continues. Why not sound W.L. as to trying this with something of yours?

Douglas the Desperate has got hold of another journal called The Plain Dealer, in which he writes savage libels on you and me and everyone he can lay his pen on. He then marks the copies and send them to us clamoring for us to take notice of them. But the silence is the silence of the grave; the poor devil is denied even the vogue of the man who got into society on the strength of having had his nose pulled by D'Orsay. He has probably read your life of Wilde. Do not break that silence.

As the composition of this letter has now spread over five months and a bit it is time for me to stop. I have just shot my last bolt in Back to Methuselah, a play in five acts, of which every act is a biggish play, with a huge preface. The MS is complete, except for the final revision of the last few pages; and most of it is already in proof. The theme is one on which fifty plays might be written: I have been able barely to touch it with the tips of my fingers. You might very well write one of the fifty.

Ever

G. Bernard Shaw

P.S. Bruno says you published my version of your essay on me. Where did it appear? I never saw it. You could have planted it here, I think.

SHAW to HARRIS [C/4]

[Mary Boyle O'Reilly was a journalist in whom Shaw sometimes confided. Kate Richards O'Hare had been the most prominent woman Socialist in the U.S.; she, Debs and others had been jailed for "sedition" during the war hysteria of 1918.]

Ayot St Lawrence, Welwyn, Herts
28 Sept. 1920

Your letter of the 14th has crossed one of mine sent from Ireland. The book has not reached me yet: perhaps it is in London.

I kept publicly refusing to go to America on the ground that I should get 23 years for agreeing precisely with Debs and Mrs. O'Hare; and Mary Boyle O'Reilly tells me that Mrs. O'Hare was released in consequence. This is Mary's blarney; but it shows that I said what I could.

Serve Larkin right for trusting himself in a country where liberty is called anarchy!

You cabled to me for a cable about something (I forget what); but either I had nothing effective to say, or had said it already (I forget which).

Of course I am a fullblooded William & Mary Irishman, and not a transplanted Catalonian pretending to be a Celt. There are no Celts in Ireland.

G.B.S.

The ice has broken at last. Full dress review of the Life of O.W. in the Times Literary Supplement, and of the Portraits in the New Statesman by Desmond MacCarthy.

G.B.S.

HARRIS to SHAW [H/4]

[A. E. Burleson, the Postmaster General, considered it a special national duty to scent sex and subversion in the mails and root it out. The Shakespearean-nicknamed Bumley may be Horatio Bottomley; Douglas is the ubiquitous Lord Alfred Douglas.

Terence McSwiney, an Irish nationalist imprisoned for his role in the 1916 Easter Rebellion, was on a hunger strike in Brixton Prison, London, at the time Harris wrote this letter. McSwiney died thirteen days later.

Johann-Heinrich Bernstorff was German ambassador in Washington until the war ended his mission in April 1917. Count Bernstorff had tried vainly through Wilson to prevent America's entry into the war but was undercut by the German submarine campaign, which finally pushed anti-German feeling far enough for Wilson to call for war.]

40 Seventh Avenue, New York.
October 12th, 1920.

My dear Shaw:

I do not know how to thank you for your great and interesting letter,

But, but, but—

Why do you say that my portraits have *maquillage* on them? They are all naturally not realistic enough, except perhaps the one of George Moore which is most astonishingly realistic without a trace of maquillage; but the Clemenceau for instance is necessarily only a sketch because if I told the truth about his sex affairs (and his sex life has been the centre of his life) I should simply be jumped on by all Puritans and prudes, yourself included. I am keeping such things for my autobiography in which, if I ever get the chance to write it, I shall tell the truth as I see it.

Burleson has been after me again holding the magazine up in the mails in order to see whether there was anything seditious in it, the consequence being that he has cut my sales to pieces and as I have put all my money into paper and printing of a complete set of my works in fifteen volumes, he has caught me at last and whether I shall get through or not is rather doubtful. However, I recognize that it was my own haste to get out of the country and do my three volumes of autobiography that led me into this trap. Do you remember Cleopatra's word to Antony:

> "Ah! infinite virtue,
> Hast thou come from the world's great snare uncaught?"

I have not infinite virtue, but I am going to stop whining; self pity is bad for anyone. The main thing is that I have my health. I am able to write all of Pearson's, or practically all, every month, and lecture twice a week besides.

I asked you sometime ago by cable for your opinion on Wilson. If you decide to send it to me after all please consider two things. Read Bernstorff's book "My Three Years in America," and you will find that when Wilson turned against the Germans he was a more virulent foe than any in Paris. The conference meetings were kept secret in spite of Clemenceau's express desire that they should be open meetings because Wilson insisted on their being kept secret. This has been established by Clemenceau's secretary and also by Secretary Lansing's testimony before the Senate Committee in 1919.

In the same way it was Wilson and not Lloyd George who was willing to give the Saar valley to France in spite of the fact that there are nine hundred thousand Germans in it and only one hundred Frenchmen.

I call him the man of the great betrayal—"*al gran rifiuto.*" He has murdered the last vestige of liberty in these United States. I want to write a great thing about him in the March number. I wish you would give me your view of him. Do not forget to read Bernstorff and Maynard Keynes on him.

You don't know what your letter has meant to me. I ventured to publish most of it without asking you because it was so interesting.

Please write me again soon and I wish you would send me a portrait of yourself or the Rodin bust and just four or five lines in your own handwriting. I should like to reproduce it as I have reproduced a little letter of Anatole France's in this last number.

I hope you will get some sense into Lloyd George's head about Ireland. He is another of my disappointments. As for Desperate Douglas your advice is right. I shall do nothing to break the great silence. I'll let the bitch-boy kick in the air and Caliban-Bumley with him. Their ravings do not excite me over much. It is not these earth-born creatures that annoy me but the idealists who fail; it is the Wilsons and Lloyd Georges who make life bitter, but never the Bumleys or the Douglases.

Sincerely ever,
Frank Harris

P.S. By the way all you say about love stories is piffle. The greatest stories in the world are love stories. Ruth and Micah in the Bible and the *Song of Solomon. Romeo and Juliet* and *Antony and Cleopatra* in Shakespeare. What does everyone remember in Dante beyond the *Paolo and Francesca* incident?

You have missed the point of these artist stories of mine. I am going to make each of them a different love story. The musician loves her boldness and honesty and is simple food enough not to see that these qualities make it certain she is not deceiving him. My painter will fall in love especially with the girl's color and perfection of form, and my man of letters will fall in love with her soul; the courage and sweetness and helplessness of her.

But it would take too long to describe them. Still, I will try to tell new things about each art while telling a love story. I cannot say they will be successful till they are done; but you praise the musician part in the musician story which is the chief thing. By the bye I wish you would send me a postcard just on the state of Ireland. I believe they must be feeding McSwiney with albumen in his water.

Your note about Larkin is right; this indeed is a land where "liberty is condemned as anarchy."

Ever
Frank Harris

HARRIS to SHAW [H/4]

[President-elect Harding did not make Lodge his Secretary of State, nor did he finally offer the post to any of his cronies, succumbing instead to pressure to name the austere Charles Evans Hughes. Harding had actually preferred Senator Albert Fall, who later as Secretary of the Interior was involved in the Teapot Dome oil swindle. Arthur Brisbane was the editor of the Chicago Herald and Examiner *and an influential editorial writer and columnist in other Hearst publications as well.]*

40 Seventh Avenue, New York
November 9, 1920

My dear Shaw:

Things are in a parlous state here. We are on the edge of Niagara and you might help to save us.

Harding and reaction are in power. Harding according to today's paper is going to make Cabot Lodge, the Massachusetts senator, his Secretary for Foreign Affairs. Cabot Lodge who is understood to have nominated Harding for President, in his speech at the opening of the Republican Convention in Chicago, plainly stated that he thought Mexico should be made to carry out all contracts, should be coerced if she tried to get out of any of the oil swindles perpetrated by American subjects.

Hearst, too, with his millions of readers a day, has always preached war with Mexico and the taking of it. The first journalist in America, Arthur Brisbane, has come out by saying that "The constructive policy consists of making the southern boundary of the United States the southern side of the Panama Canal zone." Today, (the ninth of November) he continues it in this way:

> "Prime Minister of Australia Hughes says Australia will not submit the question of 'White' Australia to the League of Nations or any other Power. This means, briefly, 'no Asiatics need apply.'
>
> "That is true also of this country, although luckily, being

now out of the League of Nations swamp, we need not consult that interesting body.

"Courtesy for Asiatics, a warm welcome for travellers, scientists, literary men, but no settlements of Asiatics on the American continent, that is the program.

"Canada means it, this country means it, and this country should make Mexico mean it also."

It seems to me certain that they are preparing for war with Mexico which will give the profiteers another chance.

I assure you I do not exaggerate the gravity of the position. Wall Street is offering odds in favor of war with Mexico within the year.

Under these circumstances could you not write me an article saying that the attempt to coerce labor by forbidding strikes, as labor has been coerced here, is against the elementary laws of individual liberty, and that if the United States proceeds to make war against Mexico after the experience of the world war, it should be regarded as the chief criminal of the world.

Harding pretends to be a Christian. All his people are Seventh Day Adventists, which fact may give your divine humor a chance to run riot.

I went out to Marion to see him to try and persuade him as a Christian to forgive and allow Debs and the forty conscientious objectors to go free. He said he could not "revoke the judgment of thirty or forty United States judges—the best in the world!" I have noticed that whenever an American says "in the world" he knows nothing outside of his own parish.

This man Harding is an inconceivable ass; a village schoolmaster in England would know more, and yet I fear that under him we shall be led into war with Mexico that will turn into a guerilla war and be waged with a savagery unknown in Europe.

I do not know if you would address a warning to the American people through me but I wish you would. Seriously it seems to me you might prevent this inhuman crime.

Really I am not making this appeal at all as a journalist but simply as a citizen of the world and a lover of mankind.

Sincerely ever,
Frank Harris

HARRIS to SHAW [H/4]

*[Murry is the critic J. Middleton Murry and Palmer is Wilson's
Attorney General, A. Mitchell Palmer. Judge Henry Neil of Chicago in 1918 had asked Shaw to write an appeal to America to
help the Irish poor, and Shaw had produced "The Children of
the Dublin Slums." George Lansbury was a leading Labour politician and would be in the first Labour government.]*

40 Seventh Avenue, New York.
January 12, 1921.

My dear Shaw:

I have not yet thanked you for the card telling me that I was
being reviewed in England. Murry did his best and Desmond
MacCarthy was even better.

Your "Heartbreak House" has had a success here among
thinking people as all your plays have; but your letters in the
New York American have been absolute sensations:—"Foolhood
suffrage"; "100 percent American, 95% village idiot"; the condemnation of Wilson and Palmer; all these things have done
good and have done much to establish your position as a thinker
with vision.

A Judge Neil has sent me from Chicago an article of yours
called "Ireland An Incorrigible Beggar." It is all true enough,
but not your best it seems to me—not the sweet-thoughted
truth you often reach.

I have called this English government the Soviet of Snobs.
Curzon, Winston Churchill, Milner and Lloyd George are tem-
porizing on the Irish matter. They found out how to make South
Africa loyal by giving it freedom and self-government. Why
don't they give complete freedom to Ireland? The poor fools! In
ten years the Irish would give up their republic and come back
into the monarchy; and if they had sense an Irish Republic
might even yet be avoided.

I wish you would write me an article on this, or a letter, as
casual as you please. Or on the Soviet Government of Russia.

Fancy Wells going to meet Lenin with the confession that he
was *"disposed to dislike him."* As if we ever get near anyone till
we are disposed to love him and do love. Silly idiot!

You probably know Lansbury and might be able to say something new about this Soviet business and Holy Russia's wonderful struggle to found a new form of society and remold existing institutions nearer to the heart's desire.

I ask you for articles on either or both of these subjects almost as a beggar for help. The Postmaster-General has found out a new trick in dealing with me. He gives orders to the Postmaster of New York not to let copies of Pearson's go out in the mails till he has passed on them for sedition and he often keeps them held up for from fifteen to thirty days and then lets them go through too late to sell. By this means he has fined me fifteen or twenty thousand dollars this year just as he did last year. But this year, owing to my getting out sets of my complete works and the rise in the cost of paper he has put me in a tight place. I don't know how to keep Pearson's going; yet I have done it as well as I can.

If you have a good word to say for Pearson's, say it and send it to me, Shaw. It will help me and I need help at the moment, sorely.

Sincerely ever yours,
Frank Harris

My wife joins me in best wishes to both you and Mrs. Shaw in this New Year.

HARRIS to SHAW [H/4]

[Irish poet George Russell signed his work "AE." A. E. Burleson, Wilson's Postmaster General and Harris's nemesis, lost his office on March 4, 1921 when he was replaced by a Harding appointee. James M. Cox was the unsuccessful Democratic nominee for president, a newspaper publisher and former Ohio governor.]

Pearson's Magazine
57 Fifth Avenue, New York City
March 16, 1921

My dear Shaw:

At last I have got something that I think will make you sit up and scratch your head.

Here is a paper by George Russell which I regard as the best thing ever written on Ireland. Yet he does not lay as much stress as I should on the loveable qualities of the Irish.

I was born and bred in Ireland and when at twelve years of age my father discovered that I was a little Fenian he shipped me off at once to an English school to cure me, and it taught me as nothing else could, the superiority of the Irish, especially the greater kindliness of them, the quicker and deeper sympathies.

I am going to publish this article of "A.E.'s" in the next number of Pearson's, but I wanted your opinion of it. It is one of the few things I have received since I have been in America that enobles the wretched trade of journalism and I would like your commendation to help to give it weight in Washington and London. If you agree with me I know you will do it. I want a real word from you about it.

Burleson, the Postmaster General nearly killed me this last year; held up all the issues in which I fought against Cox on the pretext of examining them for sedition, did not allow them to go through the mails for weeks, in some cases months, and so hurt our sales terribly. I am, however, slowly recovering, and am lecturing twice a week at my studio-shop, 57–5th Ave. to make a living.

I have not seen Chesterton since he has been out here. I don't think that verbal genius wants to see me, and as I could get nothing from him I am content to be without any personal relation.

I have to thank you for a postcard telling me of the reviews of my book in England, and I have to thank you, too, for your brave articles in the *American* some of which I reproduced and which I lectured upon. Great stuff!

Please write to me when you get a chance. I feel in utter exile here in the mills of the Philistines and am beginning to feel doubtful whether I shall ever be able to extricate myself and get back to France and do my "autobiography" which I have looked upon as my chief work for the last thirty years, but which may now never get done thanks to Burleson and this feeble-minded but strong-bodied people.

Now do write to me and tell me what you think of A.E.'s stuff.

Ever sincerely yours,
Frank Harris

SHAW to HARRIS [E/213]

[An enclosure card ("With Bernard Shaw's compliments") attached to a typewritten manuscript, corrected and signed, "The War Indemnities by Bernard Shaw." The playlet (which follows) was Shaw's view of the absurdity of attempting to extract confiscatory indemnities from defeated and prostrate Germany.

In the skit is an obvious pun on the comic novel by Montagu Glass, Potash and Perlmutter *(1910), which became a hit London play in 1914. The Belgian diplomat was Shaw's friend André Vandervelde. Dr. Walter Simons was a German delegate to the Versailles conference assigned the onerous task of negotiating reparations. Simons would write to his wife that his "predominant feeling" about the negotiations was one of "a great unreality."*

Shaw's concluding prediction was grimly accurate.

Harris happily published the skit in Pearson's *for June 1921.]*

22/3/21

I am dead beat, and can scrawl only a few lines of rubbish. However, it will fill up a column.

GBS

The War Indemnities

How it would clarify the question of the so-called indemnities if the parties would only call things by their right names! Indemnity for war is flat nonsense: you cannot shoot a man and unshoot him again by treaty afterwards. Even Mr Lloyd George sees that, and seizes the opportunity to make a magnanimous gesture of foregoing what he knows he cannot get.

War is a game in which the stakes are plunder and conquest. Germany lost; and the winners now proceed to take what they can get; and that will not be indemnity or reparation or any such nonsense, but booty pure and simple. But the simpler the language, the more apparent becomes the complexity of the fact. For example, the Germans admit that they must pay something; and they accordingly propose to pay England in coal. Hereupon ensues something like the following:

LLOYD GEORGE. Coal! Good God, no. Not a sack, not a lump. What are you dreaming of? You would throw our coal miners out of employment.

THE GERMANS. Well, will you take it in steel?

LLOYD GEORGE. Worse and worse. No country in Europe shall produce steel but England if I can help it. Steel indeed! Dont you dare to trifle with me. Your attempts to avert payment are too transparent. [*Aside to Marshal Foch*] Rattle your sabre a bit, will you, my dear Marshal? [*Foch does so*].

THE GERMANS. Well, what on earth are we to pay in? You know we cannot pay in gold.

LLOYD GEORGE [*aside to Foch*] What are they to pay in, Marshal?

FOCH [*aside to Expert*] What are they to pay in, *mon cher*?

EXPERT [*aside to Foch*] Potash.

FOCH [*aside to Lloyd George*] Potash.

LLOYD GEORGE [*aloud, menacingly, to the Germans*] You know as well as I do. You shall pay in potash.

THE GERMANS. But *Donnerwetter*, there is not five thousand millions worth of potash in the world.

LLOYD GEORGE. Come, come! No prevarication. There are other products: for example, perlmutter. So let me have no more nonsense.

DR SIMONS. *Blödsinn!*

LLOYD GEORGE [*blushing*] Oh! Nice language that! Can no German ever be a gentleman? Fie for shame, sir!

DR SIMONS. You really must propose something practicable.

LLOYD GEORGE. Must I? Pray, who won the war: you or we? "Must," as Queen Elizabeth said, is not a word that is addressed to British prime ministers. However, how would it be if you were to raise a loan to pay England?

DR SIMONS. Raise it where?

LLOYD GEORGE. In America. They have lots of money there. Or in France.

FOCH. *Comment!!!*

LLOYD GEORGE. An excellent investment for your peasant proprietors, my dear Marshal. Think of how well they did out of the 1871 indemnity.

FOCH. But why should your own people, our brave allies, be deprived of such an opening for their little savings? After all, it doesnt matter to you where the money comes from, does it? Money is money. *Non olet.*

LLOYD GEORGE. My French is shockingly bad. What does *nong olay* mean?

FOCH. It means that all money smells alike.

LLOYD GEORGE. True; but how—?

FOCH. You see, *mon cher Loi Georges*, if this German *farceur* can arrange to make the proletariat pay, does it matter greatly which proletariat it is? Yours, or ours, or theirs, or the American *canaille*: what does it matter?

LLOYD GEORGE. *Non olet*, eh?

FOCH. Well, not exactly *non olet*. But they all smell alike.

LLOYD GEORGE [*sternly to Dr Simons*] I have consulted with my illustrious friend and ally, Marshal Foch. We are agreed that you can find the money if you choose. If a satisfactory proposal to that effect does not reach us by the middle of next week, we shall occupy every city on the Rhine.

DR SIMONS. And what then?

LLOYD GEORGE. What then! You shall see what then. None of your insolence with me, if you please. What then, indeed!

DR SIMONS. The money your troops will spend will be very useful to us.

LLOYD GEORGE. Fifty per cent on every one of your exports for that speech, young man.

DR SIMONS. Ah, well! The consumer will pay.

FOCH. What does he say? What is that word?

LLOYD GEORGE. Consumer. *Le consommateur*, you know. *Le shallong*.

FOCH [*with military pith and brevity*] *Je m'en fous!*

Curtain

This is the kind of thing that we are being landed in by diplomatists and soldiers who know nothing, pushed from behind by commercial adventurers who do not know the A.B.C. of finance, but who, having got noses for money, may be depended on to sniff their way to a solution which will mean that the workers will have to support an additional burden of idleness and waste all the world over. And it is quite likely that the victors will bear the heavier share. As to asking America or any other country to trade in German promissory notes payable 42 years after date, I will only quote what a Belgian historian and diplomatist has just written to me: "I believe that ten years hence Germany and Russia will be masters of Europe."

[A postscript to Shaw's playlet may make it possible for some of the music-hall cross-talk to work its fun before such explication as is necessary is applied to the zany, tri-lingual dialogue. Well over the heads of Harris's readers, it appears to be meant more for Harris, who knew his French and German well, than for Pearson's, although Shaw knew Harris would print anything with a G.B.S. signature as gift copy. The dialogue would lose a dimension as an acted skit, needing the visual element for some of its word-play. Foch's literalness and laconic speech are made fun of, and readers (and audiences) of Potash and Perlmutter *would have recognized the title, although perhaps not that, like* potash, perlmutter *is literally a product—mother-of-pearl.* Donnerwetter! *is an ejaculation on the order of* Damn it! *while the pun in* Blödsinn! (Nonsense!) *is more subtle, for Lloyd George (who in actuality blushed at little if anything) becomes uncomfortable with Dr. Walter Simons's language because the prime minister apparently confuses the word—he says his German is weak—with the sanguinary English expletive* bloody, *with which Eliza Doolittle caused such consternation in Shaw's* Pygmalion *(1914).*

Foch's Comment!!! *is only* What?!!—*while his Latinism,* Non olet, *declaring that money (regardless of origin) does not smell, confuses Lloyd George because Foch pronounces it as if it is French (thus the* -ong *ending as Lloyd George repeats it). Before long, at least one of them is wondering if all money smells the same, or whether the reference is to the odor of the* canaille (rabble). *Since the long-suffering consumer* (consommateur) *will pay, inevitably, whatever costs of the indemnities are passed along to him in higher prices, Lloyd George's apparent attempt to explain that to Foch by Frenchifying his pronunciation of* shilling *goes awry, because Foch, misunderstanding and at a loss for words, dismisses the explanation with an* I don't give a damn!*]*

SHAW to HARRIS [H/4]

[Shaw's "few lines" to Harris were about "AE" (George Russell), whom they both admired. His opening reference to "E.E., alias A.E.," suggests how he must have pronounced the pen-name of his compatriot. Harris would publish Shaw's memoir of Russell

in the July, 1921 issue of Pearson's, *where it appeared as a response to Harris's publication in May, 1921 of Russell's analysis of the Irish problem, "The Inner and the Outer Ireland." The letter makes clear that "How Shaw and Russell Met" actually anticipated the "AE" article.]*

Ayot St Lawrence, Welwyn, Herts
29th March 1921

Dear Frank Harris

Some days ago I sent you a hasty screed about the Indemnities to 40 Seventh Avenue. In case you have left that address I mention this here, so that you may retrieve it, if possible, from Burleson.

A.E. wrote an admirable letter to The Times the other day giving the economic gist of the article he has sent you. I append a few lines which you may care to publish. I can do nothing serious for the moment, as the finishing off of my Methuselah and of the arrears of correspondence and business which it left has written me to a standstill; and now I must go away to the mountains or the sea for a fortnight or so before doing a round of speeches in the north or looking at a pen without wanting to die.

ever,
G. Bernard Shaw

How Shaw & Russell Met

George Russell, better known as E.E., *alias* A.E., better known as George Russell, is one of Ireland's chief human assets. He is a large, bearded man, an Irish equivalent to Chesterton. The two men resemble one another in their entire unaffectedness, their friendliness, their inexhaustible literary and conversational powers, and their combination of a dignified and decent appearance with an avoidance of new clothes. Their difference is very characteristic of their nationalities. Chesterton has no discoverable intellectual conscience: reasoning is with him a sport that must justify itself by entertaining results: when anything goes wrong with his sympathies or cuts off his generosity (a war, for instance) he becomes, in respect of that particular thing, a literary Nero. He hates Prussians. Russell's intellectual integrity is so scrupulous that he spends more than half his life in economic demonstrations and practical suggestions which cannot be reduced to absurdity by the keenest criticism. He does not hate Englishmen. Chesterton, when he is not writing (if he is ever in that condition) is a cheerfully roaring lion, roaming from Beaconsfield in Bucks to Ireland or Jerusalem or Boston, Mass. Russell is a hermit, though a very capable lady very properly married him and took charge of his socks. His cell is on the top floor of Plunkett House in Merrion Square, Dublin, one of the handsomest of the many handsome houses which survive in Dublin from the eighteenth century. He has painted walls in the manner of the Italian fresco painters; but his business there is not art, but the editing of The Irish Homestead, which is the best weekly paper of its kind in the world. Some day its back numbers will be treasured like Addison's Spectator and Steele's Tatler. At present Russell edits it, which means writing it almost from end to end for a dock laborer's wages. The Irish Agricultural Organization Society, which holds the handsome house, and Sir Horace Plunkett and a few of his friends, come to the rescue when the paper cannot get enough advertisements of churns and ploughs and cream separators to pay the printer. It contains always from one to three first rate political and social articles, followed by instructions how to keep bees or conduct continuous cropping or what not. When the paper is out for the week, Russell goes home and paints pictures. And they have quality, every one of them, though you can buy three or four hundred of them for the price of a single full length life size portrait of yourself (in your official robes) by the President of the Royal Academy in London. Between the paper and the pictures A.E. squeezes in poems and books. And yet he seems to have nothing to do but talk when you meet him, as you always do if you are anybody in particular, and are foolish enough to go to Ireland when it is so easy to keep out of it.

I met Russell for the first time as a man lost in the desert might catch sight amazedly of another figure on the naked horizon. To be exact, I was one day in the Dublin National Gallery, one of the best in Europe of its size, and therefore less populous than Connemara or Timgad, when lo! a man! Presently I pulled up before a lovely little modern picture. The master who painted it had suppressed his name, not in modesty, but because he found that he could get fully a hundred times as much for his work by adopting the name Correggio. The man came over to have a look at it too; and at once, without preliminaries, we entered into intimate conversation as if we had known each other all our lives. When I mentioned the incident afterwards I was told "Oh, that must have been George Russell"; and when he mentioned it he was told "Oh, that must have been Bernard Shaw." But we had both known without being told, though I never said, like H. M. Stanley when he met Livingstone in an only slightly more probable place, "Mr. Russell, I presume"; nor did A.E. dream of going through that ceremony with Mister Shaw.

I am not surprised to hear that Frank Harris thinks Russell's article on Ireland the best he ever got. A.E.'s article always is the best.

G.B.S.

SHAW to HARRIS [H/4]

[Nellie Harris's mission to London was to secure Shaw's assent to let his name be used in connection with Oscar Wilde and The Man Shakespeare *so that Harris could peddle the film rights, for which he claimed he had been offered $50,000. He was also trying to sign Lady Warwick and Queen Marie of Romania. Harris failed on all counts, but Nellie had a splendid holiday at the Savoy. Later, when Shaw permitted Harris to publish the letter, he excised the references to Lord Alfred Douglas and to Nellie Harris's innocence in business matters.]*

10 Adelphi Terrace, W.C.2
1st June 1921

Dear Frank Harris

I write in the middle of this mess about Mrs Harris's mission. I have cabled you that I do not understand the proposal and that Mrs Harris is helpless without a scenario. You have replied that you are sending one, adding at the end, "cable." But I have nothing to cable until I receive the scenario. I am, however, so apprehensive of a disappointment for you that I had better write and say certain things that you may not know.

First, I can, by lifting up my finger, get $50,000 for an Oscar Wilde film by Bernard Shaw, or with the name Bernard Shaw in the advertisement of it. I have in my desk offers to guarantee me $100,000 a year for five years if I will release two films per year during that time. Anybody can get it if he can secure my name, which is all that is wanted. Not a month—sometimes not a week—passes that some hard-up literary hack does not come to me and plead that I can rescue him from a desperate situation by writing a preface to his book or letting him make a comic opera or a film out of one of my plays. If, therefore, the offer you have had involves the announcement of my name as collaborator, or in any capacity whatever, there is nothing in it: it is really an insult to you and a thank-you-for-nothing attempt to sidetrack me.

Second, I am a married man; and my wife is a member of the firm. We have arranged our domestic affairs in such a fashion that she has put a good deal of money into my business by spending her income on the house whilst I do the saving. The $50,000 that my name is worth on a film is an asset of the firm; and I am not free to give it away with a Cyranesque gesture even if I could afford it.

Third, though I have copyright in the words of what I have written about Oscar, I have none in the events of his life; consequently a film representing the life and adventures of Oscar needs no authorization from me even when the events represented have been narrated by me for the first time, unless I prove that they are fictitious, in which case I should be proving myself a liar and impostor. Therefore my refusal to allow my name to be used, or to give any authorization in connection with the film will not prevent you from introducing all the scenes I have described into your scenario. Nothing that I can do can prevent Frank Harris from filming his Life of Wilde, and getting the full value of his work. What I can do is to prevent the film firms from throwing in the value of my name as well without paying me for it. I may add here that though the firms are right to secure the attraction of my name if they can get it, they will if they cannot help themselves, pay just as much for the film without my name as with it, however loudly they may protest the contrary.

Where I foresee the possibility of a disappointment is in the danger of representing real persons on the screen without their consent. You can make up a movie actor as Oscar, and another as old Queensberry, and another as yourself; but what about Carson and all the other still living actors in the tragedy?

Douglas would jump out of his skin with delight at the chance of taking proceedings if you "featured" him. If you avoid this by calling them Smith and Jones, and not making up the actors like the originals, you put a good deal of water into the brandy. Film firms (not to say American business men generally) never foresee these things until they break their shins over them: I am constantly receiving the very maddest proposals of moral, legal, and even physical impossibilities from America. I think it quite a good and feasible notion to take advantage of your biographical reputation to make a series of films, calling them educational, of lives of famous men by Frank Harris; but the more contemporary they are the greater will be the difficulty. Suppose Douglas anticipated you with a Wilde film in which an actor posed as Frank Harris In His Cell and so forth, what would you do?

Mrs Harris, who is almost as innocent in affairs of this sort as you are, suggested that my chapter should be published on the screen in ten line lengths for the audience to read. If I were not to squash that, the film operators would. It is ridiculously and obviously impossible.

As far as I can see, what can be done is this. The film can begin, after the usual lists of everybody employed in the film company from the office boy upward, with a portrait of F. H., followed by extracts from The Times Literary Supplement, The New Statesman &c. &c. and a sentence from one of my letters to the effect that F. H. is the greatest biographer since Plutarch or the like. No authorization is needed for these; but there must be at least three or four of them from various sources; and there must be no reference to them in the announcements: if the film people attempt to use my name, I shall be down on them instantly with all the legal thunderbolts I can throw. You must use this threat to prevent them pushing you off the stage and putting me in the centre, which they will certainly do if you or I let them.

Now you know how the case stands with me. I await further information.

G. Bernard Shaw

P.S. The £600 was unacceptable because it is far beneath my market rate.

HARRIS to SHAW [U/1]

[Harris took Shaw's declaration about what he could get for a film script seriously.]

14 June 1921

I ACCEPT PROPOSAL YOUR LETTER JUNE FIRST FIFTY-THOUSAND DOLLARS FOR YOUR RIGHTS COAUTHOR WILDE FILM STOP SAME PRICE SHAKESPEARE FILM YOU TO APPROVE BOTH SCENARIOS STOP WILL NOT INTERFERE WITH ANY ARRANGEMENTS YOU HAVE FOR YOUR OWN BOOKS OR PLAYS STOP WILL NOT LIBEL ANY ONE STOP RUSH CABLE CONFIRMATION AND I SHALL BE OVER WITHIN MONTH DELIGHTED FRANK HARRIS

SHAW to HARRIS [U/1]

[15 June 1921]

FRANK HARRIS   40 SEVENTH AVENUE   NEWYORK YOU MISUNDERSTAND MY LETTER   MY NAME IS NOT AVAILABLE ON ANY TERMS WHATSOEVER   THIS IS FINAL   TELL THEM SO POSITIVELY   SHAW

HARRIS to SHAW [H/4]

[Harris's newest effort to found a fiction magazine would be abortive.]

Pearson's Magazine
New York
September 12, 1921

My dear Shaw:

I remember your telling me once, or I dreamed it, that you had written some short stories as a young man.

I wish to God you would send me the best of them.

I have given up the fight here and am now going to make Pearson's a fiction magazine in a last try to make it pay. If I fail I am finished. A story from you, needless to say, even if it had been published before, would be a huge success and would help infinitely. If you can I think you will.

I have had pleurisy twice this year and am in bed now with grippe; so I grasp at straws.

I send you Pearson's regularly, but you never speak of it to me. Do you read it? Please tell me what you think of the new venture? I am still in these Mills of the Philistines.

Ever yours,
Frank Harris

HARRIS to SHAW [H/4]

[What Harris does not say is that he was selling Pearson's *for whatever he could get for the property, and planning to live by his wits and his writings in Europe. He would get two thousand dollars for the magazine. Hugh Weir had been behind the abortive film schemes, all of them impossible, in which Harris was to involve Lady Warwick, the ex-Kaiser, Queen Marie of Rumania, and Shaw.]*

Villa l'Aiglon, Cimiez, NICE
March 9th, 1922

My dear Shaw:

Enclosed you will find a cablegram about yourself and your work which may or may not interest you. I send it on to you, and if you find it worth answering you can answer it directly to Hugh Weir, who gives the address of "Pearson's Magazine," 96, Fifth Avenue, New York. Weir has nothing to do with Pearson's, but he is an interesting little journalist and very eager to make money. He was the man who bothered me last summer to get your permission to use your name on that movie stunt.

I broke down—worked too hard lecturing and writing, got dreadfully nervous headaches (a thing I didn't know the meaning of) and at last began to misuse words in a way that, as soon as I realized it, scared me. So I took my wife and came abroad here to Nice to rest, and thank God I am now my own man again and fairly well except that the headaches threaten to become permanent.

In April I want to go to Vienna, and Berlin, and from there to Moscow to hear the story of the revolution from Lenin and Trotzky's own lips and to give pen-portraits of them of course. No American paper wants me, and I am afraid that no English paper would have me either, though Wilson Young on the "Saturday Review" has been good enough to take some of my articles.

I don't know what you are doing, but my wife gives most fantastically flattering accounts of you. She admires you almost as much as she despises the ordinary man, so I can only think that you talked music to her or herself to her.

I wonder whether you have kept hope and heart. I have lost a great deal of both in these last two appalling years. You remember the German proverb:

"Who loses money loses little;
Who loses honor loses much;
Who loses courage has lost all."

It is not courage so much that is lacking in me as desire. The human comedy always seemed infinitely interesting to me. Today

". . . . it is a tale
Told by an idiot full of sound and fury,
Signifying nothing."

but I need not inflict you with my pessimism.

I should like to have news of you. Please commend me to your wife and tell me what you are doing. Could we meet by any chance? Is Paris too far off for you: London to me is further off than far away: but I'd give a lot to have a talk with you.

Frank Harris

HARRIS to SHAW [H/10]

[G. S. Viereck was a journalist and lobbyist for Germany through to the beginning of the Second World War.]

Pearson's Magazine
799 Broadway, New York, New York
September 16, 1922

My dear Bernard Shaw:

You left my last long letter unanswered, so I scarcely know how to write to you in terms of our ancient kindness. However, I write this to introduce to you Mr. George Sylvester Viereck, who took Germany's side in the war because his father was a German, though his mother was an American. Viereck is one of the persons you really ought to know, because he is exceedingly articulate in poetry and in prose both in German and in English. One of his poems, which I have told him to enclose to you and which he calls "Slaves," is so good that I am compelled to give it to you here.

Now be kind to him if you will, for my sake, and one of these days I will shake hands with you and thank you, for I too am returning to Paris almost immediately. My address there will be c/o American Express Company, 11 rue Scribe. My wife is there now and it would be more than kind if you wrote a word to her.

Ever yours affectionately
Frank Harris

SHAW to HARRIS [H/213]

[The two-page, typewritten letter has not been located, but an extract appears as item 201 in the Anderson Galleries Sale Catalog No. 3845, April 24, 1930. Shaw has received a presentation copy of volume one of My Life and Loves, *and lectures Harris on its unsuitability.]*

10 Adelphi Terrace
February 15, 1923

. . . it is no use remonstrating with you; you are incorrigible. So I will not argue with you: I will just tell you . . . You had better burn this letter at once: it would damage you seriously if it got loose, as all letters do sooner or later.

HARRIS to SHAW [A/4]

[Harris was answering Shaw's objections to the first volume of My Life and Loves. *Murray was the London publishing firm of John Murray.]*

c/o The American Express Co
11 rue Scribe, Paris
February 18, 1923

My dear Shaw,

I think you are right when you say that the illustrations injure the book and make it almost indefensible but if I had been asked to criticize such a mistake on the part of Shaw, I should not have thought of dismissing him as "incorrigible." I would have inferred that revolt was usually in some proportion to the injustice of the tyranny and if your revolt were unsoundly, I should have concluded that the puritannical prohibitions were plainly idiotic and oppressive. However, as you say I have given my enemies (and my friends) a weapon they will not be slow to use. Yet in spite of the illustrations (the cover appears to me harmless) I had hoped that you would see more in the book than mere pornography: there is an attempt in the book to give the woman's sensations, quite apart from the man's and different and never before even hinted at even in medical works and more important perhaps still there is a certain spiritual growth indicated and a certain mental growth as well.

Moreover if as you say the book will be burned as soon as read, it can't do much damage for your information that I wanted Murray to publish it is so far from the truth that I do not think of publishing it in England at all.

It is really my individual protest against the idiotic Anglo-American Convention which has nearly made an end of English literature. It was in this spirit that Walt Whitman rebelled in spite of Emerson's remonstrances and if my rebellion is more outspoken than his or if you will more obscure, it is perhaps because I am a Celt and less submissive than he was; or it may be that I am more familiar with the disastrous consequences of English and American prudery. If you had read "Main Street" and "Babbitt," you might be more inclined to appreciate if not to sympathize with my unlimited revolt.

However, the chief thing is that you have undoubtedly put your finger on the weak spot and for that I owe you thanks.

I can't follow you about burning your letter, I will of course do so if you wish; but I don't consider it "damaging"; it is the ordinary view put with extraordinary point and a Shavian fierceness of contempt.

I should think you had written it in haste; but to have found time to write at all to me, is an evidence of good will which I am not likely in these latter days, to underestimate.

I am curious to see what "A.E." will think of the book; but perhaps I had better wait till I can send him a copy of the second edition without the plates.

As ever yours,
Frank Harris

P.S. I am still bound to contribute to Pearson's; but without further responsibility.

Yours, F.H.

SHAW to HARRIS [H/4]

["Top shelf author" apparently meant the same thing as "under the counter" author—a writer of pornography.]

10 Adelphi Terrace
[February 21, 1923]

Dear Frank Harris,

Never mind my "fierce contempt." If a dreamy boy, at a moment when it is important that he should keep his boots clean, persists in staring at the skies and walking straight through all the deepest puddles in the road, a certain peremptoriness in chucking him back to the dry pavement is inevitable and excusable.

As to my letter, keep it if you cannot bear to part with any scrap of evidence against yourself; but if you have an atom of sense left you will withdraw all those illustrations, leave the cover unblocked, and destroy every reference to this first print-

ing that you can lay your hands on. I purposely made the letter
so unpleasant that any other man would have torn it up there
and then with an oath or two; but I reckoned without your
literary craze for keeping letters—a most mischievous habit—
and was not offensive enough. And yet you are surprised at my
calling you incorrigible!

It is not easy to guess the fortunes of this book. You have
mixed up two very different kinds of interest: the interest in
sex, which is the most impersonal interest in the world, and
that of autobiography, which is the most personal. Frank Harris as Everyman and Frank Harris as himself have a very
different appeal. And you are not a born autobiographer. You
may have noticed that though the world is now full of men who
have fought in the trenches and gone over the top and had all
the horrible experiences that active military service involves, it
is impossible to get any first hand information about it: the
men won't or can't tell. Now you, very curiously, have over-
come this shyness in recounting your gallantries, which are, as
I have just said, really impersonal; though you have not completely succeeded: it is the women's experiences which you give
rather than your own. Only a woman could tell you how far you
have divined rightly; and she wouldn't. When you come to yourself you are rather like the soldier: you tell us when you ran
away to America and virtually managed a hotel in your teens
(without a single comment on the way in which America gives
chances to boys); that you left that to become a cow puncher,
and incidentally a cattle thief with violence and murder (say
a moss-trooper); then a University student, a law student, a
practising barrister, just as the soldier tells us that he was at
Mons and Vimy and Messines, and was corporal, sergeant, and
so forth, with an incident or two thrown in, but one could have
learnt it all from a police dossier. It could have happened only
to an extraordinary man; but the man eludes us. You don't
really give yourself away as Rousseau did. You don't take much
interest in yourself, and are not disposed to tolerate inquisitiveness in others. The book interests me because I have seen
you and talked to you and read a lot of your stuff. I can therefore take any scrap of information about you and tack it on to a
portrait already in my possession. But I am quite unable to
guess whether a total stranger to you would come out with any
vision of you. I told you that what was missing in your life of

Oscar Wilde was the figure of Frank Harris the buccaneer. A faint scrap of St Francis of Assisi was perceptible, but nothing else. In a life of Frank Harris this defect is more serious, and I am disabled from estimating the extent to which it exists. What do the other people say?

I know that you did not want Murray to take up this particular book. But you suggest him as a possible publisher for all your other works; and this would be out of the question if you became known as a top shelf author.

In haste—excuse it—

G. Bernard Shaw.

HARRIS to SHAW [H/4]

[Shaw had claimed that Charlotte ordered the first volume of Harris's Life and Loves *burned. In his letter of 31 July 1928 he notes that it was done by Charlotte personally, "page by page so that not a comma should escape the flames."]*

Paris
March 2, 1923

My dear Shaw:

I do not mind your calling me names in the smallest degree. It is a trick I believe all great characters have, women as well as men, and you, like the women, do it to show your affection. But this second letter of yours interests me, because it is more critical. Of course, you begin by saying that I am not a born autobiographer. If, in the first volume, I had tried to sketch a complex character in all its intricacy, you would have been right to laugh at me. You call me at one moment a buccaneer and a gambler and a cattle thief, and then tell me that what I have really given is a touch of St. Francis d'Assisi.

As volume after volume comes, my character will appear more and more clearly. I am not anxious about it, even, because I have the truth to guide me, and I do not propose to alter it one jot or tittle.

But you say in this letter rightly that it is the woman's experience that I have given, rather than my own, and you add: "Only a woman could tell you how far you have divined rightly, and she would not." But they did, Shaw, they did! They delight in telling the truth to the people who take pleasure in hearing it.

In the same way you say that I tell you how I managed a Hotel in my teens and you add, "without a single comment on the way in which America gives a chance to boys." But I have told you that again and again. I have told you how an Irish woman on 5th Avenue took me in and mothered me and gave me food and made her husband serve me and help me. I have told you how a boot-black allowed me to work with him and went shares with me, how a hotelkeeper asked me to come to Chicago to his hotel and paid my fare. And explicitly, on page lll, I have told you that "no people in the world is so kind to children and no life so easy for the hard workers."

You have not read the book, Shaw, or rather, you have read all the naughty love passages and they have deluded you. Yet, at the end, you are beginning to see it, because you say it could all have happened only to an extraordinary man, and then you go on to show me that more than what you have said, has come to you from the book.

Have you really burnt your copy?

One part of your criticism is profoundly true and that is that the illustrations are a mistake and I have already taken what is your advice in this letter: I have already suppressed the first edition and have sent to Germany to get 1,000 copies printed without illustrations. But my second book, which takes me to London and to my memories of all sorts of people, is already half done, and when it is completely finished, I think you will better be able to judge this first volume, for I agree with Montaigne that passionate love is an affair best talked of in the years immediately after childhood.

I wish I could see you and have a real talk. Letters are unsatisfactory. Do you ever come to Paris, or rather will you be over before I leave on the 22nd of this month? I should be delighted to see you and measure the difference of the years.

Ever yours gratefully,
Frank Harris

HARRIS to SHAW [A/2]

[The play attributed in part to Shakespeare was Two Noble Kinsmen *but Harris's memory failed him here. The other play he planned to attribute to Shakespeare was probably* Henry VIII. *His memory in his first volume of* My Life and Loves *had been supplemented by imagination in the amatory episodes, which contributed to the difficulties he had with customs and postal officials as well as with the police. The date suggests that Harris did not leave Paris as early as anticipated.]*

c/o The American Express Co.
11 rue Scribe, Paris
26th March [1923]

Dear Shaw as Shakespeare said once:—"I have lost my way in life" & hardly know how to find it again: I'm getting old, too, & tired—

Perhaps you will care to help me. I could surely do an Edition of Shakespeare better than any living man: moreover—& this is the business part of the enterprise—there is a play not attributed to Shakespeare which I could *prove* to be his or touched by his hand over 300 times. Now if any publisher would bring out a Tri-Centenary of his works & include this & the "Three Noble Kinsmen" as indubitably his in part, I would write introductions to every play & I give you my word of honor I would prove the play I speak of, to be his. The publishers would thereby get an unique & definitive Edition of the best seller after the Bible in all literature & I am assured they could get besides Copyright in all my notes of the new play which would make the edition definitive in a very remarkable sense. I feel pretty sure you know some firm of publishers who would risk this venture—of course on your assurance; but I do assure you that I will be your warranty in every particular. "My Life & Loves" was stopped in France. As soon as I got your letter I agreed with it (I could tell you how the pictures came to be included) for I didn't want the pictures & such pictures! Now I've cut them all out, the book looks & is much better: but whether I shall now get through or not remains to be seen.

But you could get me this Shakespeare commission at once I feel sure & indeed I would do your commendation honor, for with the introduction you've already written to the *Dark Lady* the edition would go like wildfire.

If I'm wrong you will tell me: but my "Memories" of men & things in London in my second vol. of autobiography is going to interest even you. I'm already hard at work on it: have indeed done more than 100 pages of great stuff. Now Shaw I want not your critical but your human & humane faculty: I don't beg; but if you can help me I shall be infinitely obliged & you might easily help a worse man than your friend

Frank Harris.

PS If you knew what it cost to write this letter; but perhaps you'll halfguess. I've never been so hard up since I was twenty-three & never worked so hard!

HARRIS to SHAW [A/4]

[The letter is scrawled on several scraps of notebook paper which suggest Harris's predicament.]

c/o American Express
11 rue Scribe, Paris
[March 1923]
S.O.S.

Dear Shaw,

I want you to read this letter in as kindly a spirit as you can; I had a second shipment of "My Life" up through the Ruhr disturbance, some sent to Cologne, took your advice, cut out all the pictures, had the book pressed and returned to Paris last night with 200 but the officials stopped them then. I had orders for the 200. I spent my last pennies on this venture. Here I am now in a cheap little hotel—Hotel Haussmann, rue du Helder, Paris with $10 and no more. A shipment of "Oscar Wilde's" which I also had printed in Germany is on the way; but may not arrive for a month or more: I have a couple of thousand of my books in New York; but they must first be bound and even at 30 cents a vol. that needs money. I need a loan dreadfully. My wife is at Nice in a little hotel and I must go to her help as soon as I can.

All the friends who would have helped me, are dead or out of my ken. I have no one I can turn to except you. Time and again you helped me generously with your writings when I edited Pearson's but the Postmaster General's continual persecution and prosecutions ruined me and the magazine. I was knocked out there while fighting for what I thought was the truth, I made a foolish effort to retrieve myself and came to worse grief. But I am as full of fight as ever: I have a book of short stories nearly ready—"Undream'd of Shores"; and a volume of "Memories" dealing with my Life in London half-done (intimate portraits of de Maupassant and Ruskin and of Sarah Bernhardt and her husband Jacques Damata—whose whole family I knew well) and I'm writing it as well as I can in other words, I'm not asking you to hold up an empty sack. I should be able to get a publisher to finance me; but you know how the hard-feeling both in England and in the Benighted States has been stirred up against me. I have no friend but you able to help. And even you will hardly be able to realize the pressure; it is impossible to write well or do your best when you are half crazed with doubt and anxiety as to next week's food. If I had £500 I could repay it this year easily and it would put me on my feet again: I daresay I can get through with half [of] it or even less; but with £500 I am *sure*; for then I could get my books in New York bound and put upon the market while I should be finishing my work here. If you decide to give me another chance cable the money to me through the American Express Company in London to their Paris office, by Tuesday next if possible. If you only knew what this confession cost me; but help from you will give me new courage. To be thought worth saving by Shaw is half the battle.

I should like to save my conceit by telling you how many I helped in my good days and how willing I was always to help every artist or man of letters worth helping; but what has that to do with my extremity?

I want you to keep this letter private; no one knows yet that I am hard up; if that once gets known, the worst will follow. My wife even doesn't know that I'm writing you, indeed she doesn't know how desperate my need is.

I wish I could have seen you, a letter is so unsatisfactory: I would have told you that it is my work too that you are saving; for really I am writing better than I've ever written; but what good is it? Your sympathy may read between the lines; if it

doesn't the words will be weak. Already I owe you great kindness, help me this once more Shaw and I'll never ask again.

Ever yours
Frank Harris

P.S. I wrote this long letter & forgot to tell you that I saw
Grant Richards on his way through Paris. He was willing, he
said, to make one an offer for the 4th volume of my "Contemporary Portraits" (Brentano's gave me £100 for the American
rights, but Richards is more than cautious; he wanted to see
the book: I sent him a list of the people treated; but haven't
heard from him; he said he'd offer for the English rights of all
four of my "Contemporary Portraits"; but he did not offer. I
don't know if you know him; but I do know he thinks a lot of
your opinion and a word from you might spur his slight belief
in me to some action.

   This too I now leave with you: I told Richards I had a book of
"Short Stories" almost ready to be published; he said he'd write
me his business proposal: so far I've seen nothing.

Ever yours   S.O.S.
Frank Harris

I used to think "hard work and good," solved every economic
difficulty but now I doubt it.

SHAW to HARRIS [A/4]

*[Shaw was deploring postwar inflation, which was particularly
astronomical in Germany and Austria. His Viennese translator
was Siegfried Trebitsch, whose play,* Frau Gittas Sühne, *Shaw
had freely adapted as* Jitta's Atonement. *Fridtjof Nansen was
the Norwegian Arctic explorer, statesman and humanitarian
who after the First World War as League of Nations High Com-
missioner for Refugees developed a passport (afterwards identified with his name) for individuals whom political and military
upheavals had left stateless.]*

The Metropole Hotel, Minehead, Somerset
5th April 1923

Dear Frank Harris

   I can't afford it. Your letter, declaring that you must have
£500 on Tuesday or perish, fortunately (for me) did not over-

take me here until yesterday; and I did not read it, being tired with the journey and confronted with a mountain of letters, until today.

All I can do is to write to Grant Richards to say that if he will take up the Wilde biography and the portraits I will throw in my contributions as in America. If that fails you must drive a taxi; for you have come to a Europe where men of high academic and literary distinction are trying to keep body and soul together by writing the most piteous begging letters, and mostly failing. I cannot describe to you what this side of my correspondence is like: the poor wretches are like crying children: they pour out anything in desperate protest against the cruelty of their situation; and we who have escaped only by the skin of our teeth have to harden our hearts and let them perish, as all we have would be only a drop in the ocean of their needs. As to the unfortunate students – – – – !

Meanwhile I am a multi-millionaire. In Vienna my bank balance (I have never drawn a farthing since the war) is 30,090,000 Kronen. In Berlin I have masses of Marks on which I have paid Income Tax at 240. Their valuta is now 100,000! I have a couple of million roubles in Moscow, which cannot be sent to me because they are not sufficient to pay for a draft and a registered letter. In London my plays draw receipts undreamt of for highbrow stuff before the war, and uncommon then even for popular stuff; but theatre expenses have doubled, and left me economically impossible except in the provincial repertory companies. The net result is that since the war, every 1 Jan and 1 July, when my taxes have to be met, has been a squeeze to avoid selling out. I have had to resort to journalism in the Hearst papers to save the situation more than once. In short, I am one of the fortunate ones; and I am personally comfortable and keep two cars: but I have not a penny to spare. Some time ago the wife of one of the richest men in England, with God knows how many times my income, said to me what I have just written to you: "I have not a penny to spend."

That is what you are up against over here: culture penniless and profiteers rolling in money but indifferent to culture. Appeal to humanity, generosity, good nature; and it is the kindest man who meets you with the hollowest laugh. From starving millions in Russia or Austria, starving authors, professors, and boot blacking students in Germany, to starving relatives at home, he has had his feelings so harrowed since 1918 that he is like Macbeth, past caring for anybody in distress.

All of which will not pay your hotel bill. I know; but what am I to do? I *could* draw a cheque for £500; but here is a letter from my cousin's daughter, destitute and despairing; and here is another from an Irish gentleman whose friendship dates from the seventies, begging me to advise him as to where he can sell his pictures. Here, too, is Nansen, vainly trying to feed multitudes with five loaves and two small fishes. And my own hotel bill is about four guineas a day even here on the mud of the British Channel. There is only one chance for me—to give nothing. So you starve; and the cousin starves; and the old friend may eat his pictures; and the multitudes may perish whilst I overeat and deplore the shocking condition of the others. My Viennese translator, a Jew, would not take money. I had to translate one of his plays and get it produced in New York for him. It took me longer than an original play, and drew only £10,000. We got £400 each: a heavy loss for me; but for him the delirious sum of forty million marks pure *surcroit*. And you demand £500!

Editing Shakespear is absurd: hack work that would not keep you in bootlaces. Your bolt is shot about Shakespear: there is nothing exciting about those two old noble Kinsmen. You cannot make money by work directly: your only chance is in the exploitation of your copyrights—have you forgotten your Karl Marx?

I really do not know what is to be done with you. You should have a Civil List pension; but what Prime Minister dare give you one? You have sown dragons' teeth so liberally that the armed men are all over the place. Werner Laurie specializes in private circulation subscription editions at £2–2–0 (George Moore, for example); but the author gets only £600. As I said, I can only write to Richards. Why cannot those books be sold from Germany if the French object to their importation? 2000 at £5 ought to come to something. It will not matter to the people who have ordered them whether they come with French or German stamps. Mine came through all right as a magical present.

G.B.S.

HARRIS to SHAW [A/4]

The American Express Co.
3 rue du Congrès, Nice (A.M.)
or
boul^d Edouard Sept, Cimiez, Nice (A.M.)
28th April, 1923

Dear Bernard Shaw

Luck (the Unusual!) always runs in series with me: I have always felt that I have had more than my fair share of good runs; but these last months brought me to grinning as the fighter grins who has just got the K.C. So I wrote you that "begging letter" as you are pleased to call—a request for a loan. . . . A couple of hours later the luck had changed: I sold $200 worth of books and got paid in advance of delivery; I ran back to the hotel, hot with shame, to retrieve my letter to you; it had gone; but in its stead I received a letter from New York returning me $1250 more I had lent but given up. The luck had changed! The two telegrams enclosed; the one begging my wife for $100, the other telling her not to send any for I had won, gave you the story in brief. When you advised me to sell 200 books at £5 a piece you evidently did not know that the French authorities had confiscated the books and when I forced them to send the books into Italy, they did so but informed the Italian authorities that they were pornographic and so the books were stopped at the Italian frontier too, and in imminent danger of being burned as likely to infect the air in the Country of Aretino!! It was that kick in the behind when I was "down and out" that made me write to you. I know my Italians, I was sure to get my books with money, sure too, I'd sell'em, but without money—? I was caught as in a trap! And all this at the end of an interminable series of German extortions: one instance, a new law was passed six days before I left, charging 90% of the cost for permission to export! How could one foresee such impositions—But a friend brought in some books, or was bringing them, and in an hour I sold a few and was free! I did not write to you again at once; but resolved simply to send back your loan by return with the best letter I could write.

Well, instead of help, I got a nor'easter which may however, be partly the measure of your annoyance at having to refuse me, or merely your opinion of my deserts.

I don't think I needed the lesson, but I certainly got it. I had never asked any one in my life before for help in money & now Bernard Shaw told me he had two Rolls-Royce cars and I had better drive a taxi!—a grim humor in the proposal for I am half blind and cannot understand anything connected with machinery. Besides, I'd never have asked for money unless I was sure of being able to repay it. . . . However, I should not have written that sort of letter to you, though I recognise in your letter to Grant Richards a serious kindness of intention. By the bye, Scheffauer who has arranged a German translation of my Wilde book tells me that you gave me permission to translate (or have translated) into German your "Memories of Wilde" to publish with my book; I should like to do this; but I trust your word on the matter as Scheffauer did not show me your letter.

Now I have done: forgive me for troubling you; please don't think I'm begging you for the German rights in your "Memories of Wilde", I'm getting nothing (10,000 marks or half a dollar) out of the book but Scheffauer tells me it is adequately translated and with your well-known name may bring something in royalties which I'm quite willing to share with you. Don't think either that one rebuff could make me forget your many kindnesses to me in the States, "the Benighted States" as I now call them.

Ever Yours Sincerely in all friendship
Frank Harris

HARRIS to SHAW [H/4]

[Fenner Brockway, who was contesting a House of Commons seat in Westminster as a Labour candidate (one of his opponents was Winston Churchill), had asked Shaw for a message and a speech. He provided both, and "was absolutely brilliant," Brockway thought, but he lost the election in a close contest.

Max as before is Max Beerbohm.

Shaw's article in Comoedia *was a response, with his usual verve, to a series of questions about* Saint Joan *put to him from*

*the London correspondent of the Parisian theatrical publication.
A translation by James Graham appeared in the* New York
Times *on April 13, 1924.]*

Paris
March 17, 1924

My dear Shaw,

I have just read your letter to Mr. Fenner Brockway in the
"Daily Mail"; no one can read it without seeing the fine comedy
there is in perfect sincerity. I am waiting for your Joan of Arc,
waiting impatiently; have you printed it yet?

I've got hold of the "Paris Evening Telegram," the only evening paper in English on the Continent; there is just a chance to
make a success of it. I wish you'd increase the chance by writing
for me on this English labor government. I've no right to ask
you, but the subject or something akin to it may tempt you and
it will put me on the map, as the Americans say, here in Paris,
to have a letter from you on a matter of real interest.

I'm trying to edit the first number today, in spite of a bad
attack of grippe; I'll send you over a copy tonight of last Monday's paper and this new sheet.

I don't know whether you have seen my latest books; a fourth
series of "Contemporary Portraits" with sketches of Wagner,
Gorki and Sarah Bernhardt in it and some gargoyles of the last
three American Presidents, and my last book of short stories:
"Undream'd of Shores." My last book of stories, I say, for the
shaping spirit of imagination has left me for ever, I believe,
and this is the real reason of my return to journalism.

I've asked Grant Richards to send you copies, but if he won't
I will, if indeed you care to see them.

Max objected to a little story of his marriage told me by his
sister, probably invented by her, but humorous, I thought, and
at once Grant Richards, without consulting me, cut out the two
pages though I asked him simply to add a line saying that Max
declares the story is untrue. The incident just shows how that
book of "My Life" has made me really negligible to such men as
Grant Richards.

Ever yours,
Frank Harris

P.S. I'm treating your article in "Comoedia" on Joan (immense!)
in tomorrow's sheet.

SHAW to HARRIS [H/4]

10 Adelphi Terrace, London
25th March 1924

My dear Frank Harris,

As Saint Joan is to be produced on Wednesday the 26th, I am too busy at the theatre to send you more than a hasty acknowledgement of your letter.

Grant Richards has sent me the books; but the papers have not yet arrived—or perhaps I should say not yet reached me, as I am snatching a week-end in the country.

Don't be unreasonable about the two page cut: how could Richards possibly have refused—or suppose that you could refuse—Max's demand for its suppression? With anyone else these things go without saying. With you, the publisher, sooner than risk a volcanic row and perhaps a withdrawal of the book, takes the law into his own hands and faces the consequences. It is annoying; but it does not indicate any notion on Richards's part that you are negligible: quite the contrary.

By the way, get posted a little in French newspaper law before you begin campaigning. It has some unexpected turns: for instance, if you pitch into anyone he has a legal right to reply in your columns. Things that involve nothing worse in England than a remote possibility of a civil action seem to lead in France to summary arrest and imprisonment. When I think of the blinding and blasting indignation with which you have received proceedings which could have been foreseen by an infant of three, I shudder to think of the collisions with foreign law which may happen to you.

I have read only a few of the contemporary portraits yet. They are of your usual quality; but you are growing kinder to little people as you find that all your biggest sitters are used up. The stories I have not had time to open.

I shall put Joan through the press as soon as I can. It is already set up, preface and all; but the rehearsals have revealed several little slips; and the preface needs another dusting. My present state of senile decay produces blunders that I never used to make. You shall have a copy as soon as I can lay hands on one for you; but you will complain that Joan had no love affairs. Her military comrades—Dunois, D'Alencon, Poulengy etc—all testify that they thought her divine because she did not attract them sexually.

As to sending you an article on the Labor Party, I could get several hundred pounds for the English and American serial rights of such an article; so I have every material inducement to do it. But my sands are running out too fast to be wasted on topical journalism. So *vade retro*; open your columns to the young.

Ever
G. Bernard Shaw

HARRIS to SHAW [A/4]

[Although the second and third volumes of his Contemporary Portraits *had to be published by Harris at his own expense, Brentano's in New York and Grant Richards in London had gambled on the fourth volume. (There would be one more,* Latest Contemporary Portraits, *published by a small New York firm in 1927.) The "stories" was Harris's* Undream'd of Shores, *also published by Brentano and by Richards.*

Shaw had been polite in the extreme to Harris's biographies, especially since one of them was an inaccuracy-ridden life of Richard Wagner, about whom the author of The Perfect Wagnerite *considered himself an expert.]*

Nice
April 4, 1924

My dear Shaw,

So you too talk of the "sands running out" and yet your portrait in the "Observer" the other day was magnificent. Send me a copy if you please with your name on it!

I was deceived about the "Paris Evening Telegram" and gave it up almost as soon as I was in the saddle—promised to me without debts. I was asked to pay 50,000 francs of debts in one afternoon. I returned to Nice and went on with the second volume of "My Life."

You are the first to see anything worth noting in the 4th

series of my "Portraits": I am *kindlier* to the smaller men. All through my mature life I only wanted to know the Immortals— those who had added something to the inherited wisdom of mankind.

You tell me you have done "Joan" without love: that was for me the supreme question and I could not make up my mind how to treat it—There's a word in Saint Beuve's essay on her worth considering. I'm looking forward impatiently to your version. I've already said in print that I believed you'd beat Anatole France and that's no mean praise; but—is a satisfying portrait possible? I'm not sure! Joan is as hard to do as Jesus! And her judges were as bad as his. Send me your book and photo when you have an hour to spare and tell me what you think of "Undream'd of Shores," especially of "A Lunatic!" and the Artist Story: the "Mad Love" you've already damned!

Ever yours sincerely,
Frank Harris

HARRIS to SHAW [A/4]

[Russian General Mikhail Skobeleff was a hero of the Russian-Turkish war of 1877–78. Harris travelled with him briefly as a correspondent. Col. Frederick Burnaby was a Horse Guards officer who served in the Sudan and wrote a popular book about his adventures, The Ride to Khiva.*]*

c/o American Express
11 rue Scribe, Paris
July 27, 1924

My dear Shaw,

My publisher has suggested my editing some books of short stories such as "The Best Short Stories," and "The Best French Short Stories," and "The Best English Short Stories." It strikes me that these selections might be made very interesting if I could get you and Upton Sinclair to help me: I'm sure of Sinclair's help but would you give me yours? I'd be greatly obliged and it can't cost you more than half an hour's thought and a letter.

I've finished the second volume of "My Life" infinitely better because of wider outlook than No. 1: I give intimate portraits of Skobeleff, the hero of Plevna, of Ruskin, Col. Fred Burnaby, de Maupassant and Lord Randolph Churchill. This last closes the last chapter and is far and away the most terrible and tragic page I've ever written. To say nothing of my own experiences which I keep in six special chapters, the others are too intimate for any publisher to handle. At first I thought of publishing an edition without any of my erotic experiences; but even so the stories of Maupassant and Churchill—victims both of syphilis—are impossible.

If you feel inclined give me a word of advice. . . . These selections of short stories will give me money enough to publish this second volume of Autobiography on which I've worked hard for a year. I'm reading your Joan. Just got it yesterday—fine, your best I think since "Caesar and Cleopatra."

Yours Ever
Frank Harris

I'm writing in bed hence shaky script, only a cold.

SHAW to HARRIS [A/4]

Highland Hotel, Strathpeffer
4th August 1924

Dear Frank Harris

I am too far out of date to help you in selecting short stories. The subject reminds me of De Maupassant and Frederick Wedmore. I thought the short story boom was over, especially as I have just been reading some very good ones by one Osbert Sitwell, who is not Wedmoresque.

The difficulty is that this practice of making books out of pickings from different authors, and paying them nothing, is now being energetically blown on. American publishers have tried to land me again and again that way, in vain. You will find yourself limited to old work that is out of copyright, or, if you resort to stories that have not been copyrighted in America because of the printing clauses in the Act, the book will be contraband over here.

I should have sent you a Saint Joan had I known where you were. You are quite right to keep your second volume generally circulable. "Man's love is of man's life a thing apart," and there must be an exoteric as well as an esoteric life of F.H. I am completely puzzled by the allusions I see in print to the first volume, as if it had been regularly published in America, which seems impossible.

You should head your second volume with a synopsis of the first (virginibus puerisque) like the serial novels in the newspapers.

My regards to Nellie, so absurdly faithful.

ever

G. Bernard Shaw

HARRIS to SHAW [H/2]

Frank Harris
c/o American Express Co.
2, rue de Congres
Nice (a.m.) France
August 30th, 1924

George Bernard Shaw, Esq.
10, Adelphi Terrace,
(off the Strand),
London, England.
Dear Bernard Shaw:

I am writing this letter with one purpose and one purpose only. In my last book of Portraits I have told everyone what I think of Emma Goldman, one who has fought for the under-dog for thirty odd years, and always with distinction. She was turned out of America, and turned again out of Russia, the Germans made life unpleasant for her, the French wouldn't have her except on sufferance, and at length we got her into England and she is to be found after September 17th care of Mme. Doris Zhook, 3, Titchfield Terrace, Regents Park, London N.W. 8.

I want you to call on her and make everything as nice for her as possible. If you placed one of your numerous motor cars at her disposal you would be doing a good deed and kindly, and she would love it. If I had one she should have it.

You, too, can influence the Labor Government to make it

easy for her in every way and I want you to do it. Take my word for it she is worth all the assistance you can give her and all the comfort too. Whatever you do for her shall be reckoned unto you for righteousness.

I have done the second volume of "My Life" which brings me down to the death of Lord Randolph Churchill. I have done the greatest portrait of De Maupassant and the greatest portrait of Randolph Churchill that have ever been done—greater I think than any other portraits in all literature. But then, I was always modest. In due time, if you are not starched beyond all recognition by prosperity, I'll send you the book, though I'm beginning to fear your gray hairs and gray beard.

Yours ever,
Frank Harris

I'm off to Nice to do a third vol. of "My Life"—

SHAW to HARRIS [H/4]

[On the heels of Shaw's success with Joan, *Harris had produced his own saint's play,* Joan la Romée. *Shaw was two months short of his seventieth birthday; thus his "pre-seventy" remark was slightly premature.]*

Ayot St Lawrence, Welwyn, Herts.
20/5/26.

Dear Frank Harris

La Romée has arrived. And first I ask you how you could be so unbusinesslike, when I had just reopened the medieval theatre market for saints, and proved it to be an extremely lucrative one, as to come into that market with the one saint in whom I had made a hopeless corner.

However, the impulse was evidently an artistic one, though you misunderstood its nature. I always want to make a drama of a subject, the bigger the better. You always want to make a short story of it, the shorter the better. My making a drama of Joan outraged your instinct: you felt that you must do something quite different with her; but you did not understand that the something was a short story and not another drama. The result is a shocking hybrid. Why not throw it into the fire

and write your story? You have done the trick in everything
except the form. You have emptied out the Middle Ages and
the Church and the Inquisition and the feudal system, and
reduced the subject to a story of a young Virginian female,
a few dullards, two crooks, and a very modern American executioner cheeking an English lord and snapping his fingers at
the Holy Office (which would have burnt him in a brace of
shakes for his heresy). Just like O. Henry, with the Harrisian
style superimposed.

But when you have done it, it wont have been worth doing.
Joan's history is the wrong material for O. Henry and De Maupassant and for you. Stick to the nineteenth century. Even a
long-story man of genius, Anatole France, was beaten by the
Maid: his "Vie" was the absurdest *gaffe* in modern literature
until you came along with your idiotic La Romée, and took the
fool's cap from him. Be not deceived by people who dont want to
quarrel with you: there is nothing to be done but drop the thing
into the waste paper basket with a goodhumored laugh, and
apologize to posterity for the surviving copies.

You will remark that I have become perfectly reckless as to
your feelings or anyone else's, and just shoo you off *my* grass as
if you were a tramp. The explanation is that my health has
given way at last: I have been ill for two months, and have
only half recovered, the pre-seventy part of me being as dead
as a doornail. I am a ruin; and you may discount my opinion
accordingly.

My handwriting is not fit to be inflicted on you.

Yours, half alive,
G.B.S.

HARRIS to SHAW [H/SY]

*[Harris told Alfred Douglas in Nice in 1925 that he was writing
a St. Joan play that would "knock spots" off Shaw's.]*

Villa et Boulevard Edouard VII
Cimiez – Nice
May 27, 1926

My dear Shaw:

Your letter on "Joan La Romée" has reached me. What an
extraordinary letter for you to write to me. I remember the

shock I had when I read in your criticism of My Shakespeare that you annexed my discovery that the Countess of Rousillon was Herbert's mother, Sydney's sister, and coolly said that I wouldn't have it though my words were "I think Shakespeare had this fine model in mind when drawing the old Countess of Rousillon." You went on to poke fun at me and pretend that I said that Shakespeare had his own mother in mind—all pure invention.

Now this criticism of my Joan is just as astonishing. It is the "pre-seventy part" of you at its worst which still exists. I had written my play before I saw yours, and Joan had been in my head for twenty years with Jesus; and it wasn't until I saw from the bottom of her garden at Domremy that she could see the church that a glimpse came to me of the way her soul grew. But you see nothing of my work at all except that my Executioner is a very modern American because he dares to cheek an English lord and disagree with the Holy Office.

You talk of the "Joan ground" as being yours and you would shoo me off this grass. This inspires me to tell you something of the truth about your play in your own vein. In the interminable four hours of it there were only two moments in which you tried to realize Joan. You make the peasant girl speak to her King as "Charlie" in open court—an anachronism as glaring as your epilogue; and you make Joan tear up her renunciation, which is contrary to the historical fact but which is a fine theatrical gesture; so much for your attempt to realize the heroine; but your Chief Inquisitor gets a speech of fifteen hundred words, which an actor can make effective by giving it his own individuality and character but which otherwise simply makes one yawn to hear. Then you place three men at a table to tell all you know about France in the beginning of the fifteenth century for thirty-two intolerable minutes by the watch and they say nothing of any value to any human soul;—and yet you call this your drama!

Your ideal of a drama is to make Jesus call Pilate "old-top" and give two hours of conversation to Caiaphas and his compeers.

Our disagreement, you see, goes to fundamentals. You think the Cauchons and the Inquisitors and all ordinary persons worth depicting at length but these like the poor you have always with you. We don't need a Shaw to portray them. Pinero does that and Henry Jones and a dozen others; but here in Joan is a great character, a heroic soul if ever there was one, and we want above all to learn how she came into being and how she was treated by men. You shirk the real problem altogether; there is more creative faculty in the first three pages of my work than in all of your four hours of drama! You should have seen the effort at least in my work to realize Joan; you should have known that nothing is gained by cheap sneering.

I am sorry to hear that you have not been well. I have been troubled too by my old enemy—Bronchitis—but as the warm weather comes on I get better; and when I heard that you had gone to Madeira I thought it would have been better if you had come down here, but you had gone before I knew of it.

What a curious dearth of poets in England today in comparison with the period I am writing about of my life in the nineties. You are, to me, the chief figure from 1895 to 1900, as Oscar Wilde was in the previous years. I shall always remember the pleasure your "Candida" gave me, much the same sort of pleasure that I had hoped to give you with my Joan. I have failed, it seems, but whether the failure is yours or mine is not yet easy to determine. I remember reading once how Cervantes praised Lope de Vega for his excellent comedies and sent him "Don Quixote," and de Vega replied that he couldn't help in any way because there was no talent in the book, "Don Quixote."

Yours ever

FRANK HARRIS

SHAW to ? [A/SY]

[Either one of Harris's friends, such as Hesketh Pearson, or Harris himself had sent Shaw a petition to sign, with other Englishmen, in an attempt to influence a pending French trial of Harris on the charge of corrupting public morals with the second volume of his autobiography, which had been printed in France. Harris's friends saw the issue as one of freedom of speech as well as one of artistic freedom. Even the British government entered the case—on the opposite side—because Winston Churchill was offended by the allegation that his father had died of syphilis, and others in positions of influence also felt defamed, directly or indirectly. Shaw's response, which Harris

eventually received, urged that the defense be kept in a low key, and he refused to be party to a petition. A number of Americans, including Theodore Dreiser and H. L. Mencken, however, stood by Harris, but the most effective lobbying of the court came from French writers. Eventually the presiding judge ordered a non-lieu, declaring that there were no grounds for prosecution.]

21st January, 1927

This is calculated to damage Harris to the utmost possible. To address it to the judge is not only an impropriety which may for all I know be a punishable offence in French law, but it must in any case give him offence as a shameless attempt to tamper with the court. It draws attention quite unnecessarily to My Life and Loves, as if that were likely to improve Harris's chances instead of providing additional evidence against him. All the stuff about France and art and freedom is enough to make any lawyer sick.

I have not seen the volume in question; but Mr Harris is in possession of my view as to how the first can be defended: that is, not as a work of art but as a document. As an invention, or a display of art for the sake of art, it is clearly a contravention of the laws against indecency. As a record of fact and an authentic clinical study it can claim the toleration allowed to all legal and scientific documents. On no other ground can the author possibly succeed; and any attempt to claim that art, as such, is above the law, will only redouble the determination of the court to explode that heresy by making an example of him.

I fear that it is too late to say this now, though I have heard nothing of any trial of the case. The delay has been caused by the temporary misplacement of this paper. However, I said it for what it may be worth.

G. Bernard Shaw

To the Presiding Judge of the French Court of Justice convened for the trial and judgement of Mr. Frank Harris charged with corrupting public morals by his book entitled "My Life, Vol. 2."

We, the undersigned artists and men of letters, earnestly desire to enter upon the records of your Court, our protest and our appeal.

With unbelieving astonishment we have learned that for the first time in French history a foreign author writing in a foreign tongue is charged with corrupting public morals. It is not clear how the French-speaking public can be corrupted by English words. It is not clear why the Author's far more outspoken book, namely, "My Life and Loves, Vol. 1," was not included in the charge of immorality. With these considerations the charge appears obscure and disingenuous. We can only conclude that the organized prudes among our English-speaking peoples are attempting to use a French court to punish a kinsman artist whose work they fear and hate. This attempt is much more than an attack on the freedom of a single author. It is a blow aimed to strike at the very right of free artistic expression by all men of letters in all the world. Therefore, we protest, severally and collectively, we protest against this contemptible outrage.

For several generations, student-artists from all parts of the world have gone to France as to the hearth and home of all the liberal arts. In France they have found the freedom of speech and action which are as necessary to the growth of Art, the supreme freedom of the mind, as sunlight and air to the growth of a flower. Is France now going to surrender the proud distinction of being the intellectual centre of the world? For it is the intellectual integrity, the artistic freedom, and the illustrious leadership of France that are here on trial. Very respectfully and very sincerely we appeal to you, in our own names and in the name of all mankind, for the protection and defence of this integrity, this freedom, and this leadership, against all enemies at home and abroad.

SIGNED:_____

SHAW to HARRIS [H/4]

[Allan Dowling then was a poet and critic who later became a Hollywood producer.]

10 Adelphi Terrace
30th March 1927

Dear Frank Harris

Do you know the address of Allan Dowling? If so, write to him at once and *order* him, on pain of your implacable displeasure, to retrieve an interview which he has perpetrated, and, I fear, sent to America. The English version is now all right, as the purchasers fortunately sent it to me for my approval. I rewrote it for them, which is no doubt what they hoped. But they did not give me Dowling's address; and what you must do is to make him substitute my revised version for his original before it appears in America.

In your account I treated him as a friend, and entertained him here, talking to him without reserve. He remonstrated with me for telling you that my St Joan was all right, and yours all wrong, an opinion which I have of course taken care to keep out of print. And now he puts it into his confounded interview at great length, and winds up with a remark of yours about Sinclair Lewis (unfit for publication) which can have no other effect than to make enemies for you of S. L. and his admirers, besides making everyone here say that you are incorrigible—worse than ever—the buccaneer in full blast. Nothing more mischievously tactless could have been contrived (with the best intentions, of course: the idiot thinks he is championing you *contra mundum*) by the greenest American simpleton.

I have done what I can; but my ignorance of his whereabouts limits me to making his betrayal of my hospitality harmless for English papers. As I have left all his abuse of me unaltered he will perhaps understand, as far as he is capable of understanding anything, that I have intervened on your account. Besides, he will not have to give back the money, as he would if I had vetoed the thing flatly.

Forgive my worrying you with this ridiculous incident; but this is not the moment to make 50 more enemies for nothing.

I was very glad to hear that the French proceedings were quashed.

Your aged
G.B.S.

SHAW on HARRIS: An Unexpurgated Interview [U/1]

[Harris's young Riviera acquaintance Allan Dowling used the Harris connection to acquire an appointment for an interview with Shaw in 1927, published as "Mr. Shaw on Heroes" in the

Liverpool Post & Mercury *on October 19, 1927. In print the interview bore little resemblance to the facts of the exchange, for Dowling, as required, had sent his typescript to Shaw for verification of the quotations, and Shaw, realizing how his remarks about Harris and his* Joan la Romée *had ranged from cutting to cruel, expurgated many of his remarks. Also excised was Dowling's entire second paragraph, which was a nasty description of Shaw. Almost all that Shaw left of the Harris portion of the interview after the opening paragraph was the line, "First of all, tell me about Harris. How is he?" After that what remained— many lines later—was Dowling's expression of pious hope that he would one day write about Harris, and Shaw's declaration that Dowling should not waste his time writing about other men. But the comment which followed, about Harris's real interviews and "imaginary conversations," was expunged.*

Although the conversation then turned to other subjects than Frank Harris—in particular Strindberg, Shakespeare and Joan of Arc—Shaw's pen scratched out much of that, rewriting large passages; and when Dowling, perhaps getting even with Shaw for his disparaging remarks about Harris, deprecated Shaw as a second-hand thinker and second-rate humorist, he must have known that the lines stood no chance of publication. None of the great people in history, Shaw was interpreted as suggesting (yet no quotations here), had nearly as much brains as he had, "but the truth is that Shaw's brain has gone weak. . . ." A large X eliminated that entire page, but Shaw broad-mindedly permitted closing lines declaring that he was at heart a conventional man and—a last gesture of inferred support for Harris— that in his own play he had "missed" St. Joan. Only a thin shell of the original interview remained.

Shaw's declared motives emerged in a note at the bottom of a letter written to him by W. W. Sayer, manager of the London General Press, an extract of which appeared in the Robert Bachelder (Ambler, Pa.) Catalog 27 in 1980, dated as March 24, 1927 "en route to Oxford": "You will see that it is quite impossible as it stands. It libels Mr. Harris grossly, and represents him as libelling Mr. Sinclair Lewis very coarsely. It puts into my mouth what would be read as a malicious and envious attack on a fellow-playwright who had produced a rival St. Joan. It makes me describe a play of Mr. Masefield's as a failure. . . . I have eliminated the passages that would make trouble, and made the rest inoffensive. . . ." Shaw's problem was that he had put on his public personality and been his outrageous self. Dowling had recorded him only too well.]

Bernard Shaw and St. Joan
by Allan Dowling

The circumstances of my first meeting with George Bernard Shaw were very interesting. A few days before I met the great man I had brought him a copy of Frank Harris's play, "Joan la Romée," and had left it at his place in Adelphi Terrace, and while I waited for him in the sitting room I was full of curiosity and excitement.

As soon as he appeared I noticed that his face was not as strong as it looks in any of the photographs. The outline of the nose is very indefinite, the eyes are pale, the general aspect of the face healthy, but bloodless, weak. His voice is weak, too, but his speech carefully enunciated, like his small, well-formed handwriting.

He came into the room quickly, smiled, dropped loosely into a chair, remarking, "First of all, tell me about Harris. How is he? His mental condition must be close to idiocy."

"Oh, no!" I cried. "Far from it!"

"But this play of his! It's no play at all; it's rubbish. Just look what he's done. He's brought in Dunois and left out the army. He's brought in Cauchon and left out the church. In fact, he's left out the whole middle ages."

"But," I said, "he hasn't left out St. Joan. What do you think of the work on her character?"

"Character? It's no character at all. I can't understand why he should deliberately come into a field which I have just made my own. After all, I opened up the market for medieval saints. There are half a dozen others just as interesting. Why didn't he choose one of those?"

"Probably because he has had Joan in his mind for the last twenty years, studying her. The early scenes seem to me sentimental and not well written, but the great trial itself in the last act is wonderfully done."

"You admire him, do you?"

"I do. I wrote to you last year asking you a question about him, and you were kind enough to answer at once. I hope to write about him someday, just as I hope to write about everything that I love in life."

"Oh!" cried Shaw impatiently. "Why waste your time writing

about other men? If there's anything in you, it's you that we want to hear about. When Harris and I were young men we didn't go about in awe of our elders. Oh! Yes, he went and got interviews with various people and wrote his imaginary conversations, but that's all. At your time of life, if you were any good at all, you'd look on Harris and me as old fogies, quite passé, no good to anyone any more. I don't know, of course; perhaps you do."

"Not at all," I said. "I have great respect for Harris."

There was a moment's silence and then Shaw continued.

"What you should do is go back and live in America. It's no good living in England or France. If you're going to do anything of importance you have to be on the spot. You ought to go back and write books about the United States, like Sinclair Lewis's, only a little less difficult to read, Lewis is on the right track. Did you see what he did last spring in Kansas, when he stood up in a pulpit, declared himself an atheist, and dared God to strike him with lightning? That was very good. It caused a sensation. It wouldn't over here, but it was the right thing to do in America."

"I remember it," said I. "I was in Nice at the time, and Harris remarked that it reminded him of a bug asking to be crucified."

The conversation turned to other subjects. . . .

HARRIS to SHAW [H/4]

[Harris's reference to his "wife" was finally accurate in 1927. It was only then that Harris married Nellie O'Hara. For years, however, Shaw had referred to Nellie diplomatically as "Mrs Harris."]

> C/O The American Express
> 2 rue du Congres, Nice
> April 3, 1927

My dear Shaw,

This same post that brings me your letter brings me a letter from Allan Dowling who tells me that he is sailing for New York tomorrow and can't give me an address till he gets there; But I'll write to friends who are sure to see him in New York.

Of course I will write in the spirit you wish, but I wish you had told me or would tell me now what he has put in my mouth about Sinclair Lewis.

I confess I don't understand Dowling. He was by way of being a poet and brought me his poetry at first; when his prose came, I had to tell him that my judgment was less favourable. But I formed the opinion that he was curiously reticent. He had to tell me what was taking place in New York in regard to some of my books and I could get nothing from him. Now it appears he spills himself out in illegitimate interviews.

I am sorry for the occasion of your writing, but I was very glad indeed to get your friendly letter. I thought you had forgotten me altogether.

It is strange that when I heard from you last you had been ill and I was well; since then I have come to grief. I caught grippe early in December and had convulsive hiccoughings with it. As soon as I got well, I went out for walks and took up my usual exercises and was soon astonished by the swelling of the veins in my right leg which turned out to be phlebitis.

So I am for the last 3 months compelled to keep my leg supported high up, and to pass all my time in bed or on a sofa. Worst of all my memory for names has gone which has made any literary work extremely difficult for me.

If it were not for my wife I should make up my mind to end the silly pilgrimage from nowhere to nothing.

You are honoured and famous and rich—I lie here crippled and condemned and poor, but I can see the sunlight through my window and I can recall the gorgeous adventures of life.

I was glad to hear from you. Your writing is far better than mine.

Yours ever,
Frank Harris

SHAW to HARRIS [H/4]

[This letter was quickly scratched out in shorthand at the bottom of Harris's letter for retyping by Shaw's secretary, Blanche Patch.]

10 Adelphi Terrace, London
7th April 1927

My dear Harris

Dowling says that Lewis took out his watch and challenged God to strike him dead in five minutes, and that your comment was "A bug demanding to be crucified." Funny enough for a private smile, but obviously not for publication. Dowling is, I think, a devoted admirer of yours; but he has no notion of public manners, and thinks that as a disgruntled man of genius his business is to write scornfully and offensively about everyone whom he does not happen to admire.

Have you ever consulted an osteopath? They cannot cure everything; but they have a genuine spinal technique which sometimes enables them to release nerve strictures which produce all sorts of troubles that have no apparent connection with the spine at all. The regular doctors do not possess this technique (it takes a couple of years to learn) and are no use in such cases.

As you say, I am honored and famous and rich, which is very good fun for the other people. But as I have to do all the hard work, and suffer an ever increasing multitude of fools gladly, it does not feel any better than being reviled, infamous, and poor, as I used to be. If it were not that "My mind to me a kingdom is" (and you can say as much) I should commit some disgraceful crime to escape from my duties as Idol-Panjandrum. It was better fun when I was rated as a clown, as I rather like clowning.

My best regards to Nellie.

Ever
G. Bernard Shaw

HARRIS to SHAW [A/4]

[Harris's projected Pantopia *was published in New York in 1930.]*

Villa et Boulevard, Edouard VII, Nice
April 28, 1927

My dear Shaw,

You'll see from the enclosed cable that I wired and wrote at once to Dowling to diminish his activity, but he's *impossible*!

You talk of age but your handwriting is as good as ever whereas mine is worse and shaky.

I've done four new books in the last year and a half and as of now I'm minded to write a novel—"Pantopia"—and a play and so complete my work. I hear of you as with Wells a good deal; but his "Clissold" did not seem to me readable. This phlebitis has kept me in bed, and sofa-ridden for months and nothing but rest seems to do any good. The end of life's pilgrimage is always before me and the last act is tedious; but I am always glad to get news of you or better still a word from you.

Yours ever,
Frank Harris

P.S. I think you might send me a copy of your play Jeanne—autographed.

SHAW to HARRIS [A/4]

Hotel Beau Site, Cap d'Antibes
31st July 1928

My dear F.H.

Many thanks for the proffered lunch on Friday; but I had better come over to Nice some day instead. You will perhaps guess the reason of this evasion; and if you don't, Nellie will.

The villas here regard a set of your confounded life and loves as an indispensable item of furniture. My wife read the first volume when you sent it to me (illustrations and all), and, as mistress of a house where all the books were accessible to a highly respectable female staff, promptly burnt it page by page so that not a comma should escape the flames. Of the subsequent volumes she knows nothing except what she infers from your promise in that first one to outCasanova Casanova in them. She has no doubt that you have been as good (or as bad) as your word.

There is no arguing about these things. You are off her visiting list; and rather than be entertained by you at the Hotel du Cap with all the publicity that my limelight inflicts on her she will go home by the next blue train and take me with her. It cannot be helped. Il faut souffrir pour etre Casanova. For a Victorian lady she has given her proofs of Liberalism and even of intransigence by marrying ME. She leaves me entirely free to maintain our old relations without protest. She hopes that it will be understood that her attitude has nothing to do with Nellie. But Frank Casanova she will not entertain on any terms.

So that's that. Any attempt to disguise the situation would be an indelicacy which you would (very properly) never forgive. My explicitness may provoke you to a dozen buccaneering oaths and epithets; but they will leave no trace.

My notion is that I should lunch you and Nellie and anyone else you like at your favorite restaurant in Nice. We can then talk at large.

ever
G.B.S.

SHAW to HARRIS [A/4]

[Prince Paul Troubetskoy was a sculptor who was doing a bust of Shaw. The Saturday Shaw proposes for the luncheon is August 11.]

8th August 1928

My dear F.H.

We had better lunch at your villa, as it is impossible to talk freely in a restaurant without the risk of seeing it all, maliciously distorted, in next day's paper. You know my habits: no meat, no fish, no fowl, no wine. A single dish of haricots blancs, or risotto with a touch of saffron but absolutely without any kind of animal in it (they will put ham in unless one stands over them), or maccaroni italienne (tomatoes), or puree St Germain (peas pudding), or an omelette or eggs sur le plat, will provide for me. But remember: a *single* dish. Unless you impress this, Nellie will serve up the whole lot: I know by experience. Only one of them.

As the post is slow, the telegraph much slower, and you do not give me a telephone number I am afraid to fix a day earlier than Saturday. Will that do? I have disposed of Troubetskoy, and have no engagement so far except for Sunday.

G.B.S.

SHAW to HARRIS [A/4]

Hotel Beau-Site, Nino's Restaurant
Cap d'Antibes
10th August 1928

My dear F.H.

I can't come tomorrow. Yesterday I was smitten with the most undignified form of maladie du pays. My interior became a mere cave of the winds and waters; and I lay about unable to keep on my legs longer than ten minutes at a time.

Today, after a good night, I am able to sit up and write and take my meals (such as they are) out of doors. The winds have subsided but not the waters; and I dare not venture out of reach of the appropriate seat until I am normally decent in that respect. I therefore propose Wednesday instead of tomorrow. By that time I shall be either quite well or dead.

Ever
G.B.S.

HARRIS to SHAW [H/4]

[Like Harris's Life and Loves, *D. H. Lawrence's* Lady Chatterley's Lover *was a favorite target for confiscation by postal and customs authorities. Unpublishable in England, it had been printed privately in Italy. Shaw would later declare that "every schoolgirl of sixteen" should read the book.]*

c/o The American Express
2 rue du Congres, Nice
January 30, 1929

My dear Shaw:—

Here I am back in our home in Nice after two months in America which have given me renewed health, but not much beside. I got so tired on the voyage that I lost all power of sleep and have not yet fully recovered.

But I must write to tell you your vogue in America is extraordinary, almost incredible. The *New York Times* declares that you are the greatest Englishman since Shakespeare, and this is the opinion one hears on all sides; I thought it would give you pleasure to know it.

I am just completing a novel I have christened "Pantopia," which I think the best thing I have done yet. I hope to send you a copy within a month or so. I want to find a publisher for it in London, but whom can I get? A word from you would make it easy. Bear my necessity in mind, will you, and say if you can get me a publisher who will [print] 50,000 words. I should send you a typewritten MS; but I hate to bother you.

You promised to send me the second of the two plays that I think your best (you agreed with me) with a word or two in your hand. Don't forget this please, and please write to me and tell what you are doing.

I have been reading a stupefying book by Wells, called "When the Sleeper Wakes" which I remember reading years ago or trying to read. Now after 15 years' rest I fail again to get through it. I don't know if you have read it, but it is frankly appalling.

I am writing now on Lawrence's last book "Lady Chatterley's Lover" which I think a masterpiece, better even than "Sons and Lovers," much better. I don't know any novel in English that I would put above "Lady Chatterley's Lover." It ranks in my mind with "The Cloister and the Hearth" by Charles Reade. If you have not read "Lady C.'s Lover," for God's sake read it, and tell me what you think of it. But don't let your wife see it, she will burn the very covers of it, but I'd like to know what you think of it. Excuse my having this letter typed. I am so shaky.

Ever yours,
Frank Harris

SHAW to HARRIS [C/4]

[Desperate for money and in increasingly fragile health, Harris while in America had elicited the promise of an advance if he could produce a biography of Shaw which, if Shaw would not authorize, he would at least agree to cooperate with and afterwards not attempt to suppress. The contract with Simon and

Schuster had been for $2500 on Harris's signature, $1000 on receipt of each 25,000 words up to $4000, and a final $1000 on publication day. Harris had broached the matter without indicating that he had already pocketed the cash advance.

Harris's "cowboy record" was On the Trail: Being My Reminiscences as a Cowboy, *which had just been published by Boni in New York. Shaw kept the typescript of it all his life.]*

4, Whitehall Court (130), London, S.W. 1
11th January 1930

Abstain from such a desperate enterprise. Nobody can do it but myself. And anyhow, why collect information from aged amateurs when your own powers of invention are so much more artistic? You ask for 30 or forty pages, leaving you to do the rest. It would run to 30 or 40 volumes; and the rest would overwork you for 5 years and leave you a broken and beggared man.

Besides, you would have to read my works! Say 33 volumes of the Collected Edition on which I am now wasting the precious remnant of my days. That alone would take you several months, ending in madness and the murder of Nellie and a tombstone inscribed "F.H. guillotined 25 Dec. 1930."

I have your cowboy record, and havnt yet had time to read a thrilling word of it. I hope to tackle it before Easter.

G.B.S.

SHAW to HARRIS [H/4]

[Planning to do a GBS biography one way or another, Harris not only sent Shaw a series of open-ended questions but circularized people who might have something to contribute. "I don't want people saying later when it is published," he wrote to Shaw's friends and acquaintances, "'But you should have put in my story of Shaw' or 'Why did you leave out this postcard I got from him?' So I am hereby warning all such critics to send me their stories, quips, inscriptions, autographs, photographs, postcards, letters, telegrams, cables, interviews and such now, or forever hold their peace." Harris's reputation guaranteed that he would not elicit any response from anyone who hoped to remain on good terms with Shaw.]

4, Whitehall Court (130), London, S.W.1
18th January 1930

My dear Frank,

You really are a daisy. You put six questions to me, the replies to which would be the book: about a year's work, which you would then decorate with nonsense about impulses and resolutions and high purposes and all the rest of the literary junk which is *de rigueur* in biographies. Also you propose to endow me with a soul. Have you not yet found out that people like me and Shakespear *et hoc genus omne* have no souls? We understand all the souls and all the faiths and can dramatize them because they are to us wholly objective: we hold none of them.

The odd thing about you is that though you can write, you have all the credulities and illusions and innocences of the amateur and the collector. I wont have you write my life on any terms: Nellie would do it far better. You made Shakespear a cross between a sailor in a melodrama and a French criminal invoking the sacred memory of his sainted mother. What you would make of me not even God knows. You haven't the very faintest notion of the sort of animal I am. If I had time I would tell you the facts just to see how utterly they would disconcert you; but I haven't; so you must drop it.

This is not my humor (you idiot!) but the solid prosaic truth.

Ever
G.B.S.

SHAW to HARRIS [H/4]

[Harris's response to Shaw is easily inferred. Shaw was resisting appeals for cooperation, particularly with reference to revelations about his early love affairs. The "only two of the ladies are dead" probably refers to Jenny Patterson, who initiated him, and Florence Farr, the actress who became her successful rival. But later amorous interests of his were also dead, except for "Mrs Pat" Campbell, whose relationship with him he had recently parodied in the "Interlude" scene in The Apple Cart *(1929).]*

4, Whitehall Court, London
27th January 1930

Francis

Your explanation is unintelligent. If success had gone to my head (by the way, to what part of my person did you expect it to go?) I should have jumped at the chance of making you my trumpeter. I should have flattered you and financed the great biography. I am throwing away a opportunity which few men could resist.

The truth is I have a horror of biographers. The Shaw legend had become so troublesome at one time that in self-defence I had to supply information enough to Archibald Henderson to enable him to produce his huge volume, which is only a colossally expanded extract from Who's Who? But I could not force myself to read the proofs for him; and to this day it remains mostly a sealed book to me. However, it was useful to me, not only as a book of reference, but because since it appeared those who write about me have the external hang of my career much more comprehensively than in the old days when I seemed to be six different little men keeping six separate little oil shops instead of a gigantic multiple trader.

A book by you would be a very different affair, though, like Henderson you would find it enormously more troublesome than you think. And it is not your job. Every man has a blind side; and I should catch you just on it. I am really a detestable fellow; and you have not the necessary désinvolture to do justice to my extraordinary talents and virtues and to the odiousness produced by the fact that my heart is never in the right— meaning the expected—place.

Besides, it is premature. Only two of the ladies are dead.

Think no more of it. And forgive me.

G.B.S.

SHAW to HARRIS [C/4]

[In any case, Shaw was not going to elaborate upon his sex life on a postcard; however he was still trying to dissuade Harris, although—as the second paragraph suggests—more feebly.]

Feb. 4, 1930

I really forget. But if I could remember, how could I possibly tell you for publication? Besides, don't you see that the fact that this is the only thing in my letters that interests you disqualifies you for a job in which it is the only thing that doesn't matter.

Don't waste good ink until you get a publisher's contract. I foresee difficulties.

Do not despise friendly counsel. I am not gibing.

G.B.S.

SHAW to HARRIS [H/4]

[Shaw was obviously giving in, but flying cautionary flags as he went down.]

4, Whitehall Court, London
3rd March 1930

Dear Frank Harris,

What a chap you are! You can of course compile a life of me as half a dozen other people have done—the sort of life that can be published whilst all the parties are still alive. Something, at best, like Morley's life of Gladstone.

Also you can write an autobiography, as St Augustine did, as Rousseau did, as Casanova did, as you yourself have done, which is something more than a heavily padded Times obituary notice. A man cannot take a libel action against himself; and if he is prepared to face obloquy, and compromises no one except himself and the dead, he may even get a sort of Riviera circulation in highly priced top shelf volumes with George Moore and James Joyce. But you cannot write that way about other people. You have a right to make your own confessions, but not to make mine. If, disregarding this obvious limitation, you pick up what you can from gossip and from guesses at the extent to which my plays are founded on fact (in your Shakesperean manner), what will happen? Your publisher, believing me to be fabulously rich and an ill man to cross, will send me the MS and ask me whether I have any objection to it. Unless it is a Morley-Gladstone Who's Who job I will say that I have every possible objection and will assuredly not hold him guiltless that taketh my name in vain; and I will point out that even if I consented I could not prevent the other persons concerned from seeking their legal remedy. And then where would you be?

You must not conclude that my private life has been a very scandalous one. But I once gave some autobiographical material to an Irish American professor. He was the son of an Irish inspector of police; and he proceeded to investigate the case precisely as his father would have done. At last he produced a book about me which began by describing my mother as an adulteress and my father as a despicable fortune hunter. Of course Harpers could not dare to publish this without my consent; and equally of course I could not consent; so the unfortunate author died of disappointment, aided by pernicious anaemia, cursing me for ruining him. Now the worst of it was that I could not deny that the information I had given him bore [upon] his construction; for as a matter of fact I was brought up in a *maison à trois* (we kept joint household with a musician who was a bit of a genius as a teacher of singing and conductor, with my mother as his prima donna and lieutenant); and my father had married, at the age of 40, with nothing but a civil service pension of about £60 a year, the daughter of a country gentleman with expectations from a rich aunt who disinherited her for not marrying an earl at least. The view taken by the police inspector's son of this domestic picture was wildly off the mark; but it opened my eyes to the impossibility of conveying a truthful impression except by such a sketch of that household and those persons as I alone could attempt. In my play called Misalliance the leading young man is "the man with three fathers." I should not have thought of that if I had not had three fathers myself: my official father, the musician, and my maternal uncle. So you see, long before my own adventures began, my story took a complexion that cannot be painted at second hand. Nearly all the guessing is bound to be wrong. That is why I am afraid of your making either a ghastly mess of a biography, or a conventional affair that will add nothing to your reputation.

The prefaces to my early novels contain as much autobiography as is worth writing.

I must stop or this letter will go on for ever.

G.B.S.

SHAW to HARRIS [A/4]

[Shaw had been putting together scraps of early autobiography for prefaces to volumes of his Collected Edition, which were about to appear, especially for volume one. It would print for the first time the text (silently revised) of his autobiographical 1878– 79 novel Immaturity, *which had been refused by most of the publishers in London by the early 1880s. He offered Harris a proof of the memoir he was planning as a preface, then added a long autobiographical follow-up in a letter. When Harris wanted to publish the letter in his biography Shaw insisted on rewriting it; thus the text as it appears in chapters 3 and 4 of Harris's book is somewhat different. Some of the changes are only mild censorship based on Shaw's second thoughts—such as his changing the characterization of George Carr Shaw before his marriage from "somehow unthinkable as a married man" to "he was a celibate." The most significant alteration appeared at the close, when Shaw insisted upon his resemblance to his father and his lack of resemblance to Lee. "I do not want my mother to be the heroine of another Wagner-Geyer lie." Ludwig Geyer, according to Wagner, filled his father's "place in the family circle" when his good friend was away, and finally did so legally nine months after Frederick Wagner's death when he married the widow. Young Richard Wagner was informally adopted and was known as Richard Geyer in his schooldays. The "lie" apparently referred to rumors that Geyer was indeed Richard's actual father. Shaw appears to have worried all his life that his mother's music teacher and friend, George John Vandeleur Lee, who shared a house in Dublin with the Shaws when GBS was young, might have been his own father, and the concern (which T. D. O'Bolger had sensed) seems to have populated Shavian drama with orphans, foundlings and others of confused or dubious parentage. The subject was first exposed in depth in a landmark biographical study by B. C. Rosset,* Shaw of Dublin: the formative years *(1964).*

In 1949 Shaw, then 93, planned to publish another rewritten version of the letter in his Sixteen Self Sketches *and had it set in proof. At the last moment he decided against publishing the text in any form, even though he had added still another line (rather than the Geyer one) to his disowning any resemblance to Lee: "He came on the scene later than I."*

"When she lost the one child she was really fond of" is a reference to G.B.S.'s younger sister, Elinor Agnes, born the year before him, in 1855. One excuse for Mrs. Shaw's desertion of her husband in June 1873, was to take Agnes, a tubercular, to the salubrious air on the Isle of Wight. (Lucinda Shaw went on to London, to join Vandeleur Lee.) Agnes died at Ventnor on March 27, 1876, four days before her brother made his long-planned break with Dublin. He left for England on March 31, 1876.

Sarasate is Pablo de Sarasate y Navascues, Spanish composer and violin virtuoso; Patti is Adelina Patti, Italian coloratura soprano. The only possible connection between Sarasate and Harris would have been a swarthy complexion.

Shaw apparently wrote the long letter by hand so that his secretary would not share in the self-revelation.]

4 Whitehall Court, London S.W. 1
5th June 1930

Dear Frank Harris

You must keep this proof most sacredly private, unquoted, and unseen until it is published, which may not be until the end of the year. Meanwhile it will give you some of the information you want.

Here is some more.

A hundred years ago or thereabouts there lived at a place called Whitechurch, out beyond Rathfarnham to the south of Dublin, a country gentleman of commanding character and noble presence. He was rich; and the alliances he formed for himself and his children were strictly limited to county families. His origin was quite unknown; but he lived and found his way *en grand seigneur.*

In the poorest quarter of Dublin there was at this time a little pawnshop. The name over the door was Cullen. Cullen, however, was only an employee. Every day the seigneur of Whitechurch drove into Dublin to call Cullen to account for the previous day's business. The squire of Whitechurch was the pawnbroker of Bride St. Hence his opulence and commanding character.

The squire-pawnbroker's daughter was married by him to a Carlow squire named Walter Bagnal Gurly, whose sole notion of procuring money when he was overdrawn (his chronic condition) was to mortgage. His father-in-law extricated him from his difficulties. He was a wiry, tight, smallish hardknit open air man, able to ride horses so ungovernable that their owners were glad to sell them for £20 after rashly paying £200 for them; so handy that he could make his own boots and make his study a workshop; a dead shot; and an indefatigable fisherman; able to do anything except manage his affairs, keep his estate from slipping through his fingers, or refrain from backing bills for neighbors as thriftless as himself. A toughened face with short ginger whiskers in the Franz Josef style must complete the portrait.

Being for the moment in smooth water and prosperously married, he became the father of two children: Elizabeth (Bessie) and Walter John. Then his wife died; and his motherless daughter was brought up by a deformed but sweetfaced and most terrible aunt, Aunt Ellen, with a will of vanadium steel. She concentrated herself on making a paragon of her niece, training her to become a perfect lady and to make a match of such splendor that the three golden balls over Cullen's shop should become Hesperidian apples. The unfortunate Elizabeth consequently grew up incredibly ignorant of the value of money, of the realities of life, and of everything except how to keep her back straight, to maintain an unquenchable dignity of style, and to compose music according to the rules of Logier's Thoroughbass. She had a mezzo soprano voice of extraordinary purity of tone, and perfect taste in using it. She never lost her self control; never sang, said, or did anything coarse; walked through the streets seeing nobody and being indignant with the people she barged into; passed by shop windows full of women's finery as if they weren't there, but could not tear herself away from a naturalist's or dog fancier's display; loved flowers more than human beings, and was exceedingly humane even to human beings; was utterly indifferent to public opinion and private gossip, taking her course as if such forces did not exist, leaving scandal dead of being hopelessly ignored; was long suffering with her friends, but never revived a friendship which had been abused; was to the closest observation so sexless that it was difficult to believe that her three children had been conceived otherwise than parthenogenetically; was void of jealousy and envy; and maintained a vigorous equanimity throughout trials that would have made most women querulous and miserable. Against Aunt Ellen's training she revolted completely in her maturity, entirely rejecting the religion and the prejudices to which she was brought up, and leaving her children without any training at all. When she lost the one child of whom she was really fond she amused herself with Spiritualism in her old age to be able to play at communicating with her; but she soon got tired of this; and the next thing that happened was that the lost daughter announced that they must separate; and left her to a certain entirely imaginary Father John, described by himself as "a Cistercian monk who lived 6000 years before Christ." Communication had been achieved also with her late husband, with the then defunct Lee (who was an utter failure) and other formerly real persons; but they could get no hold of her: she must have lived always in a world imagined by herself. Her singing, which would have betrayed anything there was to betray, never expressed eroticism. I took her singing of Mendelssohn's "Hear my prayer" as a matter of course until I heard an ordinary English singer treating a concert audience to it. I was horrified: the woman produced the effect of indecent exposure on me.

For this remarkable granddaughter of the puissant pawnbroker was my motherless mother.

It came about in this way. Walter Bagnal Gurly managed to retard his relapse into money difficulties for nearly twenty years by substituting for mortgages the obtaining of loans from rich Aunt Ellen on I.O.Us. Then, to the dismay of the family, he married again. Daughter Bessie, away from home visiting, communicated the news and date of the wedding to her Uncle John, brother of Aunt Ellen, and son and heir of the pawnbroker. Uncle John acted promptly and indignantly. He had of course had to lend money to W.B.G.; and when W.B.G. on his wedding morning incautiously went out of doors to buy a pair of gloves for the ceremony he was arrested for the debt.

Believing very unreasonably that his daughter had engineered this *coup de main*, he made it impossible for her to return to his house, and, in the exercise of a power of appointment he had over certain monies left by the pawnbroker to his children, attempted to cut her off with a shilling, but was forced by

his solicitor, who flatly refused to draw the deed in such extreme terms, to leave £5000 to her children. They came in
handly in the period described in this preface.

Meanwhile what was the homeless Bessie to do? She could
not prolong her visits indefinitely. There was no family refuge
save Aunt Ellen, whose tyranny was no longer endurable.

Among her acquaintances was a mildly amusing man with a
squint, twice her age, and well spoken of because [he was]
supposed to be harmless. He proposed to her; and in her per-
plexity and ignorance of life and its values she accepted. It
seemed a simple way out of the family difficulty. Her friends
were horrified at this throw-away. They told her the man
drank. This probably meant as little to her as the fact that
his means were very far below those on which she had been
brought up. She asked why they had not told her this before,
and went straight to him and asked him was it true. He answered with passionate sincerity that he was a lifelong and
bigoted teetotaller. So he was, in theory. In fact he was so
horribly ashamed of his dipsomania that he had to deny it just
as Rousseau had to deny stealing the ribbon. There are things
that we cannot bring ourselves to confess.

They were married, and in due course found themselves somehow in Liverpool. His behavior was disquieting. One day she
opened a press and found it crammed with empty bottles. She
left the house and made for the docks with a wild notion of
offering herself as a stewardess to get away. But there were
rough men about who frightened her back again. She had to
make the best of the mess she had got herself into. Aunt Ellen
never forgave the marriage, and left the fortune she had destined for her paragon safely out of reach of the paragon's husband and progeny. There were three children of the marriage:
two daughters and finally a son destined to eclipse Shakespear
and to have his biography written by Frank Harris. This in-
auspicious infant was taken once or twice to see Aunt Ellen,
possibly on the chance of his softening her. He failed; but, oddly
enough, she softened him. The strange little hunchbacked woman with the pretty little face and everything exquisitely clean
and refined about her, had such an effect on his imagination
that when, one Sunday morning, Papa announced that Aunt
Ellen was dead, he hurried to the solitude of the garden heart-
broken, and cried convulsively for a long time, believing that

his grief would last for ever. When he discovered that it lasted only an hour and then passed completely away he had his first taste of cynicism.

Bessie endured the children as she endured their father and the poverty and the drink and everything else, leaving them to the servants (and, My God! what servants! —except my old muse Williams) and to Providence, and taking no interest in them after, say, six years old. It would be ridiculous to call her a bad wife and a bad mother, because she was not a bad woman, and was incapable of ill treating anything or anybody, however deeply they might injure or however bitterly they might disappoint her. She was simply not a wife or mother at all. Like my father she was a hopelessly uncoercive person; and we as children had to find our own way in a household where there was neither hate nor love, fear nor reverence, but always personality.

But she was rescued from failure and despair by finding a religion. As thus.

There was in Dublin then a remarkable man whose name was George John Vandeleur Lee (known as G. J. Lee) of whose antecedents I know absolutely nothing. He had fallen over the bannisters in his childhood, and walked with a deep limp of studied elegance, one of his legs being much shorter than the other. This put him to some extent out of court in the matter of sex: at all events he never married and was somehow unthinkable as a married man. There was no room in his life for gallantry. He was a black whiskered and otherwise close shaven man, with strong black hair that looked like a wig (a result of burnt night cap—now obsolete), and resembled nobody on earth except a combination of Sarasate and Frank Harris. He was a presentable gentleman; but he was uneducated, as an attempt to impose a tutor on him (school, as I guess, may have been ruled out for a lame boy) had ended in his attacking the tutor with the thick joint of a fishing rod and driving him from the house. He supported himself and a brother by teaching singing. One of my earliest recollections is the death of this brother (a vaurien) and Lee having such a paroxysm of frantic grief that for some days, a friend had to watch him constantly to prevent him from committing suicide. He had formed a choral society and collected an amateur orchestra. He was a mesmeric conductor, quite as good as Nikisch, though he conducted from a vocal score or first violin part, and had probably never seen a full orchestral score in his life. When my mother had a serious illness he came into the house; swept my father and everyone else aside; took the case in hand; nursed it and cured it; and then told my father to send for his doctor, who, on arriving most impressively, said "There is nothing left for me to do." and withdrew.

By dissecting throats until he knew exactly what a larynx was like, and observing an Italian baritone named Badaeli whose voice was still magnificent at 80, he had perfected a method of singing, known in our household as The Method.

The Method was my mother's religion. It was the bond between her and Lee. A bond of sex could not have lasted a year. The Method was eternal. While Lee remained faithful to it she remained faithful to him as his prima donna, his chorus leader, his copyist of band parts, his harmonizer, according to the rules of Logier's Thoroughbass, his lieutenant and champion. When in the later days of his London vogue and decay he dropped it and became a fashionable charlatan she dropped him as unhesitatingly as her father used to shoot a sporting dog at its first mistake. I remember two occasions on which she was seriously angry. Once with a lady who had an idle trick of pulling things to pieces, and rashly practised it on a flower. And once when I told her that Lee had made me sing the tenor part in the big concerted piece in Lucia; I being a baritone. To strain a voice was *wicked*.

When Lee's brother died he needed only a music room in a house with a good address, and a bedroom: also a housekeeper. We could not afford a house with such an address. To combine forces was an obvious economy. We moved from modest Synge St to handsome Hatch St; and behold! a *maison à trois* based, not on adultery, but on The Method. Many masterpieces of music were rehearsed in that house; and I could whistle them all from the overture to the final cadence before I was 12.

Ten years later Lee made his grand attack on London, and took a house in Park Lane, as he had always said he would do. This produced an economic crisis. We could not keep the big house without him. My sister Lucy had a voice; sang "on the method"; and had a Mozartian musical facility which was her ruin, as she never learnt what real work meant. She had to be launched as a singer, obviously from London and from Lee's matinees there. My father, poorer than ever, could not have kept his family together even if my mother could have borne a relapse into futility and nothingness without even a chorus to lead. She, with her daughters (one of whom presently died) followed The Method to London and took the house in Victoria Grove with which this printed preface begins.

It took two or three years to train a singer by The Method. London would have none of that. Lee had to undertake to make ladies sing like Patti in 12 lessons at a guinea a lesson. They did not want to sing like my mother: they wanted to sing like harlots; and they did. Lee had all the fashionable world on his list of patrons: he raked in guineas until the ague disabled him for a day or two (a relic of malaria caught in Italy). He dropped the G.J. and became Vandeleur Lee. He shaved off the powerful black whiskers and grew a waxed imperial. His mesmerism slackened. My mother had less and less use for him as his faithlessness to the method developed and she perceived that he was a finished man, almost a living corpse. He weakened into something quite common and human; made himself impossible at Victoria Grove by becoming susceptible to my sister's sexual attraction (she could not tolerate him); found his vogue waning; began to supplement teaching by letting the house in Park Lane for supper parties; and fell into the hands of a housekeeper with a daughter. My mother had not seen him for years when one night he dropped dead as he was getting into bed. The post mortem established brain mischief of long standing. Who buried him or what became of his goods we never knew. I did not fail to note the utter vanity of his great London success. His presence in our household during the years when he was really an effective man of genius made a great difference to me. With my mother he of course completely sidetracked my father; but there was no substitution whatever; and in the end she was more lenient to the husband than to the hero.

Is it now necessary to add that my resemblance to my father is quite clearly discernible, and that I have not a single trait even remotely resembling any of Lee's?

Now you can go on to the printed stuff.

communicatively
G. Bernard Shaw

SHAW to HARRIS [A/4]

[Confident enough that he did not look *like the smooth-chinned G. J. Vandeleur Lee, Shaw enclosed a photograph which also included his mother and black-bearded father. The attribution of the photo to Pigott was wrong; it was actually taken by a respectable firm in Sackville Street, Dublin.]*

4 Whitehall Court, London S.W. 1
7th June 1930

Dear Frank Harris

The photograph was taken by Dick Pigott, the forger of the Parnell letters, at a time when he was a harmless amateur photographer.

The man seated in the middle, and obviously the mesmeric master of the situation, is George John Vandeleur Lee.

On the extreme right and left are my father and mother.

The man in the sombrero is Charles Cummins, amateur tenor (a gifted one) and professional accountant.

The lady leaning over Lee is a Miss Feeny, the one behind him a Miss Ryan.

Date: the early sixties.

It will help you to visualize Lee, who is, as you see, the only face exactly focussed by Pigott's lens.

faithfully
G. Bernard Shaw

SHAW to HARRIS [A/4]

[The proofs enclosed were the galley sheets for the Immaturity *preface.]*

4, Whitehall Court, London, S.W. 1
7th June 1930

Dear F.H.

I have been unable to write for many weeks, as my wife has had a serious illness. She now seems the better for it.

I have written the information you want with my own hand on the enclosed proof. When it is no longer private—say next year—sell it and have a spree with Nellie.

ever
G.B.S.

P.S. I am addressing to the American Express, as I am not sure that you are still at the Buffa.

SHAW to HARRIS [H/4]

[Shaw added to this letter after the fact when he permitted it to be published in Harris's book. The text below is the original.]

4, Whitehall Court, London
20th June 1930

My dear F.H.

Don't be sentimental: it's dangerous at our ages; and it is not what the publishers want from you. Not bread and milk, but brandy, with a dash of vitriol, is what they drink at your bar.

What I sent you is only an advance proof of the preface to my first novel, 50 years old, which will be published for the first time in a collected edition of my works, 1000 sets of about 30 volumes at 30 guineas for the set. Later on it will be published in ordinary form at an ordinary price; and it is for this popular issue that I must hold the preface back from every other sort of publicity. Meanwhile, however, your private glimpse of it will put you wise as to some aspects of my boyhood. I made the additions about Lee in manuscript because it will give the proof a considerable saleable value as an autograph which may come in handy later on.

All that melodrama-bunk about my good heart and open hand must come out, because (a) it is not true (if you had ever read my books you would know that I loathe mendicity, almsgiving, and poverty, and hate the people I have to help almost as heartily as they very naturally hate me); (b) that, true or not, it will only set every beggar and charitable institution in Europe and America pestering me with appeals (I am already brutalized by shouting No every day of my life); and (c) because such stuff makes nauseous reading, utterly unworthy of you as an artist, and betrays the fact that Buccaneer Frank is only the camouflage of a sentimental donkey.

As to your question whether Lee's move to London and my mother's were simultaneous, they could not have been. Lee had to make his position in London before he could provide the musical setting for my mother and sister. But the break-up of the family was an economic necessity anyhow, because without Lee we could not afford to keep up the house. I was born in a small house in an unfashionable street (then half fields) at the edge of Dublin. No professional man of any standing could have received fashionable pupils or patients at such an address. The house had, in the basement, a kitchen, a servant's bedroom, and a pantry. On the *rez de chaussée* a parlor (a *salle à manger*), a nursery, and a "return room" which served as a dressing room for my father, and subsequently as also a bedroom for me when I grew out of sleeping in the nursery with my two sisters. Upstairs was drawingroom and the best bedroom; and that was all. It was 3 Upper Synge Street at my birth; and one of my early recollections—co-eval with the death of the Prince Consort, when the newspaper came out with a black border—was its change to 33 Synge St when the three Synge Streets, upper, middle and lower, were amalgamated.

The house we shared with Lee, No 1 Hatch St, was fashionably placed. Being a corner house it had no garden; but it had two areas and a leads. It had eight rooms besides the spacious basement and pantry accommodation as against five in Synge St; and the rent, of course, was much higher. Without Lee's contribution it was beyond my father's dwindling means. Lee got his foot into England at a country house in Shropshire, where the lady fancied herself as an amateur *prima donna*; and he made smart acquaintances there. He had always said that he would take a house in Park Lane; and he did. No 13, it was: a narrow house, but with one fine music room.

When it was clear that he was going to stay there, and that Dublin had seen the last of him, the Hatch St house had to be given up. So my mother took a London house in Victoria Grove, way down the Fulham Road, and settled there with her two daughters, whilst I and my father went into Dublin lodgings at 61 Harcourt St. This must have been somewhere round about 1871. In 1876 I threw over my job in the office of a very superior land agent, and joined my mother in London.

I had no love affairs. Sometimes women got interested in me; and I was gallant in the oldfashioned Irish way, implying as a matter of course that I adored them; but there was nothing in it on my side; and you, as biographer, will have to face the very unHarrisian fact that I escaped seduction until I was 29, when an enterprising widow, one of my mother's pupils, appealed successfully to my curiosity. If you want to know what it was like, read The Philanderer, and cast her for the part of Julia, and me for that of Charteris. I was, in fact, a born philanderer, a type you don't understand. I am of the true Shakespearean type: I understand everything and everyone, and am nobody and nothing.

I really must stop now.

Ever
G.B.S.

P.S. Of course you will understand that the above, typed by my lady-secretary from my shorthand draft, does not answer the modern biographer's first question nor satisfy the modern reader's Freudian curiosity, which is "How did you respond to your sexual urges?" I must find a moment presently to write to you with my own hand (or typewriter) on that subject. It is a very wide and complex subject, on which a mere record of ejaculations, like that in My (Your) Life and Loves, throws no light. A more completely reticent book was never written.

SHAW to HARRIS [A/4]

[The promised unburdening was done sans typewriter. For publication Shaw had second thoughts about the language of his revelations, changing copulation *and* copulations *to* gallantry *and* gallantries, *whore* to *mistress and making other small alterations to improve the tone of the whole. Harris would be upset at any loss of a strong word.]*

June 24, 1930

First, O Biographer, get it clear in your mind that you can learn nothing about your sitter (or Biograph*ee*) from a mere record of his copulations. You have no such record in the case of Shakespear, and a pretty full one for a few years in the case of

Pepys; but you know much more about Shakespear than about Pepys. The explanation is that the relation between the parties in copulation is not a personal relation. It can be irresistibly desired and rapturously executed between persons who could not endure one another for a day in any other relation. If I were to tell you every such adventure that I have enjoyed you would be none the wiser as to my personal, not even as to my sexual history. You would know only what you already know: that I am a human being. If you have any doubts as to my normal virility, dismiss them from your mind. I was not impotent; I was not sterile; I was not homosexual; and I was extremely though not promiscuously susceptible.

Also I was entirely free from the neurosis (as it seems to me) of Original Sin. I never associated sexual intercourse with delinquency. I associated it always with delight, and had no scruples nor remorses nor misgivings of conscience. Of course I had scruples, and effectively inhibitive ones too, about getting women into trouble (or rather letting them get themselves into it with me) or cuckolding my friends; and I understood that chastity can be a passion just as intellect is a passion; but St. Paul was to me always a pathological case. Sexual experience seemed a necessary completion of human growth; and I was not attracted by virgins as such. I preferred women who knew what they were doing.

As I have told you, my corporeal adventures began when I was 29. But it would be a prodigious mistake to take that as the date of the beginning of my sexual life. Do not misunderstand this: I was perfectly continent except for the involuntary incontinences of dreamland, which were very unfrequent. But as between Oscar Wilde, who gave 16 as the age at which sex begins, and Rousseau, who declared that his blood boiled with sensuality from his birth (but wept when Madame de Warens initiated him) my experience confirms Rousseau and is amazed at Wilde. Just as I cannot remember any time when I could not read and write, so I cannot remember any time when I did not exercise my overwhelming imagination in telling myself stories about women.

I was, as all young people should be, a votary of the Uranian Venus. I was steeped in romantic music from my childhood. I know all the pictures and statues in the National Gallery of Ireland (a very good one) by heart. I read everything I could lay my hands on. Dumas pére made French history like an opera by Meyerbeer for me. From our cottage on Dalkey Hill, I contemplated an eternal Shelleyan vision of sea, sky and mountain. Real life was only a squalid interruption to an imaginary paradise. I was overfed on honey dew. The Uranian Venus was bountiful.

The difficulty about the Uranian Venus is that though she saves you from squalid debaucheries and enables you to prolong your physical virginity long after your adolescence, she may sterilize you by giving you imaginary amours on the plains of heaven with goddesses and angels and even devils so enchanting that they spoil you for real women or—if you are a woman—for real men. You become inhuman through a surfeit of beauty and an excess of voluptuousness. You end as an ascetic, a saint, an old bachelor, an old maid (in short, a celibate) because, like Heine, you cannot ravish the Venus of Milo or be ravished by the Hermes of Praxiteles. Your love poems are like Shelley's Epipsychidion, irritating to *terre à terre* sensual women, who know at once that you are making them palatable by pretending they are something that they are not, and cannot stand comparison with.

Now you know how I lived, a continent virgin, until I was 29, and ran away even when the handkerchief was thrown me.

From that time until my marriage there was always some lady at my disposal; and I tried all the experiments and learned what there was to be learnt from them. They were "all for love"; for I had no spare money: I earned enough to keep me on a second floor, and took the rest out, not in money, but in freedom to preach Socialism.

When at last I could afford to dress presentably I soon became accustomed to find women falling in love with me. I did not pursue women: I was pursued by them.

Here again do not jump at conclusions. All the pursuers did not want sexual intercourse. They wanted company and friendship. Some were happily married, and were affectionately appreciative of my ready understanding that sex was barred. Some were prepared to buy friendship with pleasure, having made up their minds that men were made that way. Some were sexual geniuses, quite unbearable in any other capacity. No two cases were alike: William Morris's dictum "they all taste alike" was not, as Longfellow put it, "spoken of the soul."

I found sex hopeless as a basis for permanent relations, and never dreamt of marriage in connection with it. I put anything else before it, and never refused or broke an engagement to speak on Socialism to pass a gallant evening. I liked sexual intercourse because of its amazing power of producing a celestial flood of emotion and exaltation of existence which, however momentary, gave me a sample of what may one day be the normal state of being for mankind in intellectual ecstasy. I always gave the wildest expression to this in a torrent of words, partly because I felt it due to the woman to know what I felt in her arms, and partly because I wanted her to share it. But except perhaps on one occasion I never felt quite convinced that I had carried the lady more than half as far as she had carried me: the capacity for it varies like any other capacity. I remember one woman who had a sort of affectionate worship for me saying that she had to leave her husband because sexual intercourse felt, as she put it, "like someone sticking a finger into my eye." Between her and the heroine of my first adventure, who was sexually insatiable, there was an enormous range of sensation; and the range of celestial exaltation must be still greater.

When I married I was too experienced to make the frightful mistake of simply setting up a permanent whore; nor was my wife making the complementary mistake. There was nothing whatever to prevent us from satisfying our sexual needs without paying that price for it; and it was for other considerations that we became man and wife. In permanence and seriousness my consummated love affairs count for nothing beside the ones that were either unconsummated or ended by discarding that relation.

Do not forget that all marriages are different, and that a marriage between two young people followed by parentage cannot be lumped in with a childless partnership between two middle aged people who have passed the age at which it is safe to bear a first child.

And now, no romance and above all no pornography.

GBS

SHAW to HARRIS [YY/4]

[Shaw reports that before he leaves on Monday he will be free on Saturday to visit with Harris, but asks about making arrangements with a person named Goldman, who was very likely radical exile Emma Goldman, Harris's old friend.]

Antibes
27 August 1930

Frank Harris Villa
Boulevard Edouard Sept
Cimiez   Nice
NOUS PARTONS LUNDI PROCHAIN JE SERAI LIBRE SAMEDI POUR VOUS VISITER POUVEZ VOUS ARRANGER AVEC GOLDMAN

BERNARD SHAW

SHAW to HARRIS [H/4]

[This letter was a terrible shock to Harris. It implied that he could not quote from Shaw's increasingly intriguing revelations at the very time when Shaw seemed eager to press such revelations upon Harris. As Shaw had begun unburdening himself he had apparently sensed the autobiographical value of the material for a book of his own, and had begun withdrawing the implied wholesale freedom to quote. His explanation in a postscript that he was protecting the copyright of material which would appear in the Collected Edition was only a half truth. Some of it was not published until Sixteen Self Sketches *in 1949; some was never published. Shaw's only full-length memoir remains the two-volume one posthumously pieced together from his writings,* Shaw: An Autobiography *(1969, 1970.]*

4, Whitehall Court (130), London, S.W.I.
September 18, 1930

Dear Frank Harris,

What an impossible chap you are! You want stories about actresses. Don't you know that you might just as well ask a cardinal whose life you were writing to give you a few stories from the confessional as ask a playwright to give away the secrets of rehearsal? After Tree's death I wrote an essay on him in a memorial volume published by the family. In that I gave the public a very slight peep behind the scenes, the man being dead. But the rule is that nothing that happens behind the stage door must get into the press. The actor is entitled to his stage glamor. Not until Mrs. Pritchard was dead had Johnson any right to let the public know that off the stage she called her gown her gownd, and that she had never read a word of Macbeth except her own part and its cues.

Tree once, joking about my vegetarianism, said to Mrs. Campbell "Let's give him a beefsteak and see what the effect will be." "Please dont" said Stella; "he is bad enough as it is; but if he eats a beefsteak no woman in London will be safe." Now that story, which has been printed and spoiled in the printing, is quite permissible, because it is extra-professional and might have happened if they had never been inside a theatre in their lives.

Here is another incident, I once said to Tree "Have you noticed all through these rehearsals that though you and I have had twenty years stage experience, and have reached the top of our profession, you treat me as an amateur beginner and I do the same to you?" Now that story I should not be justified in publishing if Tree were alive. It is a criticism. If I published any criticisms and professional incidents of rehearsal any actor or actresss would be justified in refusing to rehearse when I was present; and the fact that they couldn't afford to do it, poor dears, makes privacy all the more binding on me.

As to personal relations with actresses, the freemasonry of the profession makes it very difficult to let the public see it without being misled. Morals and emotions are not the same on both sides of the footlights. Ellen Terry and I exchanged about 250 letters in the nineties. An old fashioned governess would say that many of them were wild love letters; and yet though we were all the time within a shilling hansom ride of one another's doors, we never saw one another in private; and the only time I ever touched her was on the first night of Brassbound, when I formally kissed her hand. For some time before the war I was on exactly the same intimate terms with Mrs. Campbell as King Magnus with Orinthia in The Apple Cart (some pages in the scene are verbatim). Yet I was as faithful a husband as Magnus; and his phrase "our strangely innocent relations" is true. I may say that from Ellen Terry to Edith Evans all the famous actresses with whom I had any personal contact have given me their unreserved friendship, but only with one, long since dead, and no great actress either, (she is hinted at in my preface to Archer's plays) had I any Harrisian adventures. From Lady Colin Campbell, whom you used to describe in your best buccaneering English as a lumbarly exuberant female dog, onward, I have been familiar with celebrated beauties and with what is by no means the same thing, really beautiful women, without either I or them moulting a feather of our integrity, I am, and always have been, an incorrigible philanderer, retaining something of the obsolete gallantry of the Irishmen of my generation; but you may count the women who have conquered me physically on less than the fingers of one hand. To these occasions I attach no importance; it is the others which endure.

You want to know what it feels like to be a rich man. Well, you should know; for if you are not a millionaire at this moment, you have been one for an afternoon, or for a week, or if rumor be true, for perhaps a year when you married a lady in Park Lane and spent all her money consorting with Randolph Churchill and Edouard Sept. As a matter of fact I am not rich as money goes nowadays. My professional income is taxed and surtaxed both in America and England. When from time to time I make, say £20,000, what does that come to when it is invested and the tax and surtax comes off both the capital and the income it produces? Between my wife's settled property and my own we are in the class that has between five and ten thousand a year, and doesn't spend it all. I am far too busy to enjoy money; I have more than I want, and I have had nothing; and the difference in happiness has been negligible. I am one of those to whom money means security and exemption from petty tyrannies; if society would only provide me with both I should throw my money out of the window because it is troublesome to take care of and attracts parasites and hatred. I loathe charity and bountifulness and patronising and so forth; if I have to relieve people financially I hate them as heartily as they hate me.

And now to the solid matter of this letter. An American firm is advertising your biography as being authorised and as containing 15000 words by me. I have written to them to say that no biography of me except Henderson's is authorised, and that yours is specially deprecated. And if you publish a word of mine I'll have the law on you. I am not going to write your book for you: its sole interest for me and value for your reputation will depend on how you write your own book yourself. I have given you a look at certain things I have written about myself, and which I intend some day to publish myself; for if you insist on writing a life of me you may as well know what you are writing about; but you must tell the story in your own way and not in my way. Any fool can get a book published if he can persuade the publishers that I have written it and the publisher can sell it on that understanding; but in that case all the reviews will quote me and be about me, and the nominal biographer will get nothing but his share of the plunder. S. and S. must withdraw their announcements of 15000 words by me, and of an authorised biography. You are personally capable of writing a worthy successor to the Wilde biography without quoting a single word from my accounts of myself; and I shall do everything in my power to force you to do so. There is no evidence in the Wilde book that you ever read a word he wrote; and as you have certainly not read more than three per cent of my stuff you will have to stick to your strong hand and paint the man and not the author. I can imagine nothing more ghastly than a literary shepherd's pie of Shaw and Harris horribly messed up together. Besides, the book should be an essay on our times and have sketches of all sorts of people in it. That is the sort of thing you can do; and if you do it in your best manner your abominable Life and Loves will be forgiven and forgotten. You must die in the odour of sanctity even if you persist in calling it the stink of respectability.

Faithfully
G. Bernard Shaw

P.S.

I should have explained that what I sent you about my mother will form part (like the Immaturity preface) of the Collected Edition of my works now trickling out in batches; and that I am under contract with the American publishers to support them in any infringement of copyright. That is why you must use the information without quoting me.

HARRIS to SHAW [H/4]

[Outraged by Shaw's seeming withdrawal of what he had been offering so freely, Harris exploded with frustration—or Frank Scully did under Harris's signature. Scully, a crippled journalist working out of Nice who later claimed to have ghosted most of Harris's cowboy "memoir," On the Trail, *had been employed to expand Harris's* Contemporary Portraits *sketch into a book, as Harris himself was now too weak and ill with asthma, phlebitis and assorted lesser ailments to do any of it himself. Shaw's letters had been planned as the means of making up most of the verbiage needed.*

Harris's reply is typed, but corrected in his shaky hand. Although Scully was not permanently behind the scenes, he was in effect waiting to piece together a book from Shaw's contributions.]

9 rue de la Buffa, Nice
September 23, 1930

My dear Shaw,

Your extraordinary letter of the 18th September has just reached me. Schuster had no business and no authority from me to say that my biography of you was authorized. When you said that it was "specially deprecated" you passed the bounds of truth. But now comes this letter of yours that goes further still. You say that "if I publish a word of yours you will have the law on me." Again you declare that I need not put a single word from your account of yourself and you add that "you will do everything in your power to force me not to do this." Such a threat is worse than unfair. I have already months ago entered into a contract and received the money from the publisher for giving him my life of you and some of your own letters. Now 6 months afterwards you forbid me to use a word. Three months ago you wrote: "I have written the information you want in my own hand, sell it and have a spree with Nellie." And now you forbid and threaten me.

I intended to send you what I have written about you and if you objected to anything, of course, I would modify it; but in view of this letter of yours and its threats I can do nothing but risk the row. Think of it, Shaw, and put yourself in my place for a moment. I wrote to you again and again asking for special informations on special points. You sent me those informations. Naturally I incorporated your letter in my book and now you tell me that if I use a word of yours you will have the law on me, if you don't, your publisher will. What am I to do? I cannot rewrite the whole book. I have received the money for some of it already. Do be sensible. You talk of Henderson's 600 pages as the only authorized biography. There is hardly a gleam of Shaw in the whole tome. I want Shaw to live in my book from the first page till the last and I wish everyone to take a new interest in you. What should I care personally for your views of actors and actresses—I know them all almost as well as you do. I hoped you would write a searching word of them which would give this book of mine an increased value. Ask yourself please how was I to know or guess that you objected to be quoted? If you had put "private" at the head of any letter I would have regarded it as an order, but no hint of any such reticence till this letter of 18th of September. I would rather quarrel with anyone than with you, but unluckily I am caught. I have put some of your letters over your name and sold the book and received some of the money for it. I cannot get out of it. You told me not to use your printed preface—I have not used one word of it but you gave me 10 pages of your writing—by your silence it was plain that I could use them. I want you to think over the matter and withdraw this letter of yours of the 18th September, and let us get back to the old footing of assured friendship, a friendship of a quarter of century. I would then of course send you my book when it is finished and use any of your criticism that I could use.

You have you say 5 to 10 thousand £s a year—I have nothing. I was about to write to Schuster for another advance, but now he will probably refuse it because of your letter and I shall be in queer street. I am getting 1500 pounds paid in installments for the book; that is what we are living on at the moment. Think, Shaw, I have never sought to injure or hurt you, on the contrary, I have done what I could to show you kindness. Why should you hurt me in this way?

Yours sincerely,
Frank Harris

HARRIS to A.L. ROSS [YY/SY]

[Via the French Telegraph Cable Company, Harris informed his attorney in New York, Arthur L. Ross, that Shaw was on the war-path. Ross would later be Harris's harried executor.]

NICE   SEP 25 1930
NLT ROSS ONE CEDAR ST NEWYORK CITY
SHAW FURIOUS SCHUSTER ADVERTISING AUTHORISED
BIOGRAPHY THREATENS LAW HAVE WRITTEN SHAW
FULLY SENDING COPY SHAWS LETTER

HARRIS

SHAW to HARRIS [A/4]

[Wise was the American publisher of Shaw's collected Ayot St Lawrence Edition*; Simon and Schuster was to be Harris's publisher of the GBS biography.]*

26th September 1930
    In great haste—can you not manage to quote within the limits of statutory "reasonable quotation" without reproducing my history of the pawnbroking great grandfather, which is absolutely reserved for Wise & Co. You can tell that story in your own way and sell the MS, which is of course what I meant by writing it out for you with my own hand and telling you to sell it. It is S & S's announcement that the book will contain 15000 words by me: virtually making me joint author, that has got across my contracts and upset the apple cart. A letter or two, if passed by me (so that I could cut out anything that might offend my friends) would be all right; but the pawnbroker's history must not be reproduced: you must tell the story in your own words and in your own way; and I must not be advertised as contributor or collaborator or accomplice. Can't you manage somehow?

G.B.S.

HARRIS to THE EDITOR, THE [London] *TIMES LITERARY SUPPLEMENT* [X/TLS]

[Obviously worried that he would have little if any copyright Shaw to publish if G.B.S. kept to his September 26 position, Harris rushed to seek anecdotal material to fill his book, advertising his needs in the October 9, 1930 issue of TLS (p. 810).]

A Life of Mr. Shaw

Sir,—Having contracted with American and English publishers to write the biography of George Bernard Shaw, I don't want people saying later when it is published, "But you should have put in my story of Shaw" or "Why did you leave out this postcard I got from him?" So I am hereby warning all such critics to send me their stories, quips, inscriptions, autographs, photographs, postcards, letters, telegrams, cables, interviews and such material, after being copied, will be returned to its owners promptly and with thanks.

> Faithfully,
> FRANK HARRIS, care of Simon and Schuster,
> 386, Fourth-avenue, New York, or 9, Rue
> de la Buffa, Nice, France.

SHAW to HARRIS [H/4]

[Obviously Harris was unable to tell his story in his own words; and Shaw's words, in any case, would sell more books. Agreeing, reluctantly, Shaw passed upon typescripts of letters which Harris wanted to use, censoring them where he felt that he had been indiscreet or where names of living people seemed risky to leave as they were. Each approved typescript was dated and marked at the top, in a circle, "O.K. from this copy as corrected. GBS."]

4, Whitehall Court, London
2nd Nov. 1930

Dear Frank Harris

I have read over these letters and initialled them in red ink to signify that I will not sue you nor your publisher if you quote them, with my few little deletions and revisions, in your confounded biography at your discretion (not that you have any).

In haste—all my time having been taken up with the reading—

G. Bernard Shaw

SHAW to HARRIS [A/4]

[Despite the new bowdlerization he requested, Shaw was now being sincerely helpful. His "I will see you through" suggests knowledge of Harris's condition.]

4, Whitehall Court (130), London, S.W.1
3rd Nov. 1930

I sent the letters back to you yesterday in a hurry. One of them contains, I regret to say, the improper expression "permanent whore." Change the second word to "mistress." Our forecastle style will not do on the quarter deck.

I give you a free hand as to these letters; but they are so condensed and so dependent on the context of our personal relations that expectation may be better than quotation. I again urge that it must be your book: you must not let me play you off the stage.

S. & S. protest that all the announcements to which I took exception came from Nice, and that they are entirely guiltless. I have told them not to be alarmed—that I will see you through with plenty of quotes.

G.B.S.

SHAW to VICTOR GOLLANCZ
[X/G-SH]

[Claiming indignation that Harris had ventured to label his book as authorized biography, Shaw told Victor Gollancz—as he wrote to Max Schuster in New York—that an appropriate title might be one in which G.B.S. noted that he had deprecated the biography rather than authorized it. As a result Gollancz suggested "something like this" to Schuster:

GEORGE BERNARD SHAW
by Frank Harris
A biography deprecated, but written with the aid
of documents voluntarily supplied,
by Bernard Shaw

The next day Gollancz received a further message from Shaw.]

7th November 1930

Dear Mr Gollancz,

All the writings of mine in Frank Harris's hands, including the printed contribution to his volume of Contemporary Portraits, belong to me. I have never parted with a copyright.

I think I have made it clear to Messrs S & S that there must be no suggestion that I have any share in the authorship of the book or any responsibility for it. The appearance of my name on the title page is quite out of the question. What I wrote to F.H. in reply to his questions must not be published as a contribution to the book, nor as a manifesto of mine under the very objectionable heading of my Sex Credo, a label which is presumably the invention of Mr Scully. The book must be Harris's book and his only. He may use the material at his disposal as any biographer uses such material and may quote sentences or reproduce sanctioned letters in the ordinary way. But the letters that I have written to him for his information and the matter which is to appear in the collected edition of my works must not be quoted *in extenso*. For instance, the so-called Sex Credo must not be so quoted. Harris may write a chapter on my sexual character and on the very absurd assumptions that have been made about it; and he may incorporate the information and quote sentences as utterances of mine; but he must not throw the whole thing in a lump in the face of the public as a sort of Rousseau's Confession contributed by me to his book. In short, if he makes a workmanlike job of it and does not put me in an intolerable position I shall not make any trouble for him, as I think I have already proved by what I have written for him. I have done more for him than for my authorised biographer Archibald Henderson; and with this you must all be content. As to footnotes I cannot promise anything. I certainly could not have such a feature announced, as that would at once make me a collaborator; but it is possible that when I see the proofs I may be provoked to make a comment or two.

I object strongly to serialisation and advise you to object too. It will bring in some ready money, of course; but it will spoil the sale of the book. It would be far better business to begin with an expensive limited collectors' edition, though I have very little patience with that game myself.

I agree with your general conclusions. F.H. is legally invulnerable: a suit against him would be costly and totally unproductive; for where there is nothing the king loses his rights. And I do not see why the book should not pay its way very handsomely within my conditions, unless you have plunged recklessly in the matter of royalties, and advances.

Faithfully,
G. Bernard Shaw

SHAW to HARRIS [C/4]

[Harris wanted to make a plea for the material he wanted in person although he was probably medically unable to make the journey. Shaw's postcard put it off in any case.]

4 Whitehall Court
20th Nov. 1930

Caricatures are innumerable, and mostly so ugly without any artistic charm that they would spoil the look of any book. Any attempt to deal with them would mean a volume all to themselves; and even a half attempt would upset the balance of your work and give it an air of triviality. Dignity is your line: you can be ruffianly, but not trivial.

As to seeing me, you *have* seen me when I was really all alive; and at Nice you saw the ghastly old ghost of G.B.S.— what is left of him. What more do you need?

Just at present my visibility is specially low as my wife has had a fall and broken some bones; and this flat is for the moment an hospital. Your interruption would probably kill the patient.

G.B.S.

HARRIS to SHAW [A/4]

[Cashel Byron's Profession was Shaw's boxing novel, written in 1882 and published in 1886. Prize fighters since James J. Corbett had exploited their fame in unauthorized dramatic adaptations of the story but Tunney, who had retired from the ring, would not.]

c/o American Express
2 rue du Congres, Nice.
January 21, 1931

My dear Shaw,

I sent you about 10 days ago a bundle of letters from you to me which I found buried in the files of Pearson's. Did you get them? If not will you let me know and I will send another set, and if you have would you be good enough to edit them and return them.

People keep asking me all sorts of questions about you and I confess that as much as I know there is some things I doubt. For instance how do you write? Do you dictate most or do you still turn out a lot by hand, either by machine or pen? What are your best working hours? What is the most you have produced in any given day or week? I am moved to ask them as I read over these prefaces. Some run 20,000 words and in all they must total millions. Writers like Bennett and Wells cannot have averaged more than a thousand words a day, I do not believe. I remember you thought 3,000 words a week for "The Saturday Review" very fatiguing, and yet you must have averaged more than that each week since.

Of course mere quality means nothing, but it frequently happens that men of great talent produce in great amounts and, I suppose you will add in order to cover your case, genius always.

A newspaper reports that Gene Tunney is coming to visit you. Why don't you have him do a talking picture vision of "Cashel Byron's Profession." Even if done badly it would bring each of you a million.

Ever yours,
Frank Harris

SHAW to HARRIS [A/4]

[Shaw had examined the typescript copies Harris had made of his letters from him and indicated what might be publishable with an "O.K. from this copy as corrected. GBS." The apparent joke about the full colon was no joke: Shaw loved that means of punctuation and used it lavishly. He refused to permit any alteration in his style.]

4, Whitehall Court
1st February 1931

Dear Frank Harris

I have at last snatched a moment to deal with the enclosed. Have them set up from these copies.

Be particularly careful not to mention the name of Lord Alfred Douglas in the book.

Tell your typist to have a colon put on her machine.

I must leave your letters unanswered for the moment. It is as much as I can do to scribble this.

G.B.S.

SHAW to HARRIS [A/4]

[Gabriel Wells, the rare books and manuscripts dealer, had been specializing in furnishing Shaw items to wealthy collectors, mostly Americans.

Philip Snowden was Chancellor of the Exchequer and thus responsible for taxation. Shaw's book manufacturing was his

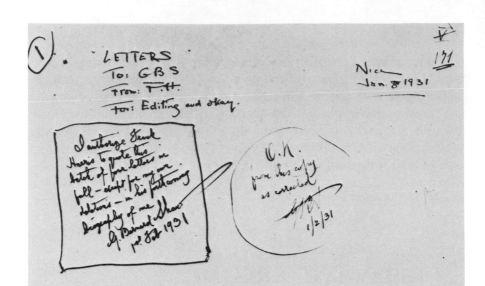

The occasion of Shaw's writing *this letter* was my objection to his calling me a "ruffian" in a previous letter; I asked him what he meant by it; here is his reply:

July 1918.

My dear Frank Harris:

You must not take my comments on your personal characteristics as sneers and disparagements. If you do you will find me an impossible man to have any relations with. I tell you you are a ruffian exactly as an oculist might tell you that you are astigmatic. I will tell you now more precisely what I mean - if I have done so already you have brought the repetition on yourself.

Somebody in London society who likes interesting people meets you and invites you to dinner. He asks you to

Shaw's imprimatur on Harris's error-ridden typescript of a G.B.S. letter to him. (Arents Research Library, Syracuse University)

shrewd method of publishing—using a recognized publisher to manufacture his books with the publisher compensated for production costs and for marketing the books. The collected edition represented a substantial Shavian capital investment.]

4, Whitehall Court
8th Feb. 1931

My dear Harris

I can't manage the thousand dollars: I am far too rich. I have just had to pay Snowden £20,000 (a thousand a year investment); and I am incurring book manufacturing expenses on a scale which obliges me to budget very stingily for current expenditure. Everyone has gone broke; and the margin I had left for rescuing shipwrecked orphans and the like is worn away. No doubt you have squeezed your publishers hard for advances; but they *must* see you through until you deliver the MS. Why not sell the originals of the letters I returned to you the other day? I know that the market has slumped; but Gabriel Wells might still fall for that set.

Besides, I always hate the people I have to give money to; and they always—very properly—loathe me.

G.B.S.

SHAW to HARRIS [A/4]

[Ellen Terry and Bernard Shaw: A Correspondence would appear in 1931 but Harris was too ill and broke to chance delaying delivery of his manuscript to Simon and Schuster.]

Grand Hotel, Venice
2nd April 1931

I think you have a natural right to "How Frank should have done it" if you want to incorporate it in that dreaded biography. It's a pity you can't wait for the Ellen Terry letters. But you can reserve that for a Vie Amoureuse de B.S. The shops here are full of Vies Amoureuses of everybody who was anybody.

G. Bernard Shaw

SHAW to HARRIS [C/4]

*[News of the Ellen Terry correspondence gave Harris the idea
that he could manufacture still another book out of his exchanges
with Shaw over the years, and he wanted Shaw to come to Nice
to discuss the proposal.]*

apcs
Hotel Lotti, Paris, France
[postmarked April 7, 1931]

My letters have been so sickeningly overdone that they have
slumped to nothing. A correspondence like the Terry one is of
course still valuable; but we have never had a correspondence
in that sense: my occasional attempts to persuade you that the
world is not populated exclusively by Frank Harrises would not
make a book even if they were fit for publication. A trip to Nice
now is impossible. My holiday has already lasted almost beyond endurance and I must hurry home when my business here
is ended.

G.B.S.

HARRIS to SHAW [H/4]

*[Since Harris by this time was far more ill than Shaw realized,
this letter may be one of those which Frank Scully referred to in
recalling that he typed out "bludgeoning letters [to Shaw] and
brought them to Harris to sign."]*

9 rue de la Buffa, Nice
April 16, 1931

My dear Shaw,

I am getting along with the biography though by no means
done with it. I had a curious idea I could finish it by March
31st, and signed contracts to that effect, but at this time of life
we all make haste slowly.

I have come to that remarkable letter of yours on this thing called "sex," and before I go on with it I want you to reconsider the absurdity of your editing. You have substituted the word "gallantries" for "copulations," thereby destroying the whole force of your opening sentence. Your original was: "First, O Biographer, get it clear in your mind that you can learn nothing about your sitter (or Biograph*ee*) from a mere regard of his copulations."

Now I note you have written above the word "copulations" the idiotic word "gallantries." They don't mean the same thing at all, and sooner or later the fact of this alteration will become public knowledge and your squeamishness at this time of life will have you laughed at as long as your name lives.

Then I observe in a note you wrote later, after initialling this letter under discussion, that you ask me to change the word "whore" to "mistress." All, this reads for all the world like some old fogey who is writing a letter to the newspapers for the first time and reads it to his maiden aunt, with a constant inquiry— "is it too strong?"

I wonder if you read modern novels at all? Your words like "copulations" and "whores" are sedate in comparison, but if you would emasculate them more the letter will have no force at all, and though I do not agree with one-tenth of it, I believe it does express your credo better than it will ever be expressed again, or ever has been expressed before. That is why I want you to leave it alone and urge you to restore the letter with all its original force.

Ever yours,
Frank Harris

SHAW to HARRIS [A/SY]

[Shaw had no idea, when he teased Harris about his forthcoming funeral, how close the event was. Later, having won his point about what words of his would be included in Harris's book, he wrote to his old friend, the sculptress Lady Kennet (once Lady Scott), ignoring Frank Scully's role in assembling the book, "The really biographical passages in Harris are inserted by me for the information of my friends. The critical part is his mostly."]

Venice—on the eve of departure for Paris
21 April 1931

Man: will nothing teach you? is Nellie to mourir sur la pleuble after spending her last sou on your funeral?

I tell you, if there is one expression in this book of yours that cannot be read aloud at a confirmation class, you are lost for ever. Your life and loves are just being forgotten, and your old reputation as a considerable and respectable man of letters reviving. This book is your chance of recovering your tall hat; and you want to throw it away for the sake of being in the fashion of O'Neill, Joyce, and George Moore. And even George does not imagine that force in literature is attained by calling a spade a f — — — — g shovel. Even if it were, that sort of thing does not belong to your generation or mine, which could say all that it wanted to say without lessons from the forecastle and the barrack guard room.

So brush up your frock coat; buy a new tie; and remember that your life now depends on your being Francis Harris, Esquire, editor of the Fortnightly and Saturday Reviews, from the great days of Victoria the Ladylike. Frank the Buccaneer is not a person with whom F.H. Esquire can have any connexion whatever. Bury him. If you dont, the parish will.

G.B.S.

SHAW to NELLIE HARRIS [A/SY]

[With the letter was a check. Shaw realized what desperate financial straits Nellie must have been in upon the death of her husband. Shaw did not expect repayment but felt that the check would be more palatable if he suggested as much. In any event, in London alone the book sold 27,000 copies on publication day.]

Malvern Hotel, Malvern
August 25, 1931

Dear Mrs. Harris

They have just telephoned me that you have finished the strange adventure of being married to Frank.

Death does not always select the convenient moment when there is plenty of ready money in the house to meet its expenses. Hence the enclosure. You can repay it out of the profits of the biography.

Now you can begin another life with the wisdom garnered from your first experiment; so run up the half-masted flag to the top of the staff, and away with melancholy.

ever
G.B.S.

PS I am working on the proofs and getting the facts straight. Will you leave it to me to see it through the press?

SHAW to NELLIE HARRIS [H/SY]

[Victor Gollancz was to be the London publisher of the Harris book. Shaw after Harris's death had taken over the manuscript from Frank Scully and rewritten most of it in the Harris style, inserting large sections of his letters to Harris—as expurgated—and removing what he felt were legally questionable statements about other living people. Frank Scully was unhappy about being largely left out of the preparation of the text but had no control over the situation, for Shaw destroyed the evidence as to what portion of the book was his and what portion had been prepared by Harris with Scully's help. As an added bonus, to help sell the book, Shaw wrote an epilogue which pretended that Harris had actually completed the book but for correcting the proof sheets.]

4 Whitehall Court, London
October 17, 1931

Dear Mr[s] Harris,

I have been hard at work on those proof sheets ever since I wrote to you, and have at last returned them to Victor Gollancz ready for press. They cannot be published until after the election and until S. & S. have had them for simultaneous publication in America; but they will be out sometime in November, I hope; and unless they are killed by an excessive price, as so many books have been lately, you may feel fairly sanguine as to a satisfactory sale. Gollancz agrees with me on this point, and having promised the booksellers the book at the price I suggested, eight and sixpence, finds them very keen about it. I am writing to S. & S. by this post to urge the same point.

You may think I have been a long time over this job; but I assure you it is only by putting everything else aside and working double shifts on it that I have been able to get it ready so soon. You see, Frank knew hardly more about my life history than I knew about yours; and the mixture of his guesses with the few things I told him produced the wildest results. I have had to fill in the prosaic facts in Frank's best style, and fit them to his comments as best I could; for I have most scrupulously preserved all his sallies at my expense.

Another difficulty was that though Frank was a member of the Kansas bar, nothing could ever knock into his head the subtle difference between legitimate criticism, including what is technically called "vulgar abuse," and actionable statements. The book contained two outrageous personal libels and three commercial ones; and these I have taken out, as they might have involved lawsuits which would put an end to all hope of any profit on the publication. The commercial libels were contained in a chapter full of gossip picked up at the film studio, which I think must have been written by Scully. Anyhow it had to go, as it was quite unworthy of Frank in style, and was almost miraculously wrong in every particular, besides overstepping the legal lines and making statements reflecting on the commercial management and finance of British International Films.

You may, however, depend on it that the book is not any the worse for my doctoring, and that Frank's opinions of me (which, between ourselves, you must often take with a grain of salt) are not softened or suppressed or evaded in any way.

If the book is a success, it may stimulate public interest on his other writings, especially, perhaps, in the life of Oscar Wilde, which has never been openly in the London market. Brentano, who handled it for some years in America, tells me that when Lord Alfred Douglas threatened proceedings a compromise was arrived at by which it was left on the market with the addition of a chapter by Lord Alfred correcting the statements made in it about himself. Would it not be possible to issue it here on the same condition? With the proofs of Frank's astonishing carelessness as to facts and evidence before me in my own case I can readily believe that he was even less particular about Lord Alfred; and if that was so it is a pity that the book should be driven underground if it can be saved by allowing Lord Alfred to justify himself in his own fashion. I have made as many references to it as possible with this in view, and also to My Life and Loves.

As to this, do you think it would be possible to make it conventionally presentable? You see, Frank, far from being the abandoned voluptuary he supposed himself to be, was really a mid-nineteenth-century Irish prude; and I think that the first volume which was the only one I read (for he was much too disgusted with me for not leaving it on the drawing room table to send me the others), could be sufficiently bowdlerized for general publication without losing any of its force or interest, or violating his intentions in any way. Fifty years ago his determination to break down the taboos and win freedom of speech about sex would have been sacred. Put nowadays, when every flapper at the dinner table and every lady novelist says things that would have made Frank and myself blush like a couple of ingenues, that particular battle is won, and indeed overwon.

Besides correcting proofs I have written a postscript which must have your approval before it goes to press. I have asked Gollancz to send you a proof. In it I have not only handled Frank almost as freely as the book handles me, but made a momentary allusion to you which you must strike out if it jars on you in any way. Frank has still some enemies surviving from old times; and I have thought it better to anticipate the worst they can say of him than to provoke them to renewal of hostilities by leaving their grievances wholly unrecognized.

Scully has just rung me up to accuse Gollancz of wanting to appropriate my MS corrections. This is nonsense; Gollancz has behaved quite correctly and amiably; but I learnt incidentally from Scully that this letter should be addressed to the American Express Co. in Paris; and though he is constitutionally incapable of making any precisely accurate statement whatever, I take a chance and address as directed. But see postscript.

As to the corrected proofs, I think I had better destroy them so that nobody shall ever know where the patches came in. If you like I will give you the MS of the postscript; but it is in shorthand.

Will you continue to live at Nice; and are you all things considered, quite well and happy?

Faithfully
G. Bernard Shaw

I have not the exact address of the American Express; and as there are three or four similar agencies—Guarantys and such like—I will address this to Nice and trust to its being forwarded.

SHAW on HARRIS: A "Self-Interview" [X/MB]

Shaw made a practice of writing out interviews for prospective interviewers. It saved a possibly annoying visit to Whitehall Court or Ayot St. Lawrence, provided quotations Shaw knew would be accurate, and a manuscript the lucky interviewer (who often never met the great man) could sell to a dealer or collector of Shaviana, of whom there were many by 1931. In the case of George W. Bishop, who actually knew Shaw, a typed copy of the "interview" exists, carefully corrected and amended in Shaw's hand.]

[November 1931]

A week after Frank Harris' book was published I called on G.B.S. at Whitehall Court and with the slightest glimmer of a smile I said to him:

"Well, you've had a fine press for your biography."

"Excuse me," he replied at once, "Frank Harris has had a fine press. Every one of our very best feuilletonists has blazed away at his best in full-dress articles, not about me but about Frank. You see, I was right: Harris, with all his vulnerability to every sort of disparagement, was not the negligible fellow you can all so glibly prove him to be. Ervine dismisses him contemptuously, but does it in two columns—almost as much as Osbert Burdett, who stands up for him manfully and justly. Read all those brilliant and earnestly interested articles, and you will understand why Frank was able to extort from me revelations which have scandalised the *Daily Mail* and made even Ivor Brown, in one of the ablest of the notices—Ivor Brown, who is one of my most generous and penetrating champions among the critics—marvel at my shamelessness. But what is a man to do nowadays when he is tackled by a writer who cannot be ignored?

"Frank Harris said in effect: 'I have walked naked through the land, just as I am, without one plea; now I am going to take Shaw for a walk.' I am not fonder than other people of being stripped in public; but if I cannot prevent the exposure at least I can effectively object to being tattooed first. I can take care that the exhibition, if the public must have it, shall be the real animal, and not a Nonesuch. And for my pains I am most ungratefully accused of exhibitionism and want of self-respect.

"Pray, how much privacy—how much self-respect of that sort—have I been allowed to enjoy in my long life? Ever since, in my first play, I astonished the critics by putting men and women on the English stage instead of heroes and heroines of romance, I have been considered fair game not only for criticism, but for amateur psycho-analyses of every possible degree of crudity; so that at last the body of public criticism became a body of pseudo-psychopathy in which every sort of abnormality was attributed to me to hide the prosaic truth.

"If all this stuff were true it would destroy all the authority of my writings, which, especially the plays, are necessarily concerned a good deal with sexual psychology. Harris was duped by it, and had set up an elaborate hypothesis of some fundamental weakness in my constitution to support a quite imaginary account of my personal conduct. I had no means of preventing him from imposing this on the public, and confirming misunderstandings that would have been a serious nuisance, not only to myself but to my family and friends for the rest of our lives, except the straightforward means of plunking down the authentic facts.

"If anyone can suggest an alternative let him do so. If not, let him thank heaven that he is not yet in my predicament, and give me his sympathy instead of reproaching me for a publicity which I can no more avoid than a searchlight can, but which I can at least try to keep clear of imposture, hypocrisy and idolatry.

"It is no use thinking about these matters in the fashion of the nineteenth century, when they were never mentioned at all—when even medical text-books of anatomy and physiology refrained from dealing with reproductive mechanisms. George Eliot, for instance, never had to expose her ankles in public to refute statements that they were striped like a zebra's, because nobody would have been allowed to hint in a review that she possessed anything so improper as an ankle at all. But nowadays public men or women may be compelled at any moment to expose their entire persons to prove that they are human beings and not monsters.

"It is a very noteworthy feature of the affair that amid all the blaze of literary brilliancy that has coruscated round Frank's last rally by far the best handling of it is the only one I have seen signed by a woman. She makes precisely the right public use of the opportunity. And she, like Frank—though heaven forbid that I should carry the comparison beyond her courage and choice of staff—is an editor in a thousand."

"And the lady is . . .?"

"Lady Rhondda, of course. If she had been a grown-up woman thirty years ago I should have contributed to *Time and Tide* and not to the *Saturday Review*."

SHAW on HARRIS: Postscript by the Subject of this Memoir [X/FH]

[By 5 October Shaw had completed his rewriting of Harris's book, including the addition of a postscript. All the galley proofs upon which he made his corrections and additions were then destroyed, including notes in his shorthand—all but the postscript, which he gave to Nellie Harris and which is now in the Humanities Research Center, University of Texas at Austin. His tracks covered, he then excised from the typescript of the "postscript" the lines "I am bound in honor not to suppress or soften any of the adverse verdicts on my case scattered through these pages. I should not greatly mind that I am accustomed to be misunderstood on this point or that and that I have yet to face a judge harder on me than I am. . . ." And he added further, and then excised, his confession that it had "cost me much self-restraint to refrain from making myself still more ridiculous than his friendship for me allowed him to make me. . . ."]

FRANK HARRIS, having finished this last chapter, died on the twenty-sixth of August, 1931, in his seventy-sixth year, leaving his proof sheets to be corrected for the press by me. I have had to do many odd jobs in my time; but this one is quite the oddest.

For Frank, famous for his pen-portraits, was the most impossible of biographers. He himself called the sketches of his contemporaries which form such a large part of his writings *Contemporary Portraits*. And that is exactly what they were: portraits, and very rapid impressionist portraits at that. In spite of the fame of his *Life of Oscar Wilde*, it is not really a biography: it is a series of impressions from successive personal contacts and directly observed incidents. And this book he describes always as a portrait, and never as that portentously exact result of laborious research and scrupulous verification implied by the word biography. The truth is that Frank was an exceedingly sensitive man, who reacted with such violence, not only to authentic facts, but to any sort of gossip that stirred up his always seething susceptibility to scornful indignation, that he could not stop to ask himself the first question of the professed biographer, which is, "What is the evidence for this?" and the cognate question of the intellectually honest judicial critic, "What else could I have done had it been my own case?"

One consequence of this was that Harris suffered deeply from repeated disillusions and disappointments. Like Hedda Gabler he was tormented by a sense of sordidness in the commonplace realities which form so much of the stuff of life, and was not only disappointed in people who did nothing splendid, but savagely contemptuous of people who did not want to have anything splendid done.

He often reminded me of a revolutionist whose rose at an obscure meeting held in a cellar near Gower Street shortly after the settlement of the great London dock strike of 1889. In that struggle the champions of the dockers were Mr. John Burns, Mr. Tom Mann, and Cardinal Manning. Mr. Burns shared with the Cardinal the credit of the settlement; and I, being the principal speaker at the meeting, gave him his due.

But this hero had been dreaming of greater things than the miserable sixpence an hour which I was claiming as a great victory for the dockers. He denounced Mr. Burns in unmeasured terms; and he denounced me similarly for supporting him. He was quite beyond argument; so I put the critical question to him, "What would you have done had you been in John Burns's place?"

He was quite equal to the occasion. "Done!" he thundered. "I would have taken the scarlet cardinal by the scruff of his gory neck and chucked him into the incarnadined river."

What else could a man say when, dazzled by millenial visions, he was invited to cheer himself hoarse over sixpence an hour for a job so heavy and dangerous that accidents requiring hospital treatment occurred every twenty minutes? I sympathised with the protest, though I knew very well what an enormous effort it had cost to get the dockers that wretched sixpence, and how utterly incapable my Boanergic denouncer would have been of getting a farthing for them.

Frank, too, was a man of splendid visions, unreasonable expectations, fierce appetites which he was unable to relate to anything except to romantic literature, and especially to the impetuous rhetoric of Shakespear. It is hardly an exaggeration to say that he ultimately quarrelled with everybody but Shakespear; and this book contains several attempts to quarrel with me. But I bear no malice, as he is at bottom trying to quarrel with a scheme of things in which fellows like me crawl between earth and heaven and snatch little successes in which there is no sort of justice and fundamentally no reality. Many of those spirits, who, like Frank, can by no means learn to live in the real world and suffer fools and humbugs gladly, have nobility of soul, though for want of adequate secular facilities—economic faculty, legal faculty, mathematical faculty, business faculty, and objective faculty generally—this nobility cannot always save them from comparatively squalid adventures in the material sphere. Harris seized his opportunities with a confident audacity that carried everything before it. His resonant voice, capable of every accent of scorn, his brilliant eyes, his ready tongue, his bold individual style, imposed him, on men and women alike, as one who was his own best credential. His knowledge and capacity were assumed without evidence at first sight. He believed himself to be a strong man and a man of action; and he was taken by everyone at his own valuation from the moment when his first marriage rescued him from some very dark days of poverty in Germany, whither he had been drawn in pursuit of literary learning, and where the only thing he learnt was that unless he had money the world would have no mercy on him. But though he took the tide in his affairs unhesitatingly at the flood, he was not thickskinned enough to hold his friendships; and the worst of it was that instead of showing his sensitiveness he made everyone believe that he was as tough as hickory.

I remember my own surprise when the late Julia Frankau

(Frank Danby) one day remonstrated with me very earnestly for treating him too roughly. She urged me to remember that he was an exquisitely sensitive man. My own early experience, which included nearly ten years of apparently hopeless failure, had hardened me to such a degree that I had lost all sensitiveness to any criticism but my self-criticism. It is impossible to acquire this hardness and retain a sympathetic understanding of how something that falls on you with the weight of a fly's foot can sting apparently tougher men like the lash of a whip. So I was somewhat incredulous at first; but I soon saw that Mrs. Frankau was right, and that Harris could not bear the spurns that patient merit from the unworthy takes with any sort of equanimity. He accumulated quarrels and tired of all his enterprises. It was at last apparent that in any concern which depended on his co-operation with and management of colleagues he would never get anywhere because he always stopped to fight somebody, and imagined every position that occurred instead of studying it. He blazed through London like a comet, leaving a trail of deeply annoyed persons behind him, and like a meteor through America, where the war betrayed him into backing the loser in his generous indignation against the Allied ambush. Then he retired to Nice and became a sort of literary sage to whom all high-souled young Americans with literary ambitions made pilgrimages in their wander years, and at last died there peacefully enough.

He really had not one career but two, simultaneous but on different planes. On the imaginative plane the invariable generosity of his transports of indignation, scorn, pity, chivalry, and defiance of snobberies, powers, and principalities enabled him to retain the regard of people who had the same sympathies. But on the prosaic plane of everyday life he got into difficulties and incurred maledictions from which it was not always possible to defend him.

These difficulties are not worth bothering about now. They were all made worse by his main delusion, which was an enormous one and sometimes highly comic. He was firmly persuaded that the human race consisted entirely of Frank Harrises and women of the sort Frank Harris idealized. Any departure from this standard was in his eyes delinquency, cretinism, unforgivable sin, diabolism. As there was only one Frank Harris in the world, and the sort of woman he idealized never completely existed except in his imagination, the effect on his social manners was often disastrous. And the matter was complicated further by his manifold nature; for his scope ranged from depths of materialism to heights of spirituality; and his ideal of womanhood varied accordingly.

As a result his dinner-table conversation was often of the most disconcerting inappropriateness. If he took in a quiet deaconess he would entertain her on the assumption that her personal morals and religious views were those of our post-war night clubs. If, knowing this, you took care to put him beside the most abandoned lady present, he would discourse to her on his favourite subject of the beauty of the character of Jesus, and his intention of writing a great book about it. And as all his conversation was uttered in a resonant and arresting voice that reached the farthest corners of the room, he was apt to produce the situation which was in Oscar Wilde's mind when he said, "Frank Harris has been received in all the great houses—*once.*" In the end it was inevitable that he should establish himself in a retreat where he could be approached only on his own terms; and this, after making London and New York too hot to hold him, he found in Nice as aforesaid. He impressed many young bloods in revolt against *bourgeois* civilization as a great man, as I have reason to know; for when they came my way afterwards I had to be careful not to shock them by the slightest levity in discussing him. He was no solitary prophet either: he could inspire and hold the devotion of his wife, who was much younger than he, and knew quite well what she was sacrificing for him. When he was editor of the *Saturday Review* he chose and held together for a while a team of contributors whom no one else had the gumption to choose or the courage to back with a free hand. I think I know pretty well all the grievances his detractors had against him; but if I had to write his epitaph it should run, *"Here lies a man of letters who hated cruelty and injustice and bad art, and never spared them in his own interest. R.I.P."*

It remains for me only to explain the extent to which I have had to revise this book in order to make its publication possible. Frank knew very little of the facts of my life, and, having no patience for the very dull work of investigation, or even for a look at Professor Archibald Henderson's monumental biography of me, put in a good deal of guesswork. His guesses were not always successful: some of them were miles off the mark. Even when he had obtained information from me directly he could not jettison the guesses that conflicted with it, and continued to write with the information and the imaginative conjecture running in his head concurrently, and coming uppermost alternately, thereby landing himself in obvious contradictions. I have got rid of the contradictions on the objective plane by simply supplying or correcting the facts, so that future writers using the work as a book of reference will not be misled. But I have made no attempt to reconcile the subjective contradictions, even when these have arisen through his slips backwards and forwards between conjectural fiction and accurate information. Many of these contradictions and inconsistencies are between the mood of one day and another as he wrote, and are none the worse for that. Nothing can be more unnatural and biographically worthless than a rigid single estimate with everything else forced into harmony with it: it is like an instantaneous photograph of a horse transfixed by the camera in the act of galloping. In one or two places, where a criticism was attached to some fable that had to be deleted, I have transposed it to a context which saved its coherence. All the criticisms, jibes, explosions of passing ill humour, and condemnations have been piously preserved; and I have taken care that they have lost nothing by a few inevitable displacements.

I could not, however, save Frank Harris from doing himself some injustice in this book. His list of the passions that life offers to the dramatic poet: "love, jealousy, envy, the will to power: passions as primitive as they are enduring," would put him out of court in dealing with humanity in its highest stage of evolution, or with society in its highest stage of civilization. If you are to rule out religious ecstasy, political utopianism, the pursuit of knowledge and of power over matter and circumstances as distinguished from vulgar ambition, the struggle in that pursuit to extend mental faculty, especially mathematical faculty, and the fixation in language, music, color and form of imaginative conceptions, thereby making their inspiration communicable, you have nothing left but savagery; and if Harris had been really limited, as he implies, to love, jealousy, envy and ambition, he would obviously have been no more competent to write a book about my work than a Hollywood scenario inventor to write a book about Einstein. His own work clears him of any such disqualification. He was a cold-blooded writer, even when his theme was sex, like the French "realist" writers who pleased him most. His impatience with artistic graces of expression, which sometimes extended to quite harmless and convenient decencies of conversation, was at bottom a scientific matter-of-factness. He rails at me for not writing like Swinburne and D'Annunzio; but you have only to turn to his stories to see that in his own work he is a hard and austere dissector of humanity, and that the only heroine who has moved him to an outstanding and touching feminine creation is not Cleopatra, but Perovskiaia (Sonia) who sacrificed herself and assassinated a Tsar in a passion of pure political *Weltverbesserungswahn* (worldbettermentcraze) which, as he rightly points out, is my own devouring malady. Note also his contemporary portraits, every one of which is of some quite hardheaded celebrity without twopennorth of love story. Evidently Cleopatra no more satisfied his soul than she satisfies mine, in spite of the thundering luxuriance of literary power with which her story is told by Shakespear.

I think that in every case where Frank Harris does not understand me, or any other of his contemporaries, the real difficulty always is that he does not understand himself. It is an old rule in business not to throw out dirty water until you get in fresh; but the extent to which men muddle themselves in applying this to affairs of the mind is disastrous. To change the metaphor, they take their loaded guns and put in a fresh charge without carefully taking out the old, with the result that at the first fire they scatter their own brains instead of those of their opponents. Frank's gun was originally loaded, one guesses, by a very old-fashioned Welsh family with Irish Catholic servants. When he rams down a supercharge of the latest high explosive on top of their ancient black gunpowder and lets fly at me—or anyone else—he blows himself to bits and leaves his adversary amazed but unharmed. But the incident is always entertaining, and sometimes more instructive than an accurate shot would have been. In truth this book is valuable, not in the least as an explanation of my works (for anyone who looks for such an explanation at second hand when my works are there to tell him all about it at first hand must be an idiot) but as a demonstration of my reactions on Harris, who was interesting enough to make his reactions very readable. Now to produce a sufficiently strong reaction there must be some incompatibility; and I find this book amusing (in the best French sense of the word) in proportion to the clash made by our two temperaments as they collide.

Naturally then I do not endorse all the judgments in this book. Its scale of values, on which my sociological work appears so insignificant, and the most negligible sex episodes—or absence of episodes—appear of supreme importance, could be justified only in a book avowedly dealing with my sex history solely. I never discussed sex with Frank Harris, because his intolerant Irish-American prudery—the last quality he ever suspected in himself—made complete and dispassionate discussion impossible. He never could understand why I insisted that his autobiographical *Life and Loves*, which he believed to be the last word in outspoken self-revelation, told us nothing about him that was distinctively Frank Harrisian, and showed, in one amusingly significant passage, that there is a Joseph somewhere in every Casanova.

This much I am obliged to say, lest it should be held that in passing the proofs for press as corrected by mc I am endorsing everything that he says about me. I am not. But no man is a good judge of his own portrait; and if it be well painted he has no right to prevent the artist exhibiting it, or even, when the artist is a deceased friend, to refuse to varnish it before the show opens. I hope this makes my part in the matter clear.

AYOT ST. LAWRENCE,
October 5th, 1931.

Index